# ESSAYS ON
# ETHICS AND POLITICS

# ESSAYS ON
# ETHICS AND POLITICS

### GORDON H. CLARK

John W. Robbins, Editor

The Trinity Foundation
Jefferson, Maryland

Cover: *The Battle of La Hogue*
Benjamin West
National Gallery of Art, Washington, D.C.
Andrew W. Mellon Fund


**Essays on Ethics and Politics**
© 1992 John W. Robbins


ISBN: 0-940931-32-X

# Contents

## Books by Gordon H. Clark

*Readings in Ethics* (1931)
*Selections from Hellenistic Philosophy* (1940)
*A History of Philosophy* (coauthor, 1941)
*A Christian Philosophy of Education* (1946, 1988)
*A Christian View of Men and Things* (1952, 1991)
*What Presbyterians Believe* (1956)[1]
*Thales to Dewey* (1957, 1989)
*Dewey* (1960)
*Religion, Reason and Revelation* (1961, 1986)
*William James* (1963)
*Karl Barth's Theological Method* (1963)
*The Philosophy of Science and Belief in God* (1964, 1987)
*What Do Presbyterians Believe?* (1965, 1985)
*Peter Speaks Today* (1967)[2]
*The Philosophy of Gordon H. Clark* (1968)
*Biblical Predestination* (1969)[3]
*Historiography: Secular and Religious* (1971)
*II Peter* (1972)[2]
*The Johannine Logos* (1972, 1989)
*Three Types of Religious Philosophy* (1973, 1989)
*First Corinthians* (1975, 1991)
*Colossians* (1979, 1989)
*Predestination in the Old Testament* (1979)[3]
*I and II Peter* (1980)
*Language and Theology* (1980)
*First John* (1980)
*God's Hammer: The Bible and Its Critics* (1982, 1987)
*Behaviorism and Christianity* (1982)
*Faith and Saving Faith* (1983, 1990)
*In Defense of Theology* (1984)
*The Pastoral Epistles* (1984)
*The Biblical Doctrine of Man* (1984, 1992)
*The Trinity* (1985, 1990)
*Logic* (1985, 1988)
*Ephesians* (1985)
*Clark Speaks From the Grave* (1986)
*Logical Criticisms of Textual Criticism* (1986, 1990)
*First and Second Thessalonians* (1986)
*Predestination* (1987)
*The Atonement* (1987)

*The Incarnation* (1988)
*Today's Evangelism: Counterfeit or Genuine?* (1990)
*Essays on Ethics and Politics* (1992)
*Sanctification* (1992)

[1] Revised in 1965 as *What Do Presbyterians Believe?*
[2] Combined in 1980 as *I & II Peter.*
[3] Combined in 1987 as *Predestination.*

# Foreword

The evening news and the daily paper testify to the collapse of morality in America. The alarming statistics on crime, abortion, taxation, and debt; the vociferous homosexual, feminist, environmentalist, and socialist movements; the lewd and violent television programs, movies, and books; the growing numbers of illegitimate births, homosexual marriages, unjustified divorces, and deaths by drunken drivers—all these things are evidence that America is caught in a moral maelstrom and may soon disappear beneath the flood.

How has this happened? How did a nation founded by Pilgrims, Puritans, and Presbyterians come to be dominated by impuritans? It did not happen overnight. It has not been only in the last two or three decades that the problem began; it has been a long time coming.

The story begins, as all stories do, with theology. America lost her ethics because she first lost her religion. Of course, there have always been unbelievers in America and they have usually been in the majority. But in the nineteenth century something new happened. Clergymen and the churches, whose duty it is to defend the truth against unbelief, not only failed to do so, they, too, became unbelievers and they began to attack the truth. The treason of the clerics became blatant in the twentieth century. Central to that betrayal was their rejection of the Bible as the infallible revelation of God. If the Bible is an untrustworthy book, a book not to be believed, all the other doctrines of Christianity— including its system of ethics—cannot stand. Gone are the promise of eternal life, the final judgment, the deity of Christ, the threat of hell, and the sovereignty of God. Gone, too, are the Ten Commandments. The prologue to the Ten Commandments states the ground of their authority: "I am the Lord." Theology, not ethics, is of fundamental importance; once an individual or a nation rejects Christian theology, he has no basis for maintaining Christian ethics. The validity of the Ten Commandments depends upon the fact that their author is indeed the Lord. Were that not the case, the Commandments would have no authority to require anyone's obedience.

Once the clerics and the churches abandoned Christianity, the moral decline of America was a foregone conclusion. Instead of churches being the salt of the earth, they became its fertilizer. We ought not be surprised that the weeds of crime, violence, greed, lust, and envy are flourishing: The churches and the clerics, by their unbelief, are feeding, watering, and cultivating them.

All of this has one rather obvious implication: If America, if the world, is to be pulled from the cesspool, it will not be accomplished by legislation, no matter how good, nor by repeated exhortations to traditional morality, nor even by preaching obedience to the moral law, no matter how vigorously. America has lost her way because she first lost her faith. And if that faith is to be recovered, it will be only through the preaching of the Gospel —the Biblical Gospel, not the various perversions taught in both liberal and conservative, Protestant and Catholic, modernist and evangelical churches today. No man or nation can save itself. No individual and no people can earn eternal or temporal salvation by good works. The Gospel alone is the power of God, and through its accurate preaching and publication, many will be granted faith.

Ironically, the cure for America's immorality is not more law, but more belief in the truth. Faith—belief—correct theology is fundamental. Anything else is treating the symptoms, not the cause, of our present condition. The ideas expressed so often in advertising and in popular culture must be rejected and replaced by Christian ideas: Atheism: "You only go 'round once, so grab all the gusto you can get." Irrationalism: "Why ask why?" "Turn on, tune in, drop out." Self-indulgence: "Gotta have it." "Buy now, pay later." Hedonism: "Try it, you'll like it." "If it feels good, do it." Our job as Christians is to replace those slogans and ideas with Christian ideas. Once people know who God is, we will have no major problems with ethics.

Dr. Gordon H. Clark was perhaps the greatest Christian philosopher and theologian America has produced. Over the course of his life he wrote hundreds of articles and essays, some of which directly concern ethics and politics. This collection of forty-three essays is a major statement of Christian ethics. In them he refutes the arguments of both secular and religious thinkers who attempt to construct ethical systems apart from revelation. He shows that there is no possibility of ethical knowledge or action apart from the Bible. The Bible alone is the source of truth: neither tradition, nor church, nor natural law, nor human opinion can provide us with the information we need to tell right from wrong.

Clark also shows that the Bible is a package deal: One cannot consistently accept the Eighth Commandment—You shall not steal—without also accepting the first—I am the Lord your God; you shall have no other gods before me. Ethics depends on theology; theology does not depend on ethics. If we pray for a recovery of Christian morality in the world, we must first pray for a recovery of Christian belief. God's law is fine, but it is inadequate: God's truth comes first.

John W. Robbins
February 1992

# 1
# Activism

Activism like its opposite, Quietism, comes in degrees. In its extreme form Quietism advocates the cessation of all volition and desire. "Absorption by God" is virtually Buddhist Nirvana in Christian dress. The extreme form of Activism would be a life all of action and volition minus any knowledge of what one is doing or should do. Obviously Christianity is neither the one nor the other. Disagreement concerning proportions oscillates between ivory-tower intellectuals and non-intellectual activists. In general European evangelicals are more intellectual while American evangelicals, even though they do not engage in the liberal's noisy demonstrations, are strongly activist.

*Baker's Dictionary of Christian Ethics*, Carl F.H. Henry, editor. Grand Rapids, Michigan: Baker Book House, 1973, p. 7.

# 2
# Altruism

Altruism as an ethical theory arose in late seventeenth century England. In reaction to Thomas Hobbes' psychological hedonism, altruism tried to prove the existence of natural impulses to do good to other people. Hobbes had held that all natural impulses and motives are self-seeking. He had expressed himself, as one critic put it, in "delightfully repulsive" terms. For example, Pity is "the imagination of future calamity to ourselves proceeding from the sense of another man's calamity." Again he asserted that "the passion of laughter proceedeth from the sudden imagination of our own odds and eminency."

Francis Hutcheson (1694-1747) argued: "Had we no sense of good distinct from the advantage or interest arising from the external senses . . . our admiration and love toward a fruitful field or commodious habitation would be much the same with what we have toward a generous friend or any noble character. . . . we should have the same sentiments and affections toward inanimate things which we have toward rational agents; which everyone knows to be false."

Hutcheson's argument is obviously unsatisfactory, and Bishop Butler (1692-1752) removed the problem by identifying the effects of self-love and conscience. "Self-love then, though confined to the interest of the present world, does in general perfectly coincide with virtue. . . . Whatever exceptions there are to this, which are much fewer than they are commonly thought, all shall be set right at the final distribution of things. . . . Conscience and self-love, if we understand our true happiness, always lead us the same way."

In the nineteenth century, Utilitarians, without the benefit of a final judgment, tried to harmonize the pleasures of all individuals, so that one's own pleasure and the pleasures of others were always consistent. They were not so successful as the good Bishop.

---

*Baker's Dictionary of Christian Ethics,* Carl F.H. Henry, editor. Grand Rapids, Michigan: Baker Book House, 1973, pp. 17-18.

# 3

# Anarchism

Anarchism is a theory that rejects government and desires society to be regulated only by voluntary agreements. Not all anarchists propose to destroy government by violence. Others do.

Some proponents of secular anarchism are [Pierre-Joseph] Proudhon [1809-1865], [Michael] Bakunin [1814-1876], [Peter] Kropotkin [1842-1921], Max Stirner [1806-1856], and the American Benjamin Tucker (1854-1939). The theory assumes that human nature is good and needs no coercive laws.

Christian anarchists claimed freedom from law on the basis of liberation by Christ. They are represented by the Levelers and Diggers of the seventeenth century, the Anabaptists and Doukhobors, and William Godwin, who published an *Enquiry Concerning Political Justice* in 1793.

Augustine argued that sin necessitates civil government. Luther and Calvin continued this Biblical position.

---

*Baker's Dictionary of Christian Ethics,* Carl F.H. Henry, editor. Grand Rapids, Michigan: Baker Book House, 1973, p. 20.

# 4

# Calvinistic Ethics

Calvinistic ethics depends on revelation. The distinction between right and wrong is not identified by an empirical discovery of natural law, as with Aristotle and Thomas Aquinas, nor by the logical formalism of Kant, and certainly not by utilitarianism's impossible calculation of the greatest good for the greatest number, but by God's revelation of the Ten Commandments. This revelation came first in God's act of creating man in his own image so that certain basic moral principles were implanted in his heart, later to be vitiated by sin; second, there were some special instructions given to Adam and Noah, which no doubt overlapped and expanded the innate endowment; third, the more comprehensive revelation to Moses; plus, fourth, the various subsidiary precepts in the remainder of the Bible.

Although the medieval church knew the Ten Commandments—in his defense of free will Pelagius even taught that it was possible to obey them perfectly, and the main body of the church came to hold that their observance earned merit toward salvation—Calvin initiated an almost completely new development in systematically using the Ten Commandments as the basis for ethics. In his *Institutes* II 8, he gives an exposition of the moral law, approximately fifty pages.

His defense of such a long exposition is that "the commands and prohibitions always imply more than the words express. . . . In all the commandments . . . a part is expressed instead of the whole. . . . The best rule, then, I conceive will be that the exposition be directed to the design of the precept . . . as the end of the fifth commandment is, that honor may be given to them to whom God assigns it. . . . [II.viii.8]."

In the main body of the exposition Calvin writes as follows on the sixth commandment:

> The end of this precept is, that since God has connected mankind together in a kind of unity, every man ought to consider himself as charged with the safety of all. In short, then, all violence and injustice, and every kind of mischief, which may injure the body of our neighbor, are forbidden to us. . . . The Divine Legislator . . . intends this rule to govern the soul. . . . Mental homicide therefore is likewise prohibited. . . . "Whosoever hateth his brother is a murderer" (II.viii.39).

Following this lead of Calvin the Westminster divines devoted questions 91-151 of the Larger Catechism to the moral law. Take question 139 as an example:

Q. 139. What are the sins forbidden in the seventh commandment?

A. The sins forbidden in the seventh commandment, besides the neglect of the duties required, are: adultery, fornication, rape, incest, sodomy, and all unnatural lusts; all unclean imaginations, thoughts, purposes, and affections; all corrupt or filthy communications, or listening thereunto; wanton looks, impudent or light behavior, immodest apparel, prohibiting of lawful, and dispensing with unlawful marriages; allowing, tolerating, keeping of stews, and resorting to them; entangling vows of single life, undue delay of marriage; having more wives or husbands than one at the same time; unjust divorce or desertion; idleness, gluttony, drunkenness, unchaste company; lascivious songs, books, pictures, dancings, stage-plays, and all other provocations to, or acts of, uncleanness either in ourselves or others.

This highlights the difference in moral standards between Calvinism and Fundamentalism. In the United States Arminian churches have often required their members to avoid the movies on the ground that Hollywood was lascivious. At present (1973) the movies are sometimes worse than that: outright pornographic. But then, some books and magazines are pornographic. Should a church then forbid all books and magazines? Calvinism stays with the Bible and outlaws neither the movies nor books in general; but prohibits "lascivious songs, books, pictures, dancings, and stage-plays."

Further reading of the Larger Catechism will show, to the surprise of some, how very ample and detailed the law of God actually is. Therefore Calvinistic ministers and writers have with some regularity expounded the Ten Commandments. An Anglican example is Ezekiel Hopkins, Bishop of Derry, (1633-1689), whose exposition occupies 300 pages.

These expositions of the detailed application of the moral law are uniformly prefaced by some remarks on sin, grace, and legalism. The Romish merit system made this necessary. Today two other views necessitate the same theological background. First there is a pietistic view that depends for guidance on the direct instructions of the Spirit. The Scriptural directives are regarded as insufficient, or even as inapplicable in the age of grace. Therefore a person must receive an answer to prayer in order to know whether a particular action is right or wrong. Calvinism stays with the Bible and disallows later claims to special revelation.

The second factor that necessitates the theological background is liberalism's novel definition of legalism. Legalism used to be the theory that man could completely or partially merit salvation by obeying the law; faith was then not the sole means of justification. But contemporary liberalism defines legalism as any attempt to distinguish right from wrong by rules, precepts, or commandments. The argument is that no rule fits every case— there are exceptions; or even that every situation is utterly unique so that rules are always impossible. Therefore each situation must be uniquely (not judged, but) perceived, and (usually) love decides what to do. Love then, of course, sanctions abortion, homosexuality, and anything one does lovingly. The Apostle Paul wrote to the Corinthians about this sort of thing.

Calvinism defines sin as any want of conformity to or transgression of the law of God. Saved by grace, that is, saved from sin and its effects, the Christian is sanctified by an ever more complete obedience to the Ten Commandments.

*Baker's Dictionary of Christian Ethics*, Carl F.H. Henry, editor. Grand Rapids, Michigan: Baker Book House, 1973, pp. 80-81.

# 5

# Can Moral Education Be Grounded on Naturalism?

Among moral prescriptions common opinion would include the sixth, seventh, and eighth of the Ten Commandments. Thou shalt not kill, thou shalt not commit adultery, and thou shalt not steal, have usually been regarded as important moral laws. An orthodox Christian or an orthodox Jew can sincerely and consistently inculcate these laws because he believes them to be the laws of God. They are right because God has commanded them. And they are laws because God imposes penalties for their transgression. Thus moral education can consistently be grounded on Biblical religion.

Humanism, naturalism, or atheism obviously does not have this ground for morality, nor does it uniformly accept these laws. Professor Edwin A. Burtt, himself a humanist, in both editions of his *Types of Religious Philosophy,* indicates the repudiation of Biblical morality by reporting that the more radical humanists regard "sex as an essentially harmless pleasure which should be regulated only by personal taste and preference." Similarly the political radicalism of many naturalists in attacking private property and advocating confiscatory taxation and the redistribution of wealth is a thinly disguised defense of legalized theft. And it is not difficult to identify godless governments which make constant use of murder. Naturalism therefore seems to be consistent with a repudiation of the Ten Commandments.

No doubt many humanists in America disapprove of the brutality and murder inherent in Communism. Some may even have a kind word for private property. And some would not condone adultery. But the problem that naturalism must face is this: Can an empirical philosophy, a philosophy that repudiates revelation, an instrumentalist or descriptive philosophy provide a ground—I do not say for the Ten Commandments—but for any moral prescriptions whatever? Or do the humanists' arguments that place sexual relations in the sphere of purely personal preference also imply that all the choices of life are equally a matter of private taste?

The empirical method in axiology can only begin with the discovery in experience of so-called values. Art and friendship, health and material comfort, are frequently so identified. The precise identification, however, is not the crucial point. These so-called values are all descriptive facts. Burtt discovers in his experience a preference for art and friendship. Someone else may not value art at all. Similarly, personal preference varies between monogamy and adultery. And Stalin shows a preference for murder. As Gardner Williams of the University of Toledo, in his volume, *Humanistic Ethics* (p. 6), says, "Selfish ambition, or the will to power, when successful, is intrinsically satisfactory." Thus murder, as much as friendship, is a value because it has been discovered as a value in experience. How then can a theory which restricts itself to descriptive facts provide ground for normative prescriptions? If the premise of an argument is the descriptive fact that someone likes something, by what logic could one arrive at the conclusion that other people ought to like the same thing? Any syllogism with a normative conclusion requires a normative premise.

Some naturalists, perhaps most naturalists today, attempt to avoid this patent fallacy by speaking of obligation as a social demand. Instead of depending on Almighty God to impose sanctions, these naturalists depend on society. However, the attempt to base morality on society not only fails to avoid the fallacy but it faces other difficulties as well. In the first place, if morality is a demand of society, one must indicate which society. Is it the demand of the family, the church, the nation, or all humanity? It can hardly be all humanity, for two reasons. There are no demands which are clearly demands of humanity. Humanity, if it speaks at all, speaks in such an indistinct and ambiguous language that no specific obligation can be proved. And second, if society is to take the place of God as the source of sanctions, then obviously humanity cannot be the basis of obligation, for humanity imposes no sanctions. Therefore an ethical theory based on social demand must appeal to family, church, or nation. Of these three the nation is most able to impose sanctions. Hence, morality becomes loyalty to the State, and murder, adultery, and theft become moral obligations when Nazism, Fascism, and Communism demand them.

In the next place, this appeal to society is itself without basis. Where is the argument to establish an individual's obligation to any society? It may be prudent to act so as to avoid penalties, but even the most totalitarian state is not totally efficient. When possible, therefore, disobedience to social custom or even an attempt to overthrow the State may be justified. In any case, a man may commit suicide. How can any society obligate an individual to continue living? Dr. Jerome Nathanson, executive secretary of the Ethical Culture Society, seeing that not everyone will be converted to Christianity, asks orthodox Christians to submerge their faith and cooperate in a moral enterprise to salvage the world from its present plight. Whether one believes in God or not, still he must go on and try to make the world a fit place in which to live. This appeal grossly begs the question. Indeed it contains an obviously false statement. It is not true that we must go on and try to improve the world. We do not have to go on. We can quit the world. It is here that Dr. Nathanson shuts his eyes to the problem. Is life worth-while if there is no God? He thinks so, but humanism seems to have no argument to support this belief. The question reappears, namely, If God be banished, how can society obligate anyone to keep on living? This question seems unanswerable, and instead of Christians being too polite to ask embarrassing questions, they should repeat this one insistently. Further, even if a person does not commit suicide, but prefers to live, how can society obligate him to sacrifice his ease for the improvement of the world? If naturalism can do no better than to call such people social sponges and other derogatory names, as W.H. Kilpatrick does, it has abandoned rational argument and can provide no basis for moral education.

In spite of the ethical speculation of the last hundred years, the best attempt to base ethics on empiricism, social demands, individual goods, and all without benefit of revelation, is still [Jeremy] Bentham's utilitarianism. Bentham thought that all men universally desire pleasure. This assertion of a single common end supposedly puts all men under a common obligation. On this general basis the right and wrong in specific instances is to be determined by calculating consequences. Murder, adultery, and theft would presumably be means to pain, and thus moral education would be possible.

Unfortunately for naturalism all such attempts are failures because there is no empirical knowledge sufficient to brand murder as wrong and private property as right. Any empirical calculation to foster the good life in all persons affected by one's conduct is a vain dream. Even if it were true that murder and theft frequently result in pain to the perpetrator, it is clear that this is not universally true. Hitler may have suffered for his murders and confiscations; but Stalin lived to a ripe old age, enjoying the almost perfect fruition of his vengeful plans. Few adherents of Biblical morality can boast of such empirical success. Indeed, even in the case of Hitler, his final catastrophe included, what purely naturalistic argument could show that his life was not better than the lives of the six million Jews he murdered? He enjoyed excitement, wealth, and power for several years, and suffered only a few moments. Is not this a better life than that of his pitiful victims? Unless there is an Almighty God to impose inescapable penalties on transgressors, why should we not praise the rich, full, stimulating, dangerous life of a dictator?

Any theory therefore which denies divine sanctions for violation of divine law not only fails to condemn murder, adultery, and theft, but in addition fails to esablish any universal or common distinction between right and wrong. Naturalism therefore cannot serve as a ground for Christian morals, nor can it serve as a ground even for the inculcation of the personal preferences of its exponents. In an empirical, descriptive philosophy, one may find the verb *is;* but the verb *ought* has no logical standing.

*Bulletin of the Evangelical Theological Society,* Fall 1958.

# 6

# Capital Punishment

Capital punishment is specified both in the Old Testament (Genesis 9:6) and in the New Testament (Romans 13:4). It is implied in Genesis 4:14 and approved in Acts 25:11. Capital punishment is therefore an integral part of Christian ethics.

Contemporary efforts to abolish capital punishment proceed on a non-Christian view of man, a secular theory of criminal law, and a low estimate of the value of life.

The low evaluation of human life occurs in the liberal penology that holds criminal law to be solely for the purpose of rehabilitation. Not only does liberalism think that the murder of a human being is too minor a crime to justify execution; the theory consistently implies that no crime should ever be punished. Justice and punishment are deprecated as "irrational vengeance." This is a basic difference between Christian and liberal ethics. As such it can be resolved only by a decision on ultimate principles, to wit, whether ethical norms are established by divine decree, and secondarily, what obligations God confers on civil government.

The liberal arguments are superficial. One is that capital punishment does not deter. Obviously it deters the executed criminal. If it does not deter others, the reply is that the law may not deter, but its enforcement will. In 1968 there were 7,000 murders and no executions, in 1969 there were about 8,500 and no executions, and in 1970 some 10,000 and no executions. But if the law had been enforced, and 5,000 murderers had been executed in 1968, and 7,000 in 1969, could anyone doubt that there would have been fewer than 10,000 murders in 1970?

A worse argument is that only the poor are convicted and the wealthy escape. Actually the courts are so lenient and the public so permissive that nearly everybody escapes. If the objection were true, however, the answer would not be to abolish capital punishment and let the number of murders keep on soaring, but it would be to put honest judges on the bench and in the box jurors who are more compassionate toward the victim than toward the criminal.

The most impressive argument is that sometimes an innocent man might be executed. Once again, with our present courts, this never or almost never happens. Even murderers like Sirhan Sirhan, whose act was seen by a dozen witnesses, are not executed. Yet if just one innocent man is executed . . . ? Do you prefer 10,000 murders to save one innocent man rather than one tragedy to save 5000 lives? But of course this type of argument is superficial and irrelevant. God gave the right of capital punishment to human governments. He intended it to be used wisely and justly, but he intended it to be used. Abolition of the death penalty presupposes the falsity of Christian principles.

---

*Baker's Dictionary of Christian Ethics*, Carl F.H. Henry, editor. Grand Rapids, Michigan: Baker Book House, 1973, p. 84.

# 7

# Capital Punishment and the Bible

In the October 12, 1959, issue of *Christianity Today*, Dr. Jacob Vellenga had an article defending capital punishment. In the present issue Dr. [John Howard] Yoder and Dr. Milligan have articles opposing it. Dr. Milligan states the question in very acceptable terms: "Is capital punishment just and right?" Since Dr. Yoder asserts, "capital punishment is one of those infringements on the divine Will which takes place in society," the wording of the question may be sharpened this way: "Is capital punishment ever right?" Dr. Yoder seems to believe that it was wrong even in the Old Testament.

Fortunately this form of the question rules out discussions on the cost of judicial procedure, the number of states that have abolished capital punishment, the (poorly founded) doubt that execution deters murder, and other extraneous details. The question is not whether murderers escape their penalty, but whether they should. The question is not the direction in which modern penology is going, but whether it is going in the wrong direction. The question is not the efficiency of American justice. We admit that American justice leaves much to be desired. Criminals receive too much favor and sympathy. But all such details would lead to an interminable discussion. The question is simply, Is capital punishment ever justified?

## The Old Covenant

Both of the opposing articles rightly center their attention on the relation of the Old Testament to the New Testament. Dr. Yoder asks whether a proper Christian understanding of any problem begins with Moses, or whether a proper approach to the Bible begins with Christ himself. To minimize the Old Testament Dr. Yoder and Dr. Milligan then press the details of stoning an adulterer, of executing an idolator, of establishing cities of refuge, of appointing a kinsman of the murdered man as the executioner, and so on.

Now, in the first place, I should like to maintain that a proper understanding of the Bible begins with Moses—not with the Mosaic law as such, but with the first chapter of Genesis. In particular, when the Old Testament lays down basic principles, such as the sovereignty of God, the creation of all things, God's control over history, the inclusion of infants in the Covenant, or other matters not explicitly abrogated or modified in the New Testament, the silence of the latter, or the paucity of its references, is not to be made an excuse for abandoning the principles of the former. As Dr. Yoder admits, there is much more information on civil government in the Old than in the New Testament. Therefore I would conclude that the Old Testament should not be minimized.

Probably every view of the controversial question of the relation between the Testaments acknowledges that the New in some respects modifies the Old. The most obvious of these modifications is the fulfillment of the ritual by the death of Christ. The Mosaic administration was superimposed upon the Abrahamic covenant 430 years afterward and was to remain in effect only until the Messiah came. Even the animal sacrifices which had been instituted before the time of Moses were types or pictorial anticipations of the one sacrifice that in truth satisfied divine justice. To offer them now would be to imply that Christ had not yet come. Because of this, Dr. Milligan's argument that the defense of capital punishment consistently requires animal sacrifice is invalid. What else could Hebrews chapter 9 possibly mean?

For this reason too, Dr. Vellenga's reference to the Crucifixion as a point in favor of capital punishment is not so irrelevant as the opposition alleges, for the death penalty was not merely Pilate's decision to be regarded as mistaken: rather it was God who had foreordained that without the shedding of blood there is no remission of sin.

Next, if the cessation of the ritual is the most widely understood modification of the Old Testament, the increase of biblical ignorance since the seventeenth century seems to have erased from memory the point that the civil laws of Israel also are no longer meant to apply. God abolished the theocracy. Such is the teaching of Jesus in Matthew 21:33-45. The Pharisees thought that any men who would kill the Messiah would be miserably destroyed,

but that God would then let out the vineyard to other High Priests
and that the theocracy would continue as before. Jesus said no.
The Kingdom would be taken from the Jews, the theocracy would
be ended, and a new order would be instituted in which the
rejected stone would become the head of the corner. So it has
happened. There is no longer any chosen nation. Therefore the
detailed civil and criminal code of Israel is no longer binding.

For this reason we do not have cities of refuge: Police and
judicial protection are sufficient. We are not required to marry our
brother's widow, because the purpose of preserving his name and
tribe is no longer in effect.

## Crime and Punishment

This does not, however, and in logic cannot imply that
capital punishment is wrong. Would one argue that since the Jews
were forbidden to lend money on interest to other Jews, it is now
wrong to obey that law and to refuse to accept interest from other
Christians? This is just bad logic. At most, the rejection of the civil
law as a whole would merely leave the individual details as open
questions. And even one who strongly deprecates the Old Testament must in honesty admit that several of those details could be
wisely adopted today. In the present depraved condition of the
United States, we might even wisely execute adulterers and
pornographers.

Where the opponents of capital punishment go astray is in
the assumption that approval of execution depends on its inclusion in the national laws of Israel. Its inclusion there is of course
quite sufficient to show the falsity of Dr. Yoder's assertion that
execution is an infringement of the divine Will. It was God who
ordered capital punishment. Therefore it is entirely incorrect to
say that capital punishment is an infringement of divine prerogatives; and the question, Is capital punishment ever right? must be
answered in the affirmative.

Of course, this much does not satisfy Dr. Milligan. The
pertinent question is, Is capital punishment ever right today?

To this question it should be replied that although the ritual
and civil laws are no longer in effect, the moral law is. I cannot
agree with Dr. Milligan that in the New Testament "we move to a

different base for law.'' The basis of moral law in all ages is the preceptive will of God. The laws against adultery and murder are not merely Mosaic enactments: They go back to creation. More to the point, capital punishment is commanded by God in his revelation to Noah, and by implication at least was applicable to Cain (Genesis 4:10, 14).

## A General Rule

God's dealing with Cain, however, indicates that it is not absolutely necessary to execute every murderer. When we say that God commanded capital punishment, the meaning is that this penalty was established as the general rule. It does not mean that there could not rightly be exceptions. Remember, the question is, Is capital punishment ever right? Therefore, the case of the woman taken in adultery has no bearing on the matter. For one thing, it should be noted that the woman was taken in the very act; but the scribes and Pharisees had arrested only the woman and not the man, whom they must also have found in the very act. Aside from Jesus' intention to reveal the hypocrisy of the religious leaders, there may have been other reasons for not inflicting the penalty on this woman. But can this one case support a theory of civil law while all the rest of the Bible is ignored? If this were so, there would be no penalties of any sort for any crimes.

It is this point that the other two authors do not discuss. Dr. Yoder, in his second paragraph, does not want to lower the standards of justice, excuse crime, or gloss over the wrongness of wrong. But he supplies no reason for inflicting prison terms instead of execution. In fact, his argument against personal responsibility, its seemingly Freudian psychology, its placing the blame on society as a whole, would rather suggest that no penalties for any crime should be inflicted. Until the opponents of capital punishment formulate their theory of civil authority, nothing more need be said on this point.

To indicate that the many details in the two articles have not been ignored, even though passed over in silence here, I shall make mention of Jesus' reading the scroll in the synagogue in Nazareth. Jesus stopped reading just before the clause on the day of vengeance. Dr. Milligan thinks that this is significant. No doubt it is. But it is not significant of the fact that the state should not execute criminals. It is significant of the fact that the ministry of Jesus at that time was to proclaim the year of Jehovah's favor. The day of vengeance is to come later when Jesus shall be revealed from heaven in flaming fire, rendering vengeance to them that know not God. Such passages have nothing to do with civil government, and to press them against capital punishment is inadmissible.

Now, finally, it is our contention that the New Testament authorizes capital punishment and war as well as the Old. Dr. Milligan does not mention the power of the sword granted to earthly governments in Romans chapter 13. Dr. Yoder tries to make this power merely a symbol of judicial authority without any reference to execution. Is not this a measure of desperation? What are swords used for? Is taxation, mentioned in the same passage, also a symbol of civil authority without any reference to extracting money from the pockets of the people? No, such an interpretation completely gives away the weakness of the case for symbolism.

In other words, the opponents of capital punishment offer no theory of civil government, they seriously misinterpret the Bible, and they are in conflict with the principles of Christian ethics.

---

*Christianity Today,* February 1, 1960, pp. 352-354.

# 8

# The Christian and the Law

Not only do denominations differ over their interpretations of various Biblical doctrines, but within each denomination individual members have their personal peculiarities. Therefore when ministers assemble for a sedate colloquium or college students get together for a friendly bull session, and a question on Biblical doctrine arises, the discussion is bound to be interesting.

Within the past year two such meetings took place—one almost exclusively of ministers and professors, the other almost exclusively of students. It may not be so surprising that the subject of divine guidance and right conduct was taken up at both meetings, but it is worthy of note that in the first meeting a minister from a liturgical and rather formal denomination and in the second meeting some students from much more informal groups, expressed similar sentiments on the Christian's relation to the law of God. It may also be worthy of note that few of the ministers agreed with the minister, while most of the students agreed with the students.

The sentiments referred to emphasized salvation by grace and God's nearness to the individual soul; but this emphasis went to the length of denying that God's commands, which of course are law, had any relevance to the Christian life.

We are not under law, but under grace, they said; and having begun in the Spirit, are we now perfected in the flesh? The law is not of faith. When we were in the flesh, the sinful passions, which were through the law, wrought in our members to bring forth fruit unto death; but now we have been delivered from the law, so that we serve in the newness of the spirit and not in the oldness of the letter. For the letter killeth, but the Spirit giveth life.

The converse of this repudiation of the law is that our daily decisions are to be directed immediately by the Spirit. The new birth has given us a new nature, and in this new nature the Spirit instructs us what to do. The Lord will guide us with his eye, and neither the law in the Old Testament nor the commands in the New Testament lay any obligation upon us. They are neither prerequisites for salvation nor guidance for life. This substantially, and without exaggeration, was the position maintained.

On more than one occasion and on more than one subject, devout men have expressed opinions from which others have later drawn distressing conclusions. I knew one man who took such a serious view of divine guidance that one evening he stood for an hour in his chicken yard waiting for the Spirit to tell him whether or not to feed the chickens. And I have heard rumors of people who pray for guidance as to whether or not they should disobey some Biblical command. In previous ages of church history (*e.g.* the early Gnostics) a repudiation of the law has led to gross sin. Someone has characterized this antinomianism by a parody on a gospel hymn: "Free from the law, O blessed condition; I can sin as I please and still have remission."

Such a conclusion was not the intention of the minister and the students above referred to; but though it was far from their intention, each one of us must determine whether or not this view of law and divine guidance leads logically to what is absurd or sinful. Each of us must also determine what significance there is for us in the Ten Commandments and the various commands and directions in the New Testament.

Perhaps a point of general agreement from which we may start is the Biblical teaching that Christ saves us not only from the penalty of sin, but from sin itself. "He died that we might be forgiven; he died to make us good." Or, in Scriptural language, "Shall we continue in sin that grace may abound? Let not sin therefore reign in your mortal bodies. For we are his workmanship, created in Christ Jesus for good works."

If this be agreed upon, if we all admit that we must no longer be the servants of sin but must present our members as instruments of righteousness unto God, the next question logically is: What is sin, what are good works, what is righteousness? We want to do good works, we want to avoid evil works; but how can we distinguish between them?

There need be no vague guessing as to the answer to these questions. The Scripture speaks very definitely. The Scripture says precisely what sin is. "Sin is the transgression of the law" (I John 3:4). "Where no law is, there is no transgression" (Romans 4:14). "Sin is not imputed when there is no law" (Romans 5:13). "Through the law cometh the knowledge of sin" (Romans 3:20). It should be clear then that sin is always defined by the law. Unless one knows the law of God, he cannot know what is wrong, evil or sinful.

Is it wrong to worship Mary and bow before angels? Is it wrong to swipe gadgets off a dime store counter? Is it wrong to work on the Lord's Day? We do not need to stand in a chicken yard waiting for an answer to these questions. Divine guidance is a wonderful thing; but more wonderful is the fact that God has already given us His guidance in easily understood sentences.

The converse also follows. If sin is what the law forbids, good works are those which the law commands. No guessing is necessary. The Scriptures say precisely what good works are. Good works are only such as God has commanded in His Holy Word, and not such as, without the warrant of Scripture, are devised by men out of blind zeal or upon any pretense of good intention. Those who vainly worship God, teaching for doctrines the commandments of men, may have a certain zeal, but not according to knowledge. "He hath shown thee, O man, what is good."

It should be evident therefore that good and evil are defined only by the law of God.

This conclusion is reinforced by the strictness with which God enjoins obedience. "This is the way, walk ye in it. Turn not from it to the right hand or to the left. Thou shalt not go aside from any of the words which I command thee this day, to the right hand or to the left." It should not be thought that these Old Testament principles do not apply to us; nor should anyone suppose that all this is inconsistent with grace. Salvation in the Old Testament is as truly of grace as salvation in the New Testament. Justification by faith is an Old Testament doctrine: Paul took it from Habakkuk. Regeneration, which Nicodemus should have known about, is explained in Ezekiel 36. If therefore grace and law are not incompatible in the Old Testament, there is no *a priori* reason why they should be so in the New Testament.

However, to make doubly sure and not to rely wholly on the Old Testament, some New Testament passages may be adduced. Jesus said, "If ye love me, keep my commandments." And further, "He that saith, I know him, and keepeth not his commandments, is a liar, and the truth is not in him. He that keepeth his commandments dwelleth in him. By this we know that we love the children of God, when we love God and keep his commandments; for this is the love of God, that we keep his commandments."

Such specific statements should be accepted as decisive.

There is one final point to be made. Someone may now admit that we are under obligation to obey God's commands, but he may argue that in addition to the Bible we need further guidance. The Bible is all right so far as it goes; but the Christian life is wider than the Bible; we meet situations that Biblical commands do not cover, and so we must look to God for additional information on what to do. After all, is there any harm in adding to the Bible, provided only that we do not subtract from it?

This type of argument, however, contradicts the express statement of Scripture, and is therefore dishonoring to God. We are all familiar, no doubt, with the phrase, "All Scripture is given by inspiration of God," but have we carefully read what follows? Of course, Scripture is profitable for doctrine, and for instruction in righteousness; but for what purpose? Note the next verse: "that the man of God may be perfect [or, perfected], thoroughly furnished [completely furnished, or equipped] unto all good works [unto every good work]." The statement is comprehensive: It includes every good work. There is no good work for which the Scripture does not prepare us perfectly. It is the law of God stated in the Scriptures that defines sin and good works.

God has given us all the guidance we need. We do not need Roman Catholic tradition; we do not need mystic visions; we do not need additional revelations. But we do need, and need sorely, a great deal of Bible study. In the Bible, and in the Bible alone, we find the rule of life.

*P.S. If you have chickens, a horse, or a pet dog, study Exodus 20:10; 23:5, 12; Deuteronomy 25:4; Proverbs 12:10; Matthew 12:11; and feed them.*

---

*HIS*, October 1957. *The Trinity Review,* March 1979.

# 9

# Christian Liberty

Freedom and liberty are grand words, but if we are to talk intelligibly, our words must be unambiguously defined. In several preceding articles unscriptural meanings of the word *freedom* and the phrase *free from the law* have been pointed out. Chapter XX of the [Westminster] Confession enumerates the factors which compose and define Christian liberty.

> The liberty which Christ hath purchased for believers under
> the gospel consists in their freedom from the guilt of sin, . . . the
> curse of the moral law, . . . [and] bondage to Satan. . . . All of which
> were common also to believers under the law . . . (sec. 1).

In addition to these elements of liberty, which particularly
concern us in our individual lives, Christian liberty includes the
liberty of conscience in the face of tyrannical ecclesiastical
organizations. Some years ago a young man presented himself to a
Presbytery for ordination. As he was known to believe that the
boards and agencies of that church were infiltrated with modernism, he was asked whether he would support the boards and
agencies. He replied that he would support them insofar as they
were true to the Bible. This answer did not please Presbytery, and
he was asked if he would support the boards regardless of what
they did. When the young man declined to make any such blind
promise, the Presbytery refused to ordain him.

One of his friends remarked that the difference between
modernism and Christianity might be stated thus: In modernism
you believe as you please but do what the officials tell you; in true
Presbyterianism you do as you please so long as you believe what
the Confession says.

As the twentieth century has seen a great increase in the
control that national governments exercise over their citizens, so
too with ecclesiastical organizations there is a trend toward
centralization, bureaucracy, and an indifference toward inalien-
able rights. Well publicized gatherings of Protestant prelates
parade in robes, and the press reports the colorful pageantry.
Impressive imitation of popery! And the same eventual results are
to be expected.

> God alone is Lord of the conscience and hath left it free from
> the doctrines and commandments of men which are in any thing
> contrary to his word, or beside it in matters of faith and worship
> (sec. ii).

The changing majorities of a Council or General Assembly
which push a conjectural translation of the Bible one year and
another year issue Sunday School lessons whose conjectures are

still worse, may boast that their theology is not static but dynamic. A different doctrine every decade—while the orthodox fuddy-duddies keep on believing the same thing all the time!

But what moral chaos there is, when the law of God is abandoned for the latest style of unbelief. It used to be [Albrecht] Ritschl's value judgments; now it is paradox; next it will be—who can guess?

The law of God is stable because God is unchangeable. Those who believe God do not need to change their moral principles with the passing years. Nor will they change their worship, push the Bible to one side, put an altar in the center, pray to the saints and the Virgin, nor as the last article recounted, engage a troupe of ballet dancers to fill an empty pulpit.

---

*The Southern Presbyterian Journal*, February 16, 1955.

# 10

# The Civil Magistrate

Godless people outside the Church of Christ, if by chance and by mistake they ever should read the previous articles on effectual calling, saving faith, assurance, and so on, would consider the topics trivial, or even nonsense, and the reading tedious. But in this age few of them would dismiss the problems of civil government as unimportant. When Dictator [Francisco] Franco [of Spain] and the Roman church attempt to force American military and civilian personnel to beg permission of a Roman bishop in order to marry one another, even a full fledged secularist develops an interest in the relation of church to state. Many non-Christians are also interested in the moral problem of war and pacifism. On these two subjects the Westminster Confession has something to say.

Any conclusion relative to church and state, war and peace, and capital punishment depends on some theory of the nature of civil authority. By what right does a government exist? Those who reject divine revelation base the state either on naked power and brutality, or on some sort of social contract, or on a natural development from the family. Elsewhere I have argued in detail that the latter two reduce to the first; with the result that secularism eventuates in dictatorship and totalitarian rule. It is only in the Hebrew-Christian revelation, *e.g.* in the account of King Ahab and Naboth's vineyard, that the rightful power of government is limited.

"God, the supreme Lord and King of all the world, hath ordained civil magistrates to be under him over the people, for his own glory and the public good; and to this end, hath armed them with the power of the sword, for the defense and encouragement of them that are good, and for the punishment of evil doers" (sec. 1).

Here the [Westminster] Confession, summarizing the Biblical position, gives the origin of the state and settles the discussion on pacifism and capital punishment. Even Christian pacifists, who in spite of their lovely character, we believe to have misunderstood the Bible, do not claim that the Old Testament forbids all war. But neither does the New Testament. Christ said, "Render unto Caesar the things that are Caesar's." Christ knew that Caesar had an army; he did not refuse to pay taxes to Rome on the ground that some of the tribute would be used to support that army. Yet in the United States today some people think it a Christian duty to refuse to follow Christ's teaching and example. They would rather go to jail than to pay one penny to support the military. Of course, in Christ's statement war is not explicitly mentioned—it is an inference, howbeit a justifiable inference, we believe. But the New Testament provides more than an inference. In Romans 13:4 the power of the sword is explicitly assigned to civil government. This disposes of pacifism and the objection to capital punishment. If the courts and the juries of our land were not so adverse to capital punishment, it is likely that brutal crimes would be fewer; and if the relatively juster governments of the west had been willing to wage war against international criminals, the lives of twenty million Chinese, Koreans, and Russians might have been saved. And the United States would have been in a much safer position today.

The relation of church to state is another lively issue at the present time. Where the Roman church controls the government, Protestants suffer oppression and physical persecution. Their churches are bombed and their ministers are murdered. The Greek church, a part of the World Council, has caused the arrest and is prosecuting two Protestants for distributing New Testaments. In our own land the Romanists are constantly attempting to divert public funds to their own purposes. A while back they were advocating an ambassador to the Vatican, and will probably push it again when they see an opportunity. In New Mexico, that is, in the United States, Protestant Indians have been denied by court order the right to hold Protestant prayer meetings even in their own homes (*United Evangelical Action*, February 1, 1954, p. 18). And bills have been introduced into Congress to honor the Virgin Mary by issuing commemorative stamps for the Marian year.

Unfortunately there are also Protestants who want a close tie-in of church and state. Some of the large denominations support lobbies for socialistic legislation. But what is worse, there are those who want the state to define the articles of religion. For example, the North Rocky Mount Baptist church, in North Carolina, by majority vote, withdrew from the Southern Baptist Convention. As to the issues involved and the wisdom of their withdrawal, I have nothing to say. It is their legal right to withdraw that is the important point. The minority went to court and the court awarded them the property. The judge claimed that he did not rule on religious beliefs. But the court defined what a *Church* is, and held that a Baptist church could not withdraw from the Convention and be independent. Now, certainly, the definition of the Church is a religious belief on which denominations differ. The Baptists, contrary to the Presbyterians, have always held to independency and have claimed that there is no ecclesiastical authority superior to the local congregation. But the news reports say that the North Carolina supreme court has made it illegal for Baptists to conduct their affairs in accordance with Baptist doctrine. In spite of the fact that the minority has won a legal case in favor of the Southern Baptist Convention, we wonder whether the Convention in good conscience can accept the verdict. Will they insist on retaining the local property at the cost of having their beliefs on the nature of the Church settled by the civil government?

It is also interesting to note that the socialistic *Christian Century* hails the decision of the court. This radical periodical wants uniformity and ecumenicity enforced by civil decree when possible. The ecumaniacs generally favor centralization of power; they want to control property; they do not object to state churches, or even to the Greek persecution of evangelicals. It would seem that the combination of church and state is a last remnant of Romanism that proves hard to part with.

---

*The Southern Presbyterian Journal,* March 30, 1955.

# 11

# Concerning Free Will

Not so long ago I attended an evangelistic service in which the evangelist introduced his prayer by a five minute talk on free will. God offers us salvation, he said, but God cannot make us accept it. The will of man is inviolable; it is free from God. Now that God has made us the offer, all that he can do is to sit back and wait and see who wills to accept it.

The evangelist thought he was preaching the Christian gospel. What is more, the great majority of the thousands of people who were listening to him doubtless thought so too. In their minds, a denial of free will would be tantamount to a denial of Christianity. They could hardly imagine the possibility of a real Christian objecting to free will. They rather clearly were ignorant that Protestantism began by denying free will. They were unaware that they had receded from the doctrines of the Reformation and had taken long steps backward to the theology of Romanism. Such is the ignorance of our day.

Therefore a series of quotations will be offered, quotations from Luther, Calvin, and others, to show what historic Protestantism really is.

The following quotations from Luther's *Bondage of the Will* are taken from the translation of Henry Cole in the Sovereign Grace Union edition, published in the United States by Wm. B. Eerdmans in 1931.

God foreknows nothing by contingency. He foresees purposes, and does all things according to his immutable, eternal, and infallible will. By this thunderbolt free will is thrown prostrate and utterly dashed to pieces. Are you not the person, friend Erasmus, who just now asserted that God is by nature just and by nature most merciful? If this be true, does it not follow that He is *immutably* just and merciful? That as his nature is not changed to all eternity, so neither his justice nor his mercy? And what is said concerning his justice and mercy, must be said also concerning his knowledge, his wisdom, his goodness, his will, and his other attributes. If therefore these things are asserted religiously, piously, and wholesomely concerning God, as you say yourself, what has come to you that, contrary to your own self, you now assert that it is irreligious, curious, and vain to say that God foreknows of necessity? Do you believe that He foreknows against his will, or that He wills in ignorance? From which it follows unalterably that all things which we do, although they may appear to us to be done mutably and contingently, and even may be done contingently by us, are yet in reality done necessarily and immutably with respect to the will of God. For the will of God is effective and cannot be hindered (pp. 38-39).

As to that other paradox you mention—that "Whatever is done by us is not done by free will but from mere necessity." [This was Erasmus's objection to Luther.] Here then I observe that if it be proved that our salvation is apart from our own strength and counsel and depends on the working of God alone, . . . does it not evidently follow that when God is not present with us to work in us, everything that we do is evil and that we of necessity do those things which are of no avail unto salvation? But of *necessity* I do not mean compulsion, but, as they term it, the necessity of immutability, not of compulsion: that is, a man void of the Spirit of God does not evil against his will as by violence, or as if he were taken by the neck and forced to it in the same way that a thief or a cut-throat is dragged to punishment against his will; but he does it spontaneously and with a desirous willingness. And this willingness and desire of doing evil he cannot by his own power leave off, restrain, or change; but it still goes on desiring and craving. And even if he should be compelled by force to anything [good] outwardly to the contrary, yet the craving will [to evil] within remains averse to and rises in indignation against that which forces or resists it. This is what we mean by the necessity of immutability—that the will cannot change itself, nor give itself another bent. . . . This would not be the case if it were free (pp. 72-73).

The third passage [which Erasmus uses against Luther] is from Moses, Deuteronomy 30:19, "I have set before thy face life and death, choose what is good."

"What words," says the Diatribe, "can be more plain? It leaves a man the liberty of choosing." I answer, What is more plain than that you are blind? How, I pray, does it leave the liberty of choosing? Is it by the expression "choose"? Therefore as Moses saith "choose," does it immediately come to pass that they do choose? Then there is no need of the Spirit. . . . [Erasmus says] "It would be ridiculous to say to a man standing in a place where two ways meet, Thou seest two roads, go by which thou wilt; when only one was open." This, as I [Luther] have observed before, is from the arguments of human reason, which thinks that a man is mocked by a command impossible: whereas I say that the man by this means is admonished and roused to see his own impotency. True it is that we are in a place where two ways meet, and that one of them only is open, yea rather neither of them is open. But by the law it is shown how impossible the one [way] is, that is, to good, unless God freely give us His Spirit, and how wide and easy the other [way] is, if God leave us to ourselves. . . . Wherefore the words of the law are spoken, not that they might assert the power of the will, but that they might illuminate the blindness of reason, that it might see that its own light is nothing and that the power of the will is nothing. . . . Man by the words of the law is admonished and taught what *he ought to do,* not what *he can do;* that is, that he is brought to know his sin, but not to believe that he has any strength in himself (pp. 153-154).

The Diatribe is perpetually setting before us such a man who either *can do* what is commanded, or at least *knows* that he *cannot do* it. Whereas no such man is to be found. If there were such an one,

then indeed either impossibilities would be ridiculously commanded, or the Spirit of Christ would be in vain. The Scripture,
however, sets forth such a man who is not only bound, miserable,
captive, sick, and dead, but who by the operations of his lord, Satan,
to his other miseries, adds that of blindness: so that he believes he is
free, happy, at liberty, powerful, whole, and alive. For Satan well
knows that if men knew their own misery, he could retain no one of
them in his kingdom. . . . But the work of Moses the legislator is the
contrary, even that by the law he might discover to man his misery.
. . . Therefore the office of the law is not ridiculous, but above all
things serious and necessary (p. 159).

Look then first at that of Jeremiah and Malachi, "If thou wilt
turn, then will I turn thee;" and "turn ye unto me and I will turn
unto you." Does it then follow from "turn ye" therefore, ye are able
to turn? Does it follow also from "Love the Lord thy God with all
thy heart" therefore, thou art able to love with all the heart? If these
arguments stand good, what do they conclude but that free will
needs not the grace of God, but can do all things of its own power?
(p. 162).

So much then for Luther. His complete argument may be read
in his excellent book, *The Bondage of the Will.* These quotations
are merely a witness to what he preached.

No one will be surprised to learn that Calvin rejected the
theory of free will. The following confirmation is not a verbatim
and consecutive quotation: While largely in Calvin's words, it is
only a broken summary of part of his *Institutes.*

The early fathers extolled human power, partly from fear of
incurring the derision of the philosophers, but principally to avoid
encouraging slothfulness. Chrysostom said, "God has placed good
and evil things in our power; he has give us freedom of choice; and
he does not constrain the unwilling, but embraces the willing. . . .
God has given us naturally a free will and imposes no necessity
upon us . . . but permits the event to depend entirely on the mind of
the patient." Succeeding writers, ambitious of fame, fell into opinions still more erroneous. The Latins have always retained the term
*free will,* as though man still remained in his primitive integrity.
The Greeks use an expression much more arrogant, *autexousion,*
denoting that man possesses sovereign power over himself (II, ii, 4).

When writers treat of free will, their first inquiry respects its power to obey the divine law (II, ii, 5).

Who, when they hear free will attributed to man, do not immediately conceive that he has the sovereignty over his own mind and will and is able by his innate power to incline himself to whatever he pleases? (II, ii, 7).

Augustine plainly confesses that the will is not free, since it is subject to lust, and cannot be free until liberated by divine grace (II, ii, 8).

The will therefore is so bound by the slavery of sin that it cannot excite itself, much less devote itself to anything good. If a necessity of doing well does not impair the liberty of the divine will, and if the devil, who cannot but do evil, nevertheless sins voluntarily, who will assert that man sins less voluntarily because he is under a necessity of sinning? (II, iii, 5).

I deny then that sin is the less criminal because it is necessary; I also deny that it is avoidable because it is voluntary. Similarly the wills of the elect angels, though they cannot swerve from good, are still wills. Those who defend free will make an improper transition from what is voluntary to what is free. These two are not the same (II, v, 1).

Through these chapters Calvin continues with long analyses of the fallacious arguments of his opponents and with frequent exegesis of the Scripture.

Jerome Zanchius was born in Italy on February 2, 1516, just a year before Luther nailed his ninety-five theses to the church door at Wittenberg. Left an orphan at twelve, he became a monk. It was largely the work of Peter Martyr that turned Zanchius's attention to the evangelical faith. While teaching in Strasbourg (1553-1562), he wrote his treatise on *Absolute Predestination,* from which the following quotations are taken. After some five years in the pastorate, he became Professor of Theology at Heidelberg, a stronghold of the Reformed faith. There he published some books on the Trinity. After ten years he resigned his professorship and became pastor at Neustadt for seven years. Old age then forced him into retirement, and he died November 19, 1590. The pagination of the following quotations is that of the edition of the Sovereign Grace Book Club.

This made Augustine say, "Evil men do many things contrary to God's revealed will, but so great is His wisdom and so inviolable His truth that He directs all things into those channels which He foreknew." And again, "No free will of the creature can resist the will of God, for man cannot so will or nill as to obstruct the Divine determination or overcome the Divine power." Once more, "It cannot be questioned but God does all things, and ever did, according to His own purpose: The human will cannot resist Him so as to make Him do more or less than it is His pleasure to do; since He does what He pleases even with wills of men" (p. 29).

After quoting Luther, Zanchius adds:

Exactly consonant to all which, are those words of Luther's friend and fellow-laborer, Melancthon, "All things turn out according to Divine predestination, not only the works we do outwardly, but even the thoughts we think inwardly," adding in the same place, "There is no such thing as chance or fortune, nor is there a readier way to gain the fear of God and to put our whole trust in Him, than to be thoroughly versed in the doctrine of predestination" (pp. 36-37).

We assert that the decrees of God are not only immutable as to himself, it being inconsistent with His nature to alter in His purposes or change His mind; but that they are immutable also with respect to the objects of those decrees, so that whatsoever God hath determined concerning every individual person and thing shall surely and infallibly be accomplished in and upon them. Hence we find that He actually showeth mercy on whom He decreed to show mercy and hardeneth whom He resolved to harden (Romans 9:18); "For His counsel shall stand, and He will do all His pleasure" (Isaiah 46:10). Consequently His eternal predestination of men and things must be immutable as Himself, and so far from being reversible, can never admit of the least variation (p. 41).

Predestination is to be preached because the *grace* of God (which stands opposed to all human worthiness) cannot be maintained without it. . . . Thus argued St. Augustine against the Pelagians, who taught that grace is offered to all men alike, that God for His part equally wills the salvation of all, and that it is in the power of man's free-will to accept or reject the grace and salvation so offered. Which string of errors do, as Augustine justly observes, center in this grand point: that God's grace is not free but the fruit of man's desert. Now the doctrine of predestination batters down this delusive Babel of free-will and merit. It teaches us that, if we do indeed will and desire to lay hold on Christ and salvation by Him, this will and desire are the effect of God's secret purpose and effectual operation, for *he* it is who worketh in us both to will and to do of his own good pleasure, that he that glorieth should glory in the Lord. There neither is nor can be any medium between predestinating grace and salvation by human merit (pp. 117-118).

Another witness to the original position of Protestantism is John Gill (1697-1771), a Baptist minister. *The Cause of God and Truth* (the work now to be quoted, the edition of the Sovereign Grace Book Club) begins with a detailed explanation of over 250 verses that are sometimes urged against Calvinism. Then there follows a series of connected articles on Reprobation, Election, Efficacious Grace, the Freedom of the Will, and so on. These studies go into great detail, and while they repay careful reading, they do not permit felicitous excerpts. To use them as a witness of the theology of the Reformation, several sentences will be strung together from the discussion on the "Freedom of the Will" (pp. 185-198). The passage in which Gill compares Stoicism and Calvinism will be chosen (p. 191ff.), and though the argument will not appear in its complete form, there is enough to indicate Gill's position.

It is said that our opinion differs very little, and in things only of little moment, from the stoical fate; and lies obnoxious to the same absurdities which the philosophers and Christians did object against it.

To which I reply; that of all the sects of the ancient philosophers, the stoics come nearest to the Christian religion has been observed by many; and that not only with respect to their strict regard to moral virtue, but also on the account of principles and doctrines; in so much as Jerome affirms that in most things they agree with us. . . . Certain it is that several of the first Christian writers were either of this sect, or much inclined to it, and greatly favored it, as Pantaenus, Clemens Alexdrinus, Tertullian, Arnobius, and others. . . . And should it appear that we agree with them in the doctrine of God's decrees, I know of no other consequence that will follow upon it but this, that our doctrine is consonant with the light of nature and far from being repugnant to the natural reason of mankind. . . . It must be allowed that there are some things said by them which have an affinity with some tenets of ours; as,

When they say that fate is God himself, to whom all things are subject and by whom they are all determined, ordered and directed as he pleases. . . . And, says Seneca, who was one of the best writers among them, "If you call God fate, you will not be mistaken, since fate is nothing else but an implicated series of causes, and he is the first cause of all on which the rest depends." . . . Now, setting aside the language in which these things are expressed (for some pagan gods had been mentioned) there is nothing but what is agreeable to our sentiments, namely, that God is he who has fixed and determined all things, in their own order, place and time, according to his good will and pleasure; and that God's decree is God himself decreeing: and therefore we also agree with them, when

They represent fate as no other than the will, purpose, and decree of God. . . . To this nothing can be excepted, but the use of the word fate. . . . And so the great Augustine allows the same thing, though he denies the name: "human governments are entirely constituted by Divine Providence," says he, "which if therefore any one will ascribe to fate, because he call the will or power of God by that name, let him hold his opinion, but correct his language."

Some of them were very careful to preserve the natural liberty of the will of man, as we are. Chrysippus, one of the principal among them, was of opinion that "the mind was free from the necessity of motion." . . . We deny any such influence of the stars which work by a necessity of nature upon the wills and actions of men.

God is a most free agent, and liberty in him is in its utmost perfection, and yet does not lie in indifference to good and evil; he has no freedom to that which is evil; he cannot commit iniquity, he cannot lie, or deny himself; his will is determined only to that which is good; he can do no other; he is the author of all good, and of that only; and what he does, he does freely, and yet necessarily. . . . The human nature of Christ, or the man Christ Jesus, who, as he was born without sin, and lived without it all his days on earth, so was impeccable, could not sin. He lay under some kind of necessity, from the purpose of God . . . to fulfil all righteousness; and yet he did it most freely and voluntarily. . . . The devils and damned spirits have no inclination to nor capacity of doing that which is good, but are wholly determined to that which is evil, and yet do all they do freely and voluntarily. . . . The liberty of the will of man, in evey state he has been, is, or shall be, lies not in an indifference to good and evil. In his state of innocence, as he was made after the image and in the likeness of God, so the bias of his soul was only to that which is good, which he performed willingly in obedience to the will of God. . . . In his regenerate state, there is, indeed, an inclination both to good and evil; but this arises from two different principles in the regenerate man. The new man, or principle of grace, is inclined, bent, and determined to that which is good only; and yet freely serves the law of sin. In the state of glorification, the saints will be impeccable, cannot sin, can only do that which is good; . . . whence it follows, that the liberty of man's will does not lie in an indifference or indetermination to good or evil; but is consistent with some kind of necessity, and a determination to one.

If liberty is not consistent with necessity in any sense, then it is not consistent with the decrees of God, nor even with the foreknowledge of God. . . . For if there is not a necessity of things coming to pass, which are foreknown and decreed by God, then his foreknowledge is uncertain, and is but mere supposition and conjecture, and his decrees must be frustrable and precarious. It is said that this was of old the chief argument of the fatalists, espoused of late by Mr. Hobbes, and is still made the refuge of the predestinarians. Be it so; if the fatalists and Mr. Hobbes meant no more by necessity than we do, namely, a necessity of the immutability and unfrustrableness of God's foreknowledge and decrees, and not of coaction or force upon the will of man; we have no reason to be ashamed of the argument they made use of; and instead of making it a refuge or mere shift, shall think ourselves obliged to defend it, and abide by it.

These excerpts from John Gill do not do justice to his argument. He does not agree so fully with the Stoics as some of these expressions might lead one to believe; nor is it necessary to maintain that he always had a correct view of Stoicism. The purpose of the excerpts is to show that he defended a natural liberty of the will against "co-action," that is, against a physico-chemical behaviorism. Natural liberty is not the liberty of indifference, nor is it inconsistent with necessity. Man wills; man acts voluntarily; but what he wills and when he wills is predetermined by the eternal and "unfrustrable" decree of God.

Augustus M. Toplady, the author of that great hymn, *Rock of Ages,* preached a sermon on May 25, 1774 against free will. It is to be found in his *Complete Works,* edition of 1869, on pages 352ff. Here the following footnote is printed:

> I was lately introduced to the acquaintance of a very learned and sensible Arminian, whose political writings and whose social virtues entitle him to no small share of public and domestic esteem. This worthy gentleman has sagacity to perceive and integrity to acknowledge the prodigious lengths to which the free will scheme if carried as far as it naturally leads, must inevitably push its votaries. He sees its consequences clearly; he swallows them without difficulty; and he avows them very honestly. "God does all he possibly can"—these were the gentleman's own words to me in conversation—"God does all he possibly can to hinder moral and natural evil, but he cannot prevail. Man will not permit God to have his wish." Then, said I, the Deity must certainly be a very unhappy being. "Not unhappy in the least," replied the ready philosopher. "God knows that in consequence of free will with which he has endued his rational creatures, he himself must be disappointed of his wishes and defeated of his ends, and that there is no help for it, unless he had made us mere machines. He therefore submits to necessity and does not make himself uneasy about it." See, on what tremendous shoals free willers, when honest, run themselves aground? Is their God the Bible God? Certainly not. Their god "submits" to difficulties which he "cannot help" himself out of, and endeavors to make himself "easy" under millions and millions of inextricable embarrassments, uncomfortable disappointments, and mortifying defeats. Whereas, concerning the God of the Bible, it is affirmed that he hath done, and will always continue to do, whatsoever he pleaseth.

It is a matter of deep regret that so little is here quoted from Augustus Toplady. It is a matter of deeper regret that his extensive works are so little read and known in our present age. His complete works run 915 pages of fine print in double columns. Much of it, and in a sense all of it, opposes the doctrine of the freedom of the will and magnifies the irresistible grace of the Almighty God.

This set of quotations does not fully explain the doctrines

alluded to. The purpose has been to present a witness to the theology of the Reformation. Perhaps some readers will be interested enough to examine the books from which these selections have been taken. The further the discussion is followed, the clearer the whole doctrine will become.

At any rate, one will soon learn that God is not so impotent as to have to sit back, after offering the gospel, and wait and see who will accept it. It will be clear that the Holy Spirit operates on the will of man, changes his likes and dislikes, takes away his heart of stone and gives him a heart of flesh, in fact gives him faith. God does not sit back and do nothing: he regenerates—he controls man's will. Such is the gospel; the other view is not.

As the Psalmist said, "Blessed is the man whom thou choosest and causest to approach unto thee" (Psalm 65:4). God *causes* men to turn to him. No one else can.

---

*The Reformed Presbyterian Advocate*, August-September 1961.

# 12

# Determinism

Determinism has many forms. The three most important are physical, logical, and theological.

Physical determinism or mechanism is most popularly associated with the term. Democritus in antiquity, Spinoza, Kant, La Place, and generally nineteenth century science, followed by behaviorism in the twentieth, hold that all motions, including the motions of human bodies, can be described by differential equations. Kant, who permitted freedom in the noumenal world, asserted clearly that men in the visible world, following their inclinations, are in no way free. Since the determinism is strictly mathematical, no statement of purpose is possible. Spinoza added, though this is not generally true of mechanists, that what does not happen is logically impossible.

The second form is logical determinism, of which the ancient

Stoics and the nineteenth century Hegelians were separate examples. They were not mechanists; they allowed for purpose; and therefore they might be called rational or teleological determinists. The universal Logos controls all that happens, or Absolute Reason unfolds itself in history. Whatever happens, must happen; and, more consistently than in Spinoza, what does not happen is logically impossible. The Stoics added their theory of eternal recurrence.

The Stoics also stressed ethics and held that the good life is a life of virtue. Mechanistic determinism may make morality meaningless (though Spinoza's great work bears the title of *Ethics*), but teleological determinism can be strongly ethical. Since too the Stoic Logos is God, this provides a transition to the third form of determinism, theological determinism; *i.e.,* God foreordains whatsoever comes to pass. Note here that Josephus (*Antiquities of the Jews,* XVIII, i, 3) reports that while the loose-living Sadducees believed in free will, the meticulous Pharisees and the strict Essenes were determinists: "The Pharisees . . . live meanly and despise delicacies in diet, and they follow the conduct of reason . . . and when they determine that all things are done by fate, they do not take away the freedom from men of acting as they think fit; since their notion is that it has pleased God to make a temperament whereby what he wills is done, but so that the will of man can act virtuously or viciously."

Romanism holds to free will, and Erasmus made this his main point against Luther, who replied in his masterpiece *The Bondage of the Will.* Melanchthon in this as in many other points repudiated Luther. Calvin, Knox, the Irish Articles of Religion, the Westminster Confession, and the Reformed position as a whole was thoroughly deterministic. Arminius in the early seventeenth century repudiated the Reformed faith and took a step backward toward Romanism.

---

*Baker's Dictionary of Christian Ethics,* Carl F.H. Henry, editor. Grand Rapids, Michigan: Baker Book House, 1973, pp. 177-178.

# 13

# Determinism and Responsibility

Unless one has been recently disgusted by a surfeit of discussion on this sometimes barren topic, a religious thinker will almost invariably be carried away into a heated argument. This is better than to denominate the question barren, for such an attitude is agnostic, and to be disgusted is merely to be exhausted. Every Christian must face this problem squarely, and especially must the Calvinist so do, since he believes that much of the learned disrespect of Christianity is owing to the loose thinking of Catholics and Arminians.

Yet for fear someone may expect too much from a paper with such a comprehensive title, it is necessary strictly to state the scope of this article. First of all it is not a discussion of the freedom of the will such as is found in Jonathan Edwards's well-known work. The arguments of that great man concern many details which, however important and interesting, may be omitted from the present subject. Naturally there is some overlapping but the direction of search is different. The investigation of innumerable intricacies runs the risk of losing all sense of proportion, of becoming entangled in a puzzling maze, and so requires an exceptionally great mind such as Edwards's was. The direction of search here, on the contrary, will be away from intricacies toward very general outlines and thus must run the risk of being superficial. Nevertheless it has seemed worth the risk. Now to state exactly the scope of the matter: Recently in books and magazines[1] of varying intellectual value there have appeared, in defence of historic Christianity as opposed to modern wanderings, attacks on "mechanistic psychology," "determinism in all its forms," and

---

1. For example, *The Defender*, which is aggressively but not very profoundly fundamental, and *Christian Faith and Life*, an equally aggressive magazine but somewhat more scholarly. The editor of the latter, Harold Paul Sloan, who has done notable practical work in his own denomination, frequently attacks the Calvinistic position. See also the confusion resulting on a non-Calvinistic view in the recent book by J. Paterson Smyth, *Myself and Other Problems*. The confusion is acute in the chapter, "Love of God and Doctrine of Hell."

other phrases of similar import. This writer fears that however much one may hold to the cardinal points of orthodoxy, it is not always clear which philosophic theories are or are not consistent with such orthodoxy. One would think that only a shallow magazine would indiscriminately condemn all forms of determinism; there might be more excuse for an attack on mechanistic psychology. The aim of this article is, then, to show that determinism is consistent with responsibility, indeed responsibility requires determinism.

The arguments on both sides are fairly well known. They so lack originality as to discourage new attempts, including this one. The determinist position is stated as well as anywhere in an article by George Stuart Fullerton, entitled "Freedom and Free Will."[2] His aim was to show that on the basis of indeterminism moral conduct in general, in so far as free or indeterminate, would lose all ethical value. The indeterminist holds that certain actions are not adequately explained, *i.e.* determined by preceding causes. Then, if benevolence, for example, is a free action, it is not determined by a benevolent personality but happens causelessly. If the will were free absolutely, then a knowledge of one's own respectable character in the past brings neither hope nor consolation. Ordinarily we consider character a determining factor, and a moral man does not become immoral except for some other determining factor. But free will allows a man to become a criminal for no reason at all. Fullerton's illustration was little Tommy who stole his mother's jam. Punishment will not prevent a recurrence of the invasion of the pantry, neither will persuasion of a gentler sort. These can have no determining power on free actions. But on a deterministic theory, punishment, persuasion and praise are all justified. "It seems, then, that Tommy's mother, and his aunts and all his spiritual pastors and masters have for years approached Tommy upon a strictly deterministic basis. They have thought it worth while to talk, and to talk a great deal. They have done what all pedagogues do—they have adjusted means to ends and have looked for results, taking no account of freedom at all."

---

2. Published December 1900, in *Popular Science Monthly.*

On the other hand, if there is no responsibility for the free-willist, is there any for the determinist? This paper aims to harmonize determinism and responsibility on the basis of Calvinistic Christianity. And if it has not been done before, the reason is that the Calvinists of today are but half-hearted followers of the prince of the theologians, John Calvin.

If we must pass by many of the details in discussions on free will, it is all the more needful to avoid embarking on the general subject of theism. Although it is the necessary foundation of the view to be explained, no one could reasonably expect it to be treated here, even in brief. We might be permitted to suggest, however, that one reason, even if only confirmatory, for assuming the being of God is precisely the more unified world which results from applying the conception of sovereignty to such problems as these.

To recall the discussion to the title of the paper and to make the present position more intelligible even if by contrast, one passage from an ancient author relative to sovereignty and omnipotence serves admirably well. Plato, in the second book of the *Republic,* says, "God, inasmuch as he is good, cannot be the cause of all things. . . . On the contrary, he is the author of only a small part of human affairs; of the larger part he is not the author: For our evil things far outnumber our good things: and the good things we must ascribe to no other than God, while we must seek elsewhere, and not in him, the causes of the evil things."[3] And as Plato here denies God's omnipotence, denies that he is the first cause of all, so Aristotle denies his omniscience.

It might now be well to turn from antiquity to some contemporary literature, not because the more recent is either better or more original than the old but because these are the living defenders of what we attack.

Dr. Arthur Holmes's *The Mind of St. Paul* provides a typical paragraph. This work is partly a description of Paul's emotional nature, partly a criticism of various psychological explanations of Paul's conversion. Theories of the subconscious or unconscious and theories of multiple personality occupy a good portion of the

---

3. P. 379 (Davies's and Vaughan's translation).

chapters. While the book as a whole does not bear on the present subject, Dr. Holmes feels called upon briefly to mention freedom and responsibility. The paragraph presents a very familiar view.

> St. Paul's system of morality avoids many pitfalls of man-made systems of ethics, but it does not eliminate one of the great problems involved in all morality and religion. This is the problem of freedom, the power of man to choose anything whatsoever. Such a liberty has been denied by predestinarian theologians and mechanistic scientists. Both contend that man's seeming freedom is illusory. Neither theory is based upon observed facts, but deduced from previous theories—the first, from the absolute sovereignty of an omnipotent God, the second from the assumed power of inductive science to predict the occurrence of future events. On the other hand, the common sense of mankind, bent on preserving the moral responsibility of men, has always favoured at least a freedom to choose between good and bad on man's part. St. Paul went thus far and no farther. He never changed from his position in this matter from the doctrine of the Pharisees (Rom. ix. 14-18, 23). He seems clearly enough to insist upon the sovereignty of God and His perfect freedom to mould men as He will. Yet, at the same time men appear free to choose both ends and means, and the Evangelist exhorts men and women to do so without a single hint that they are unable to make such choices. In all probability he would have indignantly denied the modern doctrine of determinism or physical necessity.[4]

Before quoting a second contemporary, it is well to note and emphasize that the reason—and has anyone found any other really basic reason?—for introducing the concept of freedom, either in its most extreme form of power of contrary choice or in some more modified form, is to hold man morally responsible. Could it be shown that man's responsibility does not necessarily depend upon freedom, theology would be freed from an annoying problem. Well can we imagine the groanings which cannot be uttered if generations of young theologues were to be summoned before us to describe the tortures they endured in trying to reconcile God's omniscience with free will. The Presbyterian and Reformed

---

4. Pp. 255-256.

churches do not believe in free will. They substitute the concept of free agency, meaning that a man is a free moral agent when he acts in conformity with his own nature. Even so, some have stated[5] that the reconciliation of man's free agency and God's sovereignty is an inscrutable mystery. Rather the mystery is—recognizing that God is the ultimate cause of man's nature—how the Calvinistic solution could have been so long overlooked.

But before making the solution explicit, permit a final word from the opponents. Miss Harkness, Professor of Philosophy in Elmira College, in *Conflict in Religious Thought*, offers the following:

> Throughout the whole history of philosophy and theology people have wrangled over the question of free will. In general, the idealistic philosophies have asserted that the human spirit must be in some sense free, while materialistic philosophies have denied this freedom. Theology has clung tenaciously to the belief that man is a "free moral agent" while at the same time often asserting a doctrine of predestination which, taken at its face value, would rigidly circumscribe man's acts. The problem, though complex, is too fundamental to be dodged.
>
> We have seen that the possibility of moral or immoral action depends upon the power of choice. If all one's acts are set and predetermined (either by the structure of the material world or by the will of God) in such fashion that it is impossible to act other than one does, quite obviously freedom disappears. With the power of voluntary choice goes moral responsibility. One cannot consciously choose to be good, nor choose to seek after God, unless he has the power to choose not to do so. No moral quality attaches to my failure to steal the million dollars that is outside my reach, but stealing becomes a moral question with me when I have to decide whether to tell the store clerk he has given me too much change. Likewise if I am "foreordained" to be saved or damned there is not much use of my doing anything about my fate. If I have no freedom, I am not responsible for my acts.
>
> Theological determinism, or predestination, is a cardinal

_____

5. In the *Brief Statement of the Reformed Faith* of the Presbyterian Church in the U.S.A., 1902; compare Charles Hodge, *Systematic Theology*, Vol. II, pp. 251-252; also the four questions A.H. Strong cannot answer, *Systematic Theology*, I, p. 366.

doctrine of Mohammedanism. Islam means "submission" (to the will of Allah—and a Moslem is "one who submits"—to the fatalistic decrees of an arbitrary deity. Christian theology in its earlier forms regarded God as equally peremptory (though more ethical) in His decrees. Through the influence of illustrious Christian theologians, notably Paul, Augustine and Calvin, the doctrine of predestination has profoundly influenced Christian thinking. While God's omnipotence has thus been emphasized, God's freedom has been exalted at the expense of man's, and the most inhuman acts have been glossed over as arising from the will of God. But happily the doctrine of predestination is disappearing, at least in its application to evils that are obviously preventable.

Some still hold that when the typhoid victim dies from lack of proper sanitation, it happened because it was "to be." There is a good deal of illogical comfort in such a view. But not many, even of the most rigorous of Calvinists, would now say that if a man gets drunk and shoots his family, it is the will of God that he should do so![6]

While forced to smile a bit as authors permit their animosities to give rise to disparaging circumlocutions instead of appropriate argument, one must confess to being a little irritated at insinuendo. Whether absolute predestination is happily being forgotten or not is quite irrelevant. The present question is, Can predestination and determinism be reconciled with and made the basis of moral distinctions and human responsibility? Miss Harkness thinks not.

First of all, she claims moral action requires choice and choice requires the ability to have done otherwise. This is the first thing to be denied. Choice is that mental act, that deliberate volition—I do not intend a comprehensive definition—which initiates a human action. The ability to have chosen otherwise is an irrelevant consideration[7] and has no place in the definition. It is still a deliberate volition even if it could not have been different.

---

6. Pp. 233-234.

7. All that is required to define choice or volition is that necessary and sufficient combination of factors which distinguishes it from other psychological functions. The statement of Charles Hodge, *op. cit.*, p. 285, will then be seen to be an invalid inference, for a necessary volition is as much a volition as an unnecessary one.

True we are not always conscious of our limitation. Those who appeal to the consciousness of freedom and consider that such appeal closes the issue rely on cherry or apple pie as illustrations. If illustrations be necessary we can refer to Luther's sentiments: "Here I stand, so help me God, I can do no other." The more important the decision, the less power of contrary choice we feel, and I venture to suppose that Luther's is a fairly common experience with serious, responsible persons.

But is there nothing in Kant's dictum, If I ought, I can? As stated by Kant and the Catholics it leads immediately to salvation by works. The motive which prompted this incorrect principle can, however, be better stated and so save what of truth it contains. If all ought, at least one can. If all ought to be honest, then some can and are. If all ought perfectly to satisfy divine justice, at least One has done so. At any rate we must remember that choice must be defined as a psychological function, distinct from desire or judgment for example, and nowhere in the definition can be found a place for the power to have chosen differently.

Likewise, Miss Harkness states, "if I am foreordained to be saved or damned there is not much use of my doing anything about my fate." It is strange that anyone but a novice should use this so-called "lazy argument" after the Stoics so long ago showed its fallaciousness. It is of use to do something precisely because it is the means to something else. The Mohammedan or fatalistic idea that the end is fixed independently of the means is but a caricature of Calvinism sometimes maliciously used. The end is foreordained to arrive by means of the means, and to attain the end is the value of the means. But at any rate she well illustrates that the motive for asserting man's freedom is responsibility.

After relegating theological determinism to a benighted past, Miss Harkness dismisses mechanical or scientific determinism in a footnote on the quantum theory. This is mentioned here solely to point out that Calvinistic determinism may or may not be mechanical. The rationality of the mechanical ideal is aside from the present purpose. Theological determinism neither requires nor excludes it. All one needs to maintain is that every event is determined to occur as it does and cannot be otherwise. God has foreordained whatsoever comes to pass.

The author last quoted seems in a previous page to have missed the main point. Discussing the question, Is God limited? she concludes that omnipotence is not inconsistent with freedom. God may freely limit himself and omnipotently create persons endowed with free wills. This overlooks one essential factor, *viz.* God's omniscience. If God knows what will happen, what he knows will happen will happen and nothing else. Calvinists believe God knows what will happen because he ordained it so. But aside from this, foreknowledge indicates that the future is certain. And if it is not God who made the future certain, we must return to the dualism of Plato. But let it pass; if there be an omniscient God, the future is certain. The professor in Elmira College overlooked the decisive factor.

Now then, if every event is certain, can man be responsible for deeds he could not have escaped doing? Or does determinism make good men "pious little automata" as Miss Harkness says?[8] Again neglecting to notice what is substituted for rational argument, one may very justly reply, it all depends on what is meant by automata, or more precisely, what *responsibility* means.

It seems strange that works on theology usually make no very energetic attempt to define responsibility. But if it is of such importance, one ought not to omit making it as precise as possible. Yet this attempt is noticeably lacking among determinists and free willists alike. Not all true statements are definitional. The Pythagorean theorem states a truth respecting a right triangle but it is not a definition of one. Now Charles Hodge makes certain statements about responsibility, but it is not clear whether he intended them as definitions or merely true statements. For example, "We are responsible for our feelings because they are right or wrong in their own nature."[9] In the next paragraph he makes human nature the ground of responsibility. The following looks more like a definition: "Wherever reason and the power of self-determination or spontaneity are combined in an agent, he is free and responsible for his outward acts and for his volitions."[10]

---

8. *Op. cit.*, p. 206.
9. Vol. II, p. 275, repeated on p. 304.
10. *Ibid.*, p. 286. See also *Princeton Essays* (1st series), on "Power of Contrary Choice," passim.

Definition is no easy task, and an incorrect one may deceive us frightfully. The caution of him who would not admit two plus two equals four until he knew how the admission was to be used is nothing short of exemplary. Yet those who have criticized the position to be offered at most say that the conception of responsibility involved is incomplete or restricted. Perhaps they are right, all that is needed is that the characteristics mentioned are essential elements of the definition. Let us call a man responsible, then, when he may be justly rewarded or punished for his deeds. That is, the man must be answerable to someone, to God, for responsibility implies a superior authority who punishes or rewards. Now since in theology the crux of the matter is in the eternal punishment of some sinners, we may disregard other elements in the definition and emphasize that by calling a man responsible we mean he may be justly punished by God, for this definitional truth is the key to the explanation of why a man is responsible for the act God determined him to do.

More than one person, with caution born of experience, has replied at this point, that although they did not see the trap they could always escape the disagreeable Calvinistic conclusions by clinging to the saving adverb "justly." This of course is just what is desired. For whether the adverb is an escape from Calvinism or the very essence of Calvinism itself depends on the meaning of justice. For by the echoes of Plato's *Republic* we cannot continue until we have seized Justice herself.

This leads to an illustration in the writings of Leibniz, Descartes and Calvin. Leibniz held that this was the best of all possible worlds, thus provoking the remark he must have been a pessimist. He had said that God might have chosen any one of a number of possible worlds, each more or less good, but as a matter of fact God chose the best of them. He expressly denied that this world is best because God chose it. This latter proposition, the world is good because God chose it, was Descartes's opinion.

It is at this point we must refer to and take issue with Jonathan Edwards. While he tries to avoid placing God under commands, he still seems to imply the Platonic dualism by representing God as influenced by inducements.[11] Later, when he comes to our

11. *Freedom of the Will*, I, v.

present subject, he calls the question which divided Descartes and Leibniz absurdity and nonsense.[12]

John Calvin was not of the same opinion. He anticipated Descartes's position, and in the *Institutes* has given the key to the solution:

> In the first place they inquire, by what right the Lord is angry with His creatures who had not provoked Him by any previous offence; for that to devote to destruction whom He pleases is more like the caprice of a tyrant than the lawful sentence of a judge; that men have reason, therefore, to expostulate with God, if they are predestinated to eternal death without any demerit of their own, merely by His sovereign will. If such thoughts ever enter the minds of pious men, they will be sufficiently enabled to break their violence by this one consideration, how exceedingly presumptuous it is only to inquire into the causes of the Divine will; which is in fact, and is justly entitled to be, the cause of every thing that exists. For if it has any cause, then there must be something antecedent, on which it depends; which it is impious to suppose. For the will of God is the highest rule of justice; so that what He wills must be considered just, for this very reason, because He wills it. When it is inquired, therefore, why the Lord did so, the answer must be, because He would. But if you go further, and ask why He so determined, you are in search of something greater and higher than the will of God, which can never be found.[13]

God is Sovereign; whatever he does is just, for this very reason, because he does it. If he punishes a man, the man is punished justly and hence the man is responsible. This answers the form of argument which runs: Whatever God does is just, eternal punishment is not just, therefore God does not so punish. If the objector mean he has received a special revelation that there is no eternal punishment, we cannot deal with him here. If, however, he is not laying claim to a special revelation of future history, but to some philosophic principle which is intended to show that eternal punishment is unjust, the distinction between our positions

---

12. *Ibid.*, IV, viii.
13. III, xiii, 2.

becomes immediately obvious. Calvin has rejected that view of the universe which makes a law, whether of justice or of evolution, instead of the law-giver supreme. Such a view is the Platonic dualism which posits a World of Ideas superior to the Artificer.[14] God in such a system is finite or limited, bound to follow or obey the pattern. But those who proclaim the sovereignty of God determine what justice is by observing what God actually does. Whatever God does is just. What he commands men to do or not to do is similarly just or unjust.

This much is sufficient for our solution. Granted many other things remain to be said. The necessity of means or secondary, proximate causes might be further emphasized, sin as the judicial ground of divine punishment, because God so determined it should be, might be mentioned; further appendages and replies to objections could be tacked on. Only one need be examined. Does the view here proposed make God the author of sin? Why the learned divines who formulated the various creeds so uniformly permitted such a metaphorical expression[15] to becloud the issue is a puzzle. This view most certainly makes God the first and ultimate cause of everything. But very slight reflection on the definition of responsibility and its implication of a superior authority shows that God is not responsible for sin.

It follows from this that determinism is consistent with responsibility and that the concept of freedom which was introduced only to guarantee responsibility is useless. Of course man is still a "free agent" for that merely means, as Hodge[16] says, that man has the power to make a decision. It is difficult to understand then, why so much effort should be wasted[17] in the attempt to make the power of deciding consistent with the certainty of deciding. If there be any mystery about it, as the *Brief Statement* says, it is one of the theologian's own choosing. For God both gives the power

---

14. Granted that the Neo-Platonists said Plato did not mean this. But Plato's texts are open to everyone's examination, especially the *Euthyphro*. Attention is called to the keen article of E. Gottlieb, "Zum Problem des Euthyphron," in the *Archiv für Geschichte der Philosophie*, 1926.

15. Edwards is of the same opinion, *op. cit.*, IV, ix.

16. *Op. cit.*, p. 293.

17. *Ibid.*, p. 298.

and determines how it shall be used. God is sovereign.

It seems to me that a great many objections to specific Christian doctrines, objections to the propitiatory atonement or the Incarnation, arise from a non-Christian view of God's nature. The modernists object to a vicarious sacrifice because they do not think God is that sort of a person. Theirs is not the God of the early Christians. And my sincere conviction is that if we are to retain the *Satisfactio*, if we are to promulgate a consistent Christianity, we must, among other things, reject and combat the semi-arminian-ism prevailing in so-called Calvinistic churches, and return to predestination, the perseverance of the saints, the ninth chapter of Romans, and Paul's best interpreter, John Calvin.

---

*The Evangelical Quarterly,* January 1932. *The Trinity Review,* January/February 1991.

# 14

# Egoism

Egoism is the theory that one's own good either is or ought to be the sole motive operative in human choice. The term has attracted to itself some disagreeable connotations. For example, Thrasymachus argued that the tyrant who could get away with brutality and murder is the happiest man. Plato repudiated this view and enjoined justice; but Plato was equally an egoist. He asked everyone, Do you want what is really good for you or do you want what really harms you? He expected everyone to answer in the affirmative to the first option.

Plato of course did not identify the good with pleasure. In his middle period he taught that pleasure was actually evil. Justice, wisdom, temperance, and courage are good. If therefore a man chooses injustice or intemperance, it is because he does not know what is good for him.

In the Middle Ages the problem was not acute because Christians agreed that God adjusted the interests of all men.

Thomas Hobbes sharpened the matter by insisting that by an inviolable scientific law the sole motive of choice is one's personal pleasure. To this egoistic psychological hedonism Jeremy Bentham tried, inconsistently, to add a universalism: each man ought to promote the pleasure of all. As with Plato, failure is due to lack of knowledge.

Henry Sidgwick also tried to unite egoism and universalism; but he saw that this was impossible, unless, with Bishop Butler, we assume that God eventually redresses present injustices. Sidgwick hesitates before a theistic assumption; the other utilitarians are more outspokenly anti-theistic.

Since the time of Freud the discussion has not been carried on in precisely the same terms.

---

*Baker's Dictionary of Christian Ethics,* Carl F.H. Henry, editor. Grand Rapids, Michigan: Baker Book House, 1973, p. 201.

# 15

# Ethics

I. History of ethics
  A. From the ancient period
    1. Plato (427-347)
    2. Aristotle (384-322)
  B. From the medieval period
    1. Augustine (354-430)
    2. Thomas Aquinas (1225-1274)
  C. From the modern period
    1. English ethics
      a. Thomas Hobbes (1588-1679)
      b. Ralph Cudworth (1617-1687)
      c. Henry More (1614-1688)
      d. Shaftesbury (1671-1713) and
        Hutcheson (1694-1747)
      e. Joseph Butler (1692-1752)

2. Utilitarianism
   a. Jeremy Bentham (1748-1842)
   b. Henry Sidgwick (1838-1900)
3. Categorical imperatives—Immanuel Kant (1724-1804)
4. Instrumentalism—John Dewey (1859-1952)
5. Contemporary ethics
   a. P.H. Howell-Smith
   b. W.H.F. Barnes
   c. A.J. Ayer
   d. C.L. Stevenson

II. Some Christian principles
  A. The Decalogue and its implications
  B. Christian presuppositions
    1. Authority
    2. Revelation
    3. Immutability
    4. Sovereignty of God

Ethics is the study of right and wrong, of the most desirable manner of life, and of the most worthy motivation. More profound than specific moral rules and guidance in particulars is that part of ethics that attempts to answer the question, Why? Why is stealing wrong? Why is honesty right? What makes one type of life higher or better than another?

This article is divided into two parts: First, a summary of the history of ethical theory, which is perforce largely secular; and, second, a discussion of Christian principles.

# I. History of Ethics

## A. From the ancient period

### 1. Plato (427-347 B.C.)

Plato lived at the time the Old Testament canon was complete. He was the first philosopher to discuss ethics in a somewhat systematic fashion. His ethics, far from being a mere appendage to his system or even an honorable part of it, permeated and controlled it.

In his early years he seems to have considered pleasure to be man's chief and only good, and the solution to ethical problems consisted of calculating the amount of pleasures and pains to be derived from alternative courses of action. This theory, called hedonism, reappeared in the ancient Epicureans and the modern Utilitarians.

On a journey to Italy, after the death of Socrates in 399 B.C., Plato was converted by the Pythagoreans to a vigorous belief in the immortality of the soul. The Pythagoreans, descendants of the Orphics, were a religio-mathematical brotherhood that believed in knowledge as a way of salvation. Mathematics and certain ethical and cultic rules, if followed, would guarantee a happy immortality.

Plato's conversion compelled him to repudiate hedonism and to adopt a form of asceticism. In the *Gorgias,* he argued that it is better to be the victim of injustice than to be its perpetrator. Contrary to the views of Callicles Plato held that a dictator, whose every command must be obeyed and who can be unjust with impunity, harms himself more than he harms others. This argument was supported by an appeal to rewards and punishments in the life after death. In the *Phaedo,* asceticism is more pronounced. Not only is pleasure not man's only good; pleasure is positively evil. This does not mean that pain is good. The point is that pleasures, pains, and all sensations rivet men's souls to their bodies. This is evil, for the body is a tomb; life on earth is a punishment for previous sins; and a philosopher strives to free his soul from contamination with the body. A philosopher is one who loves truth, but truth is not obtainable by sensation. Hence, love of truth and hatred of evil are both motives for wishing to die. A philosopher must try to die. He may not, however, commit suicide, *i.e.* deliberately escape from his prison house, for the gods have put man on earth for a purpose, just as the Athenians imprisoned Socrates, and it is unjust to defeat the purposes of proper authority. But by philosophic study, by the avoidance of pleasures, and by a disregard for the body, a philosopher can prepare for death, gently loosen his soul from its rivets, and anticipate a pure intellectual or spiritual existence in the higher world.

In the *Republic,* Plato described man's soul as divided into three parts. The lowest of the three is the appetitive function, concupiscence, or, simply, desire; the next may be named "spunk," or the spirited principle; and the highest is reason, or the intellect. This psychology is Plato's key to his theory of virtues. Temperance is the virtue of the lowest part of the soul and consists in its obedience to the higher functions. Similarly, courage is the virtue of the second part, and wisdom is the virtue of the intellect. Then there is a fourth virtue, justice, which consists in each part minding its own business and not interfering with or disobeying the principles above it.

Plato had a parallel theory of politics. The lowest social class, the businessmen, must be temperate and obedient to superiors. The soldiers must be courageous and obey the rulers. The rulers are the philosophers, who alone possess wisdom. And justice is the harmony between all the classes.

In addition to such definitions of virtue, ethics must provide some implementation of morality. How is it that not all people are virtuous? Plato included the story of Leontius, who, on a walk, observed some dead bodies and the executioner standing by them. Leontius immediately had a desire to look at them, but at the same time loathing the thought, he tried to divert himself, and covered his eyes. At length he was overmastered by desire; he opened his eyes wide with his fingers and exclaimed, "There, you wretches, gaze your fill at the repulsive spectacle."

Vice then occurs when desire, either alone or with the help of the spirited element, usurps the rule of reason. A deeper question, however, is, why does not reason always rule? What enables desire to usurp the soul's throne?

Plato's answer to this question seems to have been inherited from Socrates; it is given in the early dialogue, *Lesser Hippias,* and though never later emphasized, it was never retracted.

Socrates and Plato thought that no one ever does wrong voluntarily. Evil always harms him who commits it, and no one wants to harm himself. If he does so, it must be involuntarily. That is to say, the person who does wrong does so because he thinks an evil act is good. In this he is mistaken. If he knew what was good for him, he would choose it. Choosing evil is evidence that he does not know. Ignorance therefore is the cause of vice; knowledge guarantees moral action.

In the case cited above, Leontius desired to gaze upon the corpses, and he experienced a loathing at the same time. The loathing derived from the common opinion that it is degrading to enjoy brutality, tragedy, or death. This opinion may well be true, but as long as it is merely common opinion, it is not knowledge. Therefore Leontius's desire conquered the loathing. Desire could not have conquered knowledge.

To this, the reply is often given that men and women know that cigarettes cause cancer, and yet they continue to smoke. This reply, however, is superficial because it fails to understand Plato's strict view of what knowledge is.

Christian moralists, going beyond this superficiality, often criticize Plato's theory, not only as an inherent defect of paganism, but also as a defect in Plato's analysis of the will. It is held, and with fair reason, that the peculiar function of the will remained unrecognized until the advent of Christianity.

Another Christian objection is that Plato made the norms of morality independent of the will of God. His World of Ideas, which contains moral concepts as well as mathematical and zoological concepts, is an eternal reality superior to and independent of God. Because of the fundamental nature of this question, its discussion will be reserved for the second part of this article. Though it is easy to criticize Plato, it is more profitable at this point to consider something in Christianity that resembles what is taken to be a defect in his view of knowledge and the will. Of course, Christianity recognizes the conflict of reason and desire. This conflict is in fact sharpened by regeneration, so that Paul wrote, "For I do not do what I want, but I do the very thing I hate. . . . For I do not do the good I want, but the evil I do not want is what I do" (Romans 7:15, 19).

In addition to this psychological observation, there is something akin to Plato's view of knowledge in the doctrine of justification by faith. Romans 6 teaches that faith inevitably produces sanctification. Other passages say that faith without works is dead, and a dead faith is simply not faith at all. Therefore when a man says he has faith, but he is devoid of works, others judge that he has no faith. This situation is sometimes called dead orthodoxy. An orthodoxy that is dead is simply not orthodoxy, which is synonymous with right thinking.

So also would Plato argue. The man who does wrong may say he knows, but he does not know; for if he knew, virtuous action would be forthcoming.

## 2. Aristotle (384-322 B.C.)

Aristotle, unlike Plato, had very little interest in religion. Morality for him had no connection with a future life; in fact his few references to "immortality" are so vague, it is unlikely that he had any belief at all in the future existence of an individual person. For Aristotle, morality was social custom, refined of its inconsistencies by reason, and based on a view of human nature.

Aristotle formulated the problem of ethics as the search for the Good—the Good for man. In other words, there is a desire to know *that for which* man does everything else. It is the end, or purpose, of all human action.

Purposes are ordered in series. A man walks to his garage for the purpose of getting his car for the purpose of driving downtown for the purpose of getting to work on time. Whereas ethics gives proper consideration to immediate purposes, which then become the means to a more distant end, the culmination of the study is the absolutely final end, the end that is never a means to anything else, namely, happiness.

Happiness does not mean pleasure. It is true that men choose pleasure for its own sake, as they also choose health for its own sake, but they choose health and pleasure for the sake of other things as well. Amusement and pleasure are forms of rest, and men rest, or take recreation, because they cannot go on working without relief. Pleasure, therefore, is a means to further activity. Some pleasures actually cause harm; these should be avoided. Thus it is clear that pleasure is not happiness; the absolutely final end—happiness—is never chosen as a means to anything else.

To ascertain the nature of happiness, one must analyze, rather than simply accept pleasure. The way to arrive at its meaning is to see that the Good for man is related to man's ultimate purpose. Happiness is not a matter of individual choice; it is determined by human nature; it is defined by the function of man as man. The goodness of a flautist or a shoemaker resides in his function. If the flautist plays well, he is a good flautist. If flautists and shoemakers have definite functions, would it not seem strange if man as man has none and is not designed by nature to fulfill any function? If also each part of the body, the eye or the hand, has a particular function of its own, surely the human being as a whole must have a function. The good man, then, as the example of the flautist shows, is the man who performs his function well.

In a generic sense, man has many functions, including nutrition, growth, and sensation. Man, however, has these in common with plants or animals. Ethics must determine the function peculiar to man; and this is to be found, not in mere life nor even in sensation, but in rationality. Because reason, therefore, is the specific function of man, and because a thing is good if it performs its function well, it follows that the good for man is the active exercise of his soul's faculties in conformity with reason.

Such active exercise has two forms: moral and intellectual virtue. Moral virtue is not a natural property, but one acquired by habit. Since it is the nature of a stone to fall downward, and since it cannot be trained to fall upward, it is clear that natural properties cannot be altered by habit. But morality is produced, altered, and brought to maturity by habit. In the case of natural actions, the capacity precedes the activity; for example, no one acquires the faculty of sight by repeatedly seeing. It is the reverse: Man first had the senses and then used them. But with virtue man first goes through the motions and by doing so acquires the capacity, just as one does in learning to play the piano. By acting courageously or temperately, a man becomes courageous or temperate.

Action thus produces character. If anyone practices bad fingering on the piano, he becomes a poor musician. No one begins as either a good or bad musician. Habituation determines what he becomes.

Moral virtue is a mean between two extremes, for morality has to do with feelings and actions, of which a man may have an excess or a deficiency. For example, if in a given situation a man is too fearful, he is called a coward; on the other hand, if he has no fear at all, when bullets are whistling by, he is considered foolhardy. Courage consists in feeling the right amount of fear, neither too much nor too little. This right amount is relative to the situation and to the person. More fear is proper in battle, less in a less dangerous situation. Similarly, what is courageous for an elderly person may be cowardly for a young athlete whose physical powers are so much greater.

For this same reason, practical advice on how to become virtuous would be to counteract one's inclinations. Usually this would require a greater risk of being a little too rash than a little too cowardly. If, however, anyone knew he was inclined to rashness, he should run the risk of a little cowardice, and so possibly hit the mean. The same considerations apply to temperance, liberality, and all the moral virtues.

Higher on the scale than moral virtue is intellectual virtue; for the highest level of human nature is reason, and its proper functioning is the highest purpose of man. Contemplation, therefore, is the highest activity. Its objects are the highest objects, and its exercise is more continuous than any other human function can be. It is also most self-sufficient; for whereas the moral virtues require either the presence of other people, as in the case of justice, or the possession of goods, or both, as in the case of liberality, the wise man can think and contemplate by himself, and the more he does so, the wiser he becomes.

Furthermore, contemplation is the only activity that is loved for its own sake alone. It produces no result beyond the actual act of contemplation. The moral virtues are, to be sure, loved for their own sakes; they are ends, but they are also means to other good ends, and therefore are not absolutely final as is contemplation.

Once again, contemplation is the most god-like virtue. It is man's nearest approach to immortality. Obviously the gods cannot be moral; they cannot make contracts, restore deposits, endure terrors, run risks, or temperately restrain evil desires. Contemplation can be their only activity. Hence, contemplation is man's greatest source of happiness.

In the section on Plato, the problem of the will and its relation to knowledge was discussed. Aristotle also examined the subject. Christians may be a little disappointed because his interest was more political than theological or metaphysical, or even psychological; yet his arguments are well worth studying.

Feelings and actions, which constitute the area of morality, may be voluntary or involuntary. The former are praised or blamed, the latter pardoned and sometimes pitied. Therefore ethics must study volition and choice.

Involuntary actions are those done through (1) force or (2) ignorance. A forced action is one whose principle of initiation is entirely external to the man, who contributes nothing. Compulsion by threat or by fear is not pure compulsion; a tyrant may threaten, or a storm at sea may "force" one to throw the cargo overboard. Such actions are partly voluntary, but are more similar to involuntary actions. They are given a measure of praise or blame according to the circumstances because the initiation of the motion is in the man.

The claim that pleasure forces a man into immorality implies that all action would be compulsory, and no one would be responsible for anything.

Ignorance is the second cause of involuntary actions, but there is a distinction. All acts done through ignorance are nonvoluntary; only when pain and repentance follow do they become involuntary. Further, acting in ignorance is not the same as acting through ignorance. The drunk acts in ignorance but through drunkenness. Every wicked man is ignorant of what he ought to do. This ignorance does not cause involuntary action; it causes wickedness. The ignorance that causes involuntary action needs further specification.

An action is involuntary if the agent is ignorant of who is doing the act. This point of ignorance occurs only in insanity. The action is involuntary also if the agent is ignorant of the thing done, as in the case of Aeschylus who did not know he was revealing the mysteries, or in the case of a man who did not know the gun was loaded; similarly, if the agent does not know the object of the action, whether a person or a thing, as, for example, a man mistakes his son for a robber in the night, or mistakes a rapier for a foil, or poison for medicine.

Therefore, "Since that which is done under compulsion or through ignorance is involuntary, the voluntary would seem to be that of which the moving principle is in the agent himself, when he is aware of the particular circumstances of the action."

In this discussion Aristotle insisted on distinguishing between an act being voluntary and its being good or evil. There is a common tendency to dodge responsibility by blaming evil actions on force or ignorance, while taking credit for good actions. Similarly, modern liberal penology tends to excuse the criminal because he was either raised in a slum or pampered in a wealthy home. But, to be consistent, this destroys responsibility for evil actions and credit for good actions alike, and dehumanizes everybody.

Next, a subspecies of the voluntary, called deliberate choice, is a better criterion of morality than feelings and actions. Children and some animals act voluntarily, but never by choice. Sudden actions also may be voluntary, but they are not deliberately chosen. What then is choice?

Choice is a subdivision within the area of the voluntary because both children and animals can act voluntarily, but not by choice. Acts done on the spur of the moment also are voluntary, but they are not chosen. Nor is choice the same as desire, anger, wish, or opinion, for animals experience desire and anger. Similarly an incontinent man acts from desire, but not from choice. Conversely, the continent man acts from choice, not from desire.

Choice is not the same as wish because one may sometimes wish for the impossible, but he never chooses it. Further, wish relates to the end of an action, whereas choice selects the means; for example, one may wish to be happy, but one must choose the method to obtain that happiness.

Nor is choice opinion. Opinion is concerned about everything, including both the impossible and the eternal. Opinion is true or false, not good or bad. Character is the result of choice, but not of opinion. Man chooses to take or avoid something, but man holds an opinion of what a thing is. Indeed, some people have fairly sound opinions, but by reason of vice choose what they should not.

Choice, then, is what is decided upon by previous deliberation. To make the concept clearer, it is necessary to describe deliberation.

Aristotle discussed the objects of deliberation and its mode of operation. The objects do not include the impossible, the eternal, nor the invariable laws of astronomy, for they cannot be altered. Nor does a man deliberate about chance events, nor about many human affairs beyond his control. Deliberation, therefore, concerns things that are in man's power, not those that occur always in the same way, but those that are variable—matters of medicine, business, and navigation, but not mathematics and spelling.

This identification of the objects of deliberation is the key to the manner or mode of deliberation. If deliberation concerns the variable, and centers on means rather than on ends, the process consists of a search for the series of means that will produce an end. In a temporal sense, the search goes backward. For example, a man decides to purchase a necklace (the object of his deliberation) as an anniversary gift for his wife. Working backward, he next selects the store where he will purchase the necklace. The store selected, he then chooses the means of transportation, to drive his car or go by bus. The goal determines the choices.

The object of deliberation and of choice is the same object, except that the object of choice has already been determined as the result of deliberation. A man stops thinking how to act when he has brought the moving principle back to himself.

Aristotle continued in much more detail which cannot be included here. To conclude this section, a comparison with the Bible may be made. The Bible does not work out a theory of voluntary action and deliberate choice. It does, however, base responsibility on knowledge, and allows for greater responsibility, greater sin, and greater punishment in proportion to the amount of knowledge. The idea is clearly expressed in Romans 1:18, 19, 32; 2:12, 13, 15. Also, Christ said, "that servant who knew his master's will, but did not make ready . . . shall receive a severe beating. But he who did not know, and did what deserved a beating, shall receive a light beating. Every one to whom much is given, of him will much be required" (Luke 12:47, 48).

## B. From the medieval period

### 1. Augustine (354-430)

In patristic and medieval Christianity, Augustine and Aquinas developed full-fledged theories by interpreting Scripture, contrasting it with and defending it against the pagan theories, but sometimes utilizing pagan theories in combination with Biblical teachings.

Aristotle's view that the highest type of life is contemplation of truth is sometimes exaggerated, if not caricatured, as a withdrawal from the practical activities of life. Augustine's view, determined by Scripture and to a certain extent also influenced by Plato, rejects this exaggerated position. Knowledge itself is a means to an end, and this end is blessedness. This basic Augustinian principle is embedded in the Protestant phrases, "Truth is in order to goodness," and "The chief end of man is to glorify God and to enjoy Him forever."

If knowledge were for the sake of knowledge only, it would have no purpose, no end, and therefore no direction—for example, one could spend one's time counting the blades of grass on the front lawn or measuring the lengths of random bits of string. If knowledge has a purpose, however, one will not waste time contemplating useless information.

Philosophy is not the love of knowledge, but the love of wisdom. Though wisdom is a kind of knowledge and must possess the certitude of science, there is a distinction between them, as hinted in 1 Corinthians 12:8. Not all knowledge leads to blessedness; wisdom does.

Man is both corporeal and spiritual. If the mind were divorced from the body, it would no doubt attend only to the divine Ideas; but actually one of the soul's functions is to rule the body. Therefore man must know not only the divine Ideas, but things and bodies as well. He must act, and this requires thought of inferior objects and lower ends. Of course, even Aristotle did not deny the need for moral virtues as distinct from intellectual virtues.

The concern with corporeal affairs, however, is a means to higher intellectual activity. Thought leads to action only to prepare for contemplation. Action is work, effort, pursuit. Contemplation is reward, rest, vision. The distinction is illustrated in Scripture in the persons of Mary and Martha (Luke 10:38-42). During a Christian's earthly life, there is action in view of heavenly contemplation. Morality is the preparation for the vision of God.

Attention to bodily things is legitimate, if this interest is kept in proper perspective. If a man restricts himself to the lower sphere, he is guilty of pride, avarice, and personal cupidity. Instead of subordinating himself to God, he tries to subordinate the universe to himself. Science itself is good, but man easily abuses science.

Wisdom, on the other hand, turns man from things to God. Pride is replaced by humility. Science is necessary to arrange temporal affiars, but when people subordinate themselves to God, they put their various activities in their proper places.

Why isn't everyone wise? Plato had tried to answer this question in terms of a conflict between reason and desire. Christianity, however, although it does not deny a conflict between desire and reason, has a different psychology that requires a profounder explanation of evil. This difference in psychology is revealed in an emphasis on the will. Such emphasis was lacking, or at most, rudimentary, in Plato and Aristotle; although the Stoics advanced over their predecessors in the matter of the will, there are other differences.

All things, man included, are subject to the order God has imposed on the world. Each thing, so Augustine teaches, has its proper place in the universal hierarchy. Nevertheless, for morality, man must act and act voluntarily. Even intellectual learning depends on the will. One can almost say that a man is his will. In sensation the will is required to sustain attention. A person's fingers may be in contact with an object, or his eyes may be fixed on an object, yet if he does not attend to it, he does not perceive it. Memory also requires attention, and neither understanding nor belief takes place without an act of will.

Modern terminology might define volition as a natural drive. It is a principle of action. According to Aristotle, earth, air, fire, and water have a natural tendency to seek their proper places. Earth naturally falls, and fire by nature rises. As earth has weight, Augustine felt, so man has love. Love is man's natural motor power.

Parenthetically, it should be noted that in orthodox theology, love is a volition, not an emotion. Contemporary references to God's love and man's love for God often go astray because of faulty psychology. Love toward God consists in voluntary obedience to His laws (John 14:15, 21, 23; 1 John 2:4, 5). Emotion has little to do with it.

Accordingly, Augustine argues that the moral problem is not whether to love or not to love. This would be like asking whether earth should have weight or not have weight. The problem is to love what one ought to love, for this is virtue. Because men continually fail, the problem arises whether a natural principle of motion can go astray.

The difficulty was sharper for the Christian Augustine than it was for the pagan Plato, for in addition to the psychology of the will, Augustine had to operate with the theological concept of sin. This does not refer simply to the fact that men choose evil. The pagans knew that much. The Christian concept of sin is based on original sin and the inheritance of it. Aristotle had explained evil actions as the result of bad habits, such as poor fingering on a piano. At the start, a prospective musician has neither good nor bad habits. He is neutral, but practice makes him what he becomes. But Christianity teaches that man is born in sin; he has bad habits at the outset, and this together with guilt is inherited from Adam. Therefore, sin is a much more radical defect than is acknowledged by the pagan view of evil.

Augustine gives a memorable example. When he was a boy, he and his gang stole some pears from a nearby orchard. He did not steal because he was hungry, for he had pears at home; in fact, much better pears, for the stolen pears were so bad that the boys threw them to the pigs. It is wrong to steal, but if one steals because he is hungry, or even because the pears taste good, there is some superficial plausibility in the theft. Augustine's theft, however, was not so motivated. He stole simply for the fun of stealing; he enjoyed evil for its own sake; and he enjoyed it all the more because he did it with his friends who also enjoyed evil just because it was evil. Stealing pears may not be a great sin, but what depravity could be greater than a love of evil for its own sake?

The passage (*Confessions*, Book II) containing this psychological analysis of the motives of sin does not itself refer to original sin. The immediate point is merely the perversity of the human heart. This depravity cannot be accounted for on Aristotelian principles, though even at this late date some professing Christians still say that a child becomes sinful only upon committing a voluntary transgression at or after the so-called age of accountability.

Those who deny that men are dead in sin hold also that sin is not merely voluntary, but is particularly an act of free will. Volition and free will are not the same, as the article on Stoicism shows. Free will, that is, a choice that is not caused either by God, by character, by motives, or anything else, is substituted for knowledge as the basis for responsibility. Moreover, the problem is complicated by the fact that God is omnipotent. He could have made men sinless, had he so desired. This is not the case in Platonism, where god is conceived as limited in power; Plato's god does his best to restrain evil and impose order on the visible world, but the opposing forces are sometimes too much for him. Christianity teaches that God is omnipotent, so that He could even now eradicate evil. Superficial thinking attempts to say that God limited himself. The infinite made itself finite. God undeified himself, and hence there is sin. This reply is inadequate because limited omnipotence is a contradiction in terms, but also because it does not answer the original question: Why does not God now unlimit himself and make all men sinless? The problem is difficult, and Augustine changed his views, beginning as a new Christian with a certain form of free will and then developing a more consistently Christian and Biblical solution.

Augustine's first attack on this basic problem of ethics, *On Free Will*, was written about A.D. 390. The question is, "If sins come from the souls which God has created, and these souls are from God, how explain that sin is not borne back upon God *(referantur in Deum)*?" Or in other words, How is God not responsible for sin?

By A.D. 390, Augustine had made such little progress in grasping Christian doctrine and was still so under the influence of Plato that he denied the sovereignty of God by adopting the Platonic view that an action is wrong, not because God forbids it, but God forbids it because it is wrong. This error subtly influenced his arguments, but gradually he was able to discard Platonism.

He next contended that things superior to the human mind, *i.e.* God, cannot subject a man to sin or lust because, being superior, they are good and would not do so. Things inferior to the mind cannot do so because they are inferior and weaker. Therefore the mind or will itself causes sin, and God is not responsible.

Yet if God created the will of man good, how could man ever choose evil? Conversely, if men are born unwise and never have a good will, why are they punished? Augustine replied with another bit of Platonism that he later discarded. He wrote that perhaps souls lived in a preexistent state before birth, and that this fact (somehow, not too clearly) answers the questions (Book I, 12). In fact he soon repeated the question (I, 16): If God gave men free will, is he not responsible for their sins; for if he had not given them free will, they would not have sinned?

This is an unfortunate flaw in Augustine's argumentation. He nowhere defined free will, and without an explicit definition, one can only guess what he means. Presumably he meant an uncaused or unmotivated will. But if so, the flaw takes the form of assuming without proof that a will can operate without a cause. Therefore Augustine's immediate remark is irrelevant: God gave man a free will so that he might live righteously (which contradicts the previous statement that without a free will no one would sin), and God is not to blame if man uses free will for the wrong purpose (II, 1), just as one cannot object to wine because some use it wrongly (II, 18).

The argument becomes more theological as it progresses. If God foreknew Adam's sin, was it not inevitable? And must not man will as God foreknows? No, replied Augustine, because *must* means *no will;* therefore foreknowledge does not conflict with human ability. For example, if one man foreknows that another will sin, the former's knowledge is not the cause of the sin. As memory of the past does not exert force on the past, so knowledge of the future does not determine the future.

Apparently Augustine assumed that a man can know the future and that God discovers an independent future the way a man does. Neither of these assumptions seems sound.

For such reasons as these, Augustine concluded that it is unwise to seek a cause of volitions. When one asks what causes the will to choose, one is led into an infinite regress. The will itself is the cause, and further search is useless.

Nevertheless, Augustine went further. He admitted that sinning is inevitable, for he could not escape Romans 7:18. Therefore man does not have free will; strictly speaking only Adam had free will (III, 18). Adam's descendants are punished as Adam himself was, because the descendants of a sinner are of necessity sinful. If all souls have descended from one soul, then all have sinned and deserve punishment. Furthermore, because virtue can be acquired by God's grace, the sinful state is a stimulus to progress.

Late in life, after he had gone through the Pelagian controversy, Augustine wrote two more books on the same subject: *Grace and Free Will* in A.D. 426, and *Predestination of the Saints* in A.D. 429. In the former, he still used the phrase "free will," but the discussion no longer denied a divine cause of the will's action. Chapter 29 stated that God is able to convert opposing wills and to take away their hardness; otherwise, if God could exercise no causative power on the will, it would be useless to pray for the conversion of anyone. It is certain, he continued, that it is men who will when they will, but it is God who makes them will what is good. It is God who makes them act by applying *efficacious* power to their wills. The Scripture "shows us that not only men's good wills, which God converts from bad ones . . . but also those who follow the world are so entirely at the disposal of God that he turns them whithersoever he wills and whensoever he wills. . . . For the Almighty sets in motion even in the innermost hearts of men the movement of their will so that he does through their agency whatsoever he wishes to perform through them" (chs. 41, 42).

In the latter book he wrote against semi-Pelagianism and insisted that faith is a gift of God. God causes men to believe. Augustine confessed that he had not always understood the doctrines of grace: He had thought that Romans 7 referred to the unregenerate; he had denied prevenient grace; but now he retracted his earlier errors, for he obtained mercy to be a believer—not because he had believed.

Christ himself is the best example of predestination, for if he had had free will, he could have sinned; but Christ could not have sinned, therefore he did not have free will, but was predestinated in all that he did. In fact, in both of these books, but especially in the last one, Augustine taught the full Protestant position, forgotten during the Middle Ages, but rediscovered by Luther and Calvin.

After Augustine, the Roman empire in the West disintegrated under the advances of the barbarians, and learning became almost extinct. As church superstitions multiplied, theology became semi-Pelagian or worse, though what philosophy survived was mildly Augustinian.

## 2. Thomas Aquinas (1225-1274)

In the 13th century, however, Thomas Aquinas succeeded in overthrowing Augustinianism and in establishing Aristotelianism.

His ethics is based on the fact of a similarity and a difference between human beings and inanimate objects. The similarity, on which the difference is built, lies in the possession of a natural tendency or inclination. Earth has a natural tendency to fall. In inanimate things these tendencies are unconscious and are not subject to the being's control. Man also has a natural inclination, but it is a higher form because man is rational and volitional. He inclines to what he knows, and he controls his own conduct.

Appetite or desire is proportionate to knowledge. In animals, the knowledge is merely sense knowledge, and since this requires a bodily organ, it follows that if a dog sees or smells a bone, he automatically desires it. Man, however, has rational knowledge, which does not immediately depend on any bodily organ; therefore the will or rational appetite does not act automatically. Nevertheless the object chosen must be known.

The will naturally or automatically inclines toward the good. Just as each plant or animal naturally tends to the preservation of itself and of the species, so too man is directed to the good. In actual life, however, a man is not confronted so much with the Good as with particular goods. These are not completely satisfying, and hence they do not compel the will.

In fact, not even God can compel the will. The reason is that

what is done voluntarily is not done of necessity. Now, whatever is done under compulsion is done of necessity, and consequently what is done by the will cannot be compelled. . . . The will can suffer violence insofar as violence can prevent the exterior members from executing the will's command. But as to the will's own proper act, violence cannot be done to the will. . . . God, who is more powerful than the human will, can move the will of man. . . . But if this were by compulsion, it would no longer be by an act of will, nor would the will itself be moved, but something else against the will *(Summa Theologica* II i, 2.6, Art. 4).

On a later page (2.10, Art. 4). Thomas considered the objection,

It would seem that the will is moved of necessity by God. For every agent that cannot be resisted moves of necessity. But God cannot be resisted, because his power is infinite; and so it is written (Romans 9:19) "who resisteth his will?"

In reply to this quotation from the canonical Bible, Thomas uses a verse from an apocryphal book:

On the contrary, it is written (Ecclesiasticus 15:14) "God made man from the beginning and left him in the hand of his own counsel."

Natural inclinations, as in inanimate things, tend toward a form existing in nature; the sensitive appetite and all the more the rational appetite tend toward an apprehended form. Therefore the will chooses, not the universal good as such, but an apparent good. The agent intends the good; he never voluntarily chooses evil; when he chooses a particular apparent good that turns out to be evil, the evil is unintentional.

The intellect therefore moves the will, but not necessarily, by presenting an object to it. If the intellect offered to the will an object good universally and from every point of view, the will would choose it of necessity, if it chose at all, for it cannot choose the opposite. If, on the other hand, the will is offered an object that is not good in every respect it will not tend toward it of necessity. Hence the will can either accept or reject particular goods.

Choice is an act of both the intellect and the will. The matter of the choice comes from the intellect, but the form of the choice comes from the will. Intellect and will interact, but their acts are not to be confused. The intellect may even command the will and say, "Do this!" Even when the will obeys, it does so freely.

With all their interaction, more complicated than this brief essay indicates, Thomas steadfastly maintained the distinction between intellect and will. Augustine, as said above, virtually identified man with his will, in which case intellectual acts are simply particular volitions. After the time of Thomas, the discussion intensified. Descartes, at the beginning of the modern period, returned to a position somewhat similar to Augustine's, but these intricacies can be followed no further here.

One who has not read Thomas can have no idea of the immense amount of detail he incorporated into his writings. Basing his views on Aristotle, he argued that habit is a quality, a species of quality which applies order to an act; it is necessary that there be habits; some habits are bodily, some exist in the soul; some habits, such as temperance and fortitude, belong to the sensitive and irrational part of the soul; science and wisdom are habits of the intellect; justice, however, is a habit of the will; and even angels have habits.

Thomas then discussed whether any habit is from nature; whether any is caused by acts; whether a habit can be caused by one act; whether any habits are infused by God; whether habits increase (which he answers in the affirmative, for faith is a habit and faith increases); and so on until he is able to show that virtue is a habit. He then continued for many long pages on virtue' in general, and had something to say about a few particular virtues.

One basic factor in the ethics of Thomas, a factor that seems to deal more closely with the particular decisions of everyday morality, is the theory of natural law.

There are several types of law: eternal law, natural law, and civil law. A law is a rule that prescribes or forbids an action; it is an obligation founded on reason. There is no other regulative principle of action than reason. The unreasonable commands of a tyrant are not laws, but merely usurp that appellation.

So completely is reason the source of law that a private person is not competent to make laws. He can give advice but he cannot efficaciously lead anyone to virtue. Coercive power is vested in a public power. A father cannot give laws even to his family, for a family is part of the state. The father can indeed issue certain commands to his children, but they do not have the nature of law.

Furthermore, although there are various precepts of prudence, the first principle in practical affairs is the highest end—happiness or beatitude. Therefore law is chiefly ordained to the common, rather than to the individual, good.

The first of the three types of law is the eternal law. Since this is the plan of government laid down by God, the Chief Governor, all the plans of inferior governors must be derived from this eternal law.

Insofar as the eternal law applies to the conduct of men, it has been inscribed in man's substance and is called natural law. Because this law causes men to be what they are—it takes the form of a human inclination toward certain ends—they obey it when they yield to the legitimate tendencies of their nature.

The first and basic principle is that good should be done and evil avoided. All other precepts depend on this. Since good has the nature of an end, "all those things to which man has a natural inclination are naturally apprehended by reason as being good, and consequently as objects of pursuit" (*Summa Theologica* II, I, 2. 94 Art. 2). Thus self-preservation is the basic inclination; next comes reproduction and the care of children; in short, all virtuous acts are covered by natural law.

These laws are indelibly written in the human heart. They cannot be effaced. Men need only to observe themselves to discover them, or in Thomas's own words, "The natural law is promulgated by the very fact that God instilled it into man's mind so as to be known by him naturally" (*ibid.,* Q. 90, Art. 4). Thomas also extended the details of what man ought to do by including the theological virtues taught by revelation. These make his good life more Christian than that of an Aristotelian gentleman, but they are not logically deduced from this philosophic system.

Two criticisms of Thomism should be considered—one theological, one philosophical. The first is that Christian theology is inconsistent with Aristotelian ethics. The discussion of ethics depends on an assertion of free will with the assumption that man is able by practice to make himself virtuous. Man may "naturally" seek the good, but since the fall no one is "natural." All are born in sin and are in need of grace. Therefore they cannot will to be virtuous. Although Thomas never achieved the full Christian vision of Augustine's later works, he nevertheless had some notion of predestination and reprobation. Whether the latter can be consistently combined with free will is the question. At least the consistency is not clear in the following: "When it is said that the reprobated cannot obtain grace, this must not be understood as implying absolute impossibility; but only conditional impossibility; just as it was said above that the predestined must necessarily be saved, yet by a conditional necessity that does not do away with liberty of choice" (*Summa Theologica* I, Q.23, Art. 3). Also, "Man's turning to God is by free choice; and thus man is bidden to turn himself to God. But free choice can be turned to God only when God turns it . . . man can do nothing unless moved by God. . . . It is the part of man to prepare his soul, since he does this by free choice. And yet he does not do this without the help of God moving him and drawing him to himself (*ibid.*, II, I, 2. 109, Art. 6).

The inconsistency involved here seems to be that Thomas made a good case for freedom from coercion, and that this freedom is compatible with predestination, for God is not a mechanical agent. Yet Thomas also held that for responsibility and morality, the freedom of an uncaused cause is required, and this is not compatible with predestination. Until a theologian clarifies himself on these points, neither his theology nor his ethics will escape confusion.

The second objection to be considered is philosophical and ethical—the question whether Aristotle or Thomas can build an ethics on natural law. Is it actually true that men can observe what is written on their heart and discover that adultery and theft are forbidden?

It is plausible that natural law would prescribe the care and education of children. Animals instinctively care for their young, but they are not for that reason monogamous. If it be replied that a human child requires a longer period of care and that therefore a human family ought to remain together for this longer period, neither monogamy nor permanent union is thereby established. Indeed, since the state, on Thomistic principles, is to spell out most of the details left obscure in natural law, would not a rational ruler establish communal nurseries? Who is to say that Soviet laws are less rational than American?

This includes the question of theft. If property is a creation of the state, confiscatory taxation is as reasonable as Jeffersonian democracy, and laissez faire as collectivism. Thomas admits that it is always dangerous to rebel, even when a tyrant violates natural law, but how can one distinguish between a just rebellion and an unjust usurpation?

Even self-preservation is not clearly an inviolable law of nature. Military service is considered a duty, but this can lead to death. If natural law obliges, a young man would be obliged to dodge the draft. Or, on the other hand, why must suicide be considered wrong? There may be an instinct of self-preservation, but some unfortunate people have concluded that the conditions of life were so onerous that it was rational to kill themselves. This was a definite part of Stoic philosophy, and the Stoics prescribed a life of reason as strongly as Aristotle did. But if natural law cannot absolutely prescribe self-preservation, it would seem that ethics needs to find a better foundation.

## C. From the modern period

### 1. English ethics.

#### a. Thomas Hobbes (1588-1679)

In the history of English ethics, the modern approach differs from that of medieval times and antiquity. Thomas Hobbes aimed to make ethics scientific. Thus he held that all forms of life are but complicated relationships among particles of matter in motion. This materialism serves as a basis for his psychological hedonism. Hobbes professes to have discovered by scientific observation that all men naturally desire and are motivated only by personal pleasure. Man is essentially self-seeking. "Pity is imagination or fiction of future calamity to ourselves proceeding from the sense of another man's calamity"; and "The passion of laughter proceedeth from the sudden imagination of our own odds and eminency; for what is else the recommending of ourselves to our own good opinion by the comparison of another man's inferiority or absurdity."

For Hobbes, ethics is descriptive rather than normative. He did not say what men ought to do; he described their actual conduct. Surreptitiously, perhaps, he made some recommendations.

Thus he argued that the condition most unfavorable to obtaining pleasure is political anarchy. To be sure the war of each against all is man's natural state; but it is an intolerable one. No one's life is safe; and without life pleasure is impossible. Therefore everyone must surrender all his rights to the government, preferably by selecting one man and making him an absolute monarch.

This is a form of the social contract theory of government. The people enter into a covenant with each other to set up a king. Forever after it will be wrong to rebel: By the contract they retain no rights at all—therefore no right to rebel. Nor can they later claim that the king has broken the contract, for the king was never a party to the contract.

The king now, as selfish as anyone else, protects his property, *i.e.* his subjects, for his own good. He enforces laws that preserve life and protect property, and under such a totalitarian government man can best enjoy himself. To rebel against the king and to diminish his authority would be to revert to anarchy and misery.

Hobbes had some reason to be apprehensive of social disturbances. His age was one of confusion in England—the disaffection of the Scottish army toward the perfidious Charles I in England and the Puritans' hostility toward the Arminian and Romish tendencies in the Anglican Church. Civil war was on its way. Foreseeing this, Hobbes contended that the principle of private conscience, by which the Puritans read the Bible for themselves, conflicted with governmental authority. Similarly, the independent conscience of the Pope was destructive of peace. Therefore Puritans and Romanists were both to be repressed, and the king by his supremacy could not only legislate the rules of morality as he saw fit, but he could even decide what books make up the Bible and what they mean.

The immediate reaction to Hobbes, on the surface at least, was an attack on his egoism. More fundamental was a rejection of scientific observation as a basis for morality. If a sense of obligation is to be maintained, if the concept of duty and the authority of normative principles is to be defended, mere factual descriptions of *what is* are not enough; something more is needed to show *what ought to be*.

## b. Ralph Cudworth (1617-1688)

Therefore Ralph Cudworth returned to a Platonic or Neoplatonic theory of suprasensible Ideas. For him as for Plato, the Good—and its derivative forms—are independent of both human and divine volition: An action is not wrong because God forbids it, but God, himself subject to the Ideas, forbids it because it is wrong.

## c. Henry More (1614-1687)

Henry More based morality on intuitions. As one knows a rock or a mountain simply by seeing it, so in somewhat similar fashion he can have an intellectual vision of first principles. They are not deduced from anything prior or more certain: They are simply seen. Most philosophers, except the most extremely scientific, will acknowledge the legitimacy of undemonstrable axioms, but More's two dozen moral intuitions seem unnecessarily abundant.

## d. Shaftesbury (1671-1713) and Hutcheson (1694-1747)

Shaftesbury and Hutcheson paid more attention to the conflict between egoism and altruism. If men had no sense of good distinct from personal advantage, is their argument, they would hold in equal esteem a fruitful field and a generous friend. One would hold in equal esteem a man who serves him with delight and a man who brings him the same advantage by constraint. But one does not esteem these equally. Therefore we have a sense of good other than egoistic advantage.

## e. Joseph Butler (1692-1752)

A much more important writer was Bishop Joseph Butler. His most influential work, used as a textbook for over a century in many seminaries, was *The Analogy of Religion, Natural and Revealed, to the Constitution and Course of Nature*. His system of ethics is expounded in *Fifteen Sermons*. Neither of these is founded on Platonic or intuitionist principles. Bishop Butler believed that moral obligation, and the basic theses of Christianity too, can be established by observation. Whereas not so attached to the materialistic mechanism of Thomas Hobbes, he still depended on scientific methods. This procedure served him well in his *Analogy*, for he was able to destroy English Deism on its own grounds. He could show, for example, that the immortality of the soul was a reasonable conclusion, at least as reasonable as the opposite. This, however, may be the fallacy in his thinking. Pure, unmixed observation can just as reasonably arrive at either of two incompatible positions, and arrive at them by equally reasonable, that is equally unreasonable, arguments. Similarly, in ethics one must always scrutinize an argument that professes to deduce what ought to be from what merely is.

In the second of his *Fifteen Sermons*, using the text, "For when the Gentiles, which have not the law, do by nature the things contained in the law, these, having not the law, are a law unto themselves" (Romans 2:14 KJV), Joseph Butler, not noticing the intuitional or *a priori* thrust of the verse, argues that the purpose of man can be discovered by observation, or, more particularly, introspection, and that his purpose reveals man's nature and fixes his obligations.

Man has a conscience as truly as he has eyes; and as the purpose of the eye is to see trees and houses, so the purpose of the conscience is to see right and wrong. Furthermore, man's instincts lead him to contribute to the happiness of society in a way and with a force that no inward principle leads him to evil. Hence, man is at least more altruistic than selfish.

If it be replied that evil and selfish instincts are also natural, and that we therefore follow nature in following them, the reply is, first, that such an argument would destroy all distinctions between good and evil—everything would be indifferently natural; and, second, that observation of human nature did not result merely in the discovery that both altruistic and selfish inclinations equally exist, but rather that conscience exists as a superior, governing principle—its purpose is to sit in judgment over the others.

Butler is quite confident of the rectitude of conscientious judgments: "Let any plain, honest man, before he engages in any course of action, ask himself, Is this I am going about right, or is it wrong? Is it good , or is it evil? I do not in the least doubt, but that this question would be answered agreeably to truth and virtue, by almost any fair man in almost any fair circumstance."

A person, whose viewpoint is not so restricted to English common opinion in the 18th century, may wonder whether all the world in all ages has enjoyed such a universal agreement. Without pressing the Scriptural revelation of the total depravity and desperate wickedness of the human heart, but adhering solely to observation "exclusive of revelation" as Butler insists (Sermon II, paragraph 20), an observer of humanity also notes that some widows have conscientiously mounted the funeral pyres of their husbands, that some military nations have taught that suicide is honorable, that Congolese savages regard cannibalism as normal. Observation, it would seem, allows for incompatible results.

Butler next considered a most important objection. Suppose, the objection runs, that conscience prescribes for a person a line of action that would injure him. Why should he be concerned about anything other than his own personal good? If he discovers in his makeup certain restrictions of conscience, why should he not endeavor to suppress them?

Butler's answer is that personal happiness and the good of other people coincide. All the common enjoyments of life, and, even the pleasures of vice, depend on a person's regard of his fellow creatures. The satisfactions of selfishness are not to be assumed superior to the satisfaction of acting justly and benevolently. Butler wrote, "It is manifest that, in the common course of life, there is seldom any inconsistency between our duty and what is *called* interest: it is much seldomer that there is an inconsistency between duty and what is really our present interest. . . . But whatever exceptions there are to this . . . all shall be set right at the final distribution of things. It is a manifest absurdity to suppose evil prevailing finally over good, under the conduct and administration of a perfect mind (Sermon II, paragraph 28).

Some puzzles emerge in the study of Butler's arguments. Altruism and selfishness, conscience and "reasonable self-love" may coincide, but when they do not seem to—and in the 20th century, duty does not speak so clearly as it did in his day—should a man follow what seems to be his interest or what seems to be his duty? Is duty in fact more clearly discernible than interest? Again, "a final distribution of things" that will equalize the temporary inconsistencies is not a principle to be derived from observation. Butler's argument is circular: He must appeal to divine Providence to save his ethical theory, although he cannot prove the existence of Providence except by observing the uniform and inviolate coincidence of conscience and self-love.

## 2. Utilitarianism
### a. Jeremy Bentham (1748-1832)

In 19th century England Jeremy Bentham propounded the theory of utilitarianism. Based on psychological hedonism, as was the theory of Thomas Hobbes, it, too, claimed to be observational, descriptive, and scientific. From the thesis that everyone as a matter of fact seeks nothing but pleasure, Bentham somehow arrived at the position that one ought to seek, not only his own pleasure, but the greatest pleasure of the greatest number.

"Nature," writes Bentham, "has placed mankind under the governance of two sovereign masters, *pain* and *pleasure*. It is for them alone to point out what we ought to do, as well as to determine what we shall do. . . . They govern us in all we do, in all we say, in all we think."

The pleasure to be expected from prospective lines of action is to be measured by seven parameters: intensity, duration, certainty, propinquity, fecundity, purity, and extent. The latter is the number of persons to whom the pleasure extends. By calculating the amounts of pleasure to be produced from alternate lines of action, anyone should know which action he should choose.

The right action is enforced by four sanctions. Consequences, painful or pleasurable, derived through the ordinary course of nature, presumably physiological, issue from or belong to the *physical* sanction. Consequences derived through the actions of the police, the courts, and the state form the *political* sanction. Pleasures and pain received at the hands of such chance persons who spontaneously react to our conduct form the *moral* or *social* sanction. Bentham also makes religion a fourth sanction; but this *religious* sanction operates only through the other three. Bentham gives lip service to the possibility of divine rewards and punishments in a future life, but these can have no effect on man's present choices. Such consequences are not open to observation; men cannot calculate the amounts—whether those pains and pleasures are like or unlike the present kind is something beyond the realm of discovery by observation.

Bentham's utilitarianism provides a good opportunity for showing the weakness of many secular systems. In the first place, the calculation of future pleasures, on which choice and the knowledge of obligation depend, is impossible. Only in a few simple instances, and in these only roughly, can anyone estimate the amount of pleasure he as an individual will enjoy from a particular choice. To suppose that anyone can calculate the sum total of pleasures accruing to the whole human race is utterly and obviously impossible. Let anyone who wishes, try measuring along the seven parameters.

The principle of the greatest good for the greatest number is one by which dictators can justify their cruelty. When the Communists starved to death millions of Ukrainians, massacred thousands of Polish officers, murdered possibly twenty million Chinese, and slaughtered the Tibetans, they could justify themselves on the ground that the pleasure of future generations of Communists would outweigh the temporary pain. Certainly no scientific observation can prove the contrary.

Less gruesome but even more fundamentally destructive of utilitarianism is the fact that descriptive science can discover no reason for aiming at the good of all society. Plato, Aristotle, Butler, all agree that men should seek their own good; who can urge them to seek their own harm? Why should anyone govern his actions by the good of another person? If perchance, as Butler asserted, there is never any conflict between a man's good and the good of every other human being, then self-seeking and altruism will both prescribe the same choices. But this utopian assumption contradicts observable evidence. Personal jealousies and international conflicts alike demonstrate the incompatibility of goods. Actual life is much more like Hobbes's war of each against all than like a perfect universal harmony.

## b. Henry Sidgwick (1838-1900)

To avoid this disastrous argument against utilitarianism, Henry Sidgwick, whose *Methods of Ethics* is the best analysis of ethical methodology so far written, relinquished the descriptive basis Bentham used, and tried to found utilitarianism on intuitions. He urged his readers to look at the matter "from the point of view, if I may say so, of the Universe." But unfortunately no one man is the universe, and therefore no one man can see things from its point of view; nor is it easy to learn why anyone ought to take any other point of view than his own. Another person's pleasure, enjoyment, or good cannot be mine.

Sidgwick was honest enough to admit that the compatibility of all individual goods can be maintained only on the basis of God's rewards and punishments. It is incapable of empirical proof. Therefore, much to his distaste, he is forced to admit the question whether a theory of ethics can be constructed on an independent basis, or whether it is forced to borrow a fundamental principle from theology (*Methods of Ethics,* pp. 506-509). His modesty, his honesty, and his almost superhuman effort to save utilitarianism seal its doom.

Hedonism in any of its forms is a teleological system. Moral acts have the purpose of producing pleasure, and they are tested by their actual consequences.

## 3. Categorical Imperatives— Immanuel Kant (1724-1804)

A century earlier Immanuel Kant, of Germany, constructed a nonhedonistic, non-teleological system, in which the moral quality of an act was entirely independent of actual consequences.

One of Kant's chief objections to an ethics of calculation was that on such an arrangement only those who are brilliant mathematicians can be moral. On the contrary, morality ought to be within the abilities of every humble person. Furthermore, common opinion never regards a man as immoral just because he fails to obtain a great deal of pleasure. He may be imprudent or stupid, but if his intentions are sincere and good, he is considered moral. Conversely, successful calculation may prove a man clever, but is no basis for judging him to be particularly moral.

In opposition to empirical ethics, therefore, Kant put forward a theory of *a priori* duty. A moral precept is such because it is a categorical imperative. Some imperatives are merely hypothetical: To bisect a line, one must draw certain arcs. Such imperatives are scientific, and if anyone does not wish to bisect an arc, no obligation exists. Moral, or categorical imperatives, however, do not depend on *ifs*. It is "immoral" to say that if a person wants a good reputation, he should be honest and tell the truth. One ought to be honest and tell the truth regardless of consequences, and even without being so motivated. A moral act must be motivated only by reverence for duty.

Duty then is determined, not by any pleasure accruing to the individual, but by maxims that can be universalized. If I tell a lie by making a promise I do not intend to keep, I make myself an exception to a universal maxim. The only reason I can deceive anyone by a false promise is that people expect promises to be kept. If all or even most promises were broken, there would be no promises at all because no one would believe them. Hence the intent to deceive depends on the maxim of non-deception. An individual cannot universalize the maxim of false promise because such an attempt is self-contradictory. A false promise is always and of necessity an exception and can never be a general rule. Universalization therefore, or the absence of self-contradiction, is the test of morality. The results of the action have nothing to do with it.

Kant's example of truth-telling is the best one he could have used. Others are not so convincing. For example, the maxim, "Be a miser," can be universalized; so also "Be a spendthrift." Neither of these require the agent to be an exception to the general rule; neither is self-destructive. Similarly the maxim, "Commit suicide," contains no self-contradictions. Or, if the maxim applied to children so that the human race would become extinct, in which case suicides would no longer be possible, the maxim can be replaced: "Commit suicide on your forty-fifth birthday." Kant tried his best to show that suicide is immoral, but if he succeeded it is because of an appeal to God and not because of a categorical imperative. Kant's ethics can be saved, then, only by an admission that suicide is right and that a miser and a spendthrift are morally equal.

However, Kant's thesis faces even greater difficulties. Morality seems to presuppose freedom. Ask a man, wrote Kant, whether he can refuse to bear false witness in court when his king requires it; and the man might doubt that he would refuse, but he would not doubt that he could refuse. Duty and the categorical imperative depend on freedom.

At the same time, Kant, to escape Hume's empirical skepticism, worked out a system of epistemology, by which every atom, every motion, every physiological change, every natural desire is determined by mathematical, mechanical law. Freedom is physically, scientifically impossible. How then can freedom and morality be saved?

It must be insisted upon that free will is not the ability to indulge one's desires and natural impulses. Natural impulses are natural; they are caused by physiological conditions. A will is free only when self-caused—independent of all influences external to itself. Such freedom is impossible in the physical, visible world.

In this predicament Kant asserts that men are citizens of two worlds. Beyond the visible world there is an intelligible world, where neither matter nor mechanism can corrupt, and where causality does not break through and steal man's freedom. In that world, morality is possible.

In this world, where men's bodies are and where men's actions occur, is morality possible? Consider a particular act of theft. A man breaks the lock on a door, enters a house, and steals some cash and jewelry. All these actions are physical actions in time and space. Now Kant is adamant. There can be no freedom, he says, for bodies or actions in time; all temporal factors are mechanically determined. Some moralists have tried to preserve freedom by denying that the motions of the theft are physically necessitated, by asserting that they are produced by some sort of psychological causation. The thief is said to be free because he acts according to his own character. Kant calls this theory a wretched subterfuge. Psychological states are as much necessitated as physical motions. Logically, it follows therefore that the theft itself could have been avoided in the higher world, although the motions of the theft could not have been avoided in this world.

This conclusion is paradoxical, to say the least; and Kant refused to explain it. He wrote, "Reason would therefore completely transcend its proper limits, if it should undertake to explain how pure reason can be practical, or what is the same thing, to explain how freedom is possible . . . while therefore it is true that we cannot comprehend this practical unconditioned necessity of the moral imperative, it is also true that we can comprehend its incomprehensibility; and this is all that can be fairly demanded of a philosophy which seeks to reach the principles which determine the limits of human reason" (*Critique of Practical Reason*, T.K. Abbot's tr., pp. 189-191).

## 4. Instrumentalism—John Dewey (1859-1952)

For American readers something needs to be said about John Dewey. He offered an empirical, scientific ethics, and therefore the criticism must center on points previously discussed; but he is not a utilitarian and his details are significantly different.

In fact, his details and their practical application may overshadow the pure theory. For example, much of the agitation against capital punishment, which is a Biblical provision for the administration of justice, stems from Dewey's teaching. Capital punishment, he argued, ignores the fact, or alleged fact, that society is as much to blame for crime as is the criminal. Criminals should not be punished—this is irrational vengeance—they should be rehabilitated and paroled. (That the solicitude of the liberals for criminals and their callousness toward the victims result in a sharply rising crime rate never occurs to such penologists.)

This loose attitude toward crime seems to contrast with an insistence of stringent government controls over all business transactions. Rejecting the ideal of liberty, Dewey, the liberal, wrote, "Find a man who believes that all men need is freedom *from* oppressive legal and political measures, and you have a man who, unless he is merely obstinately maintaining his own private privileges, carries at the back of his head some heritage of the metaphysical doctrine of free will, plus an optimistic confidence in natural harmony" (*Human Nature and Conduct*, IV. iii). That power corrupts and that politicians are as depraved as other men, and that therefore the extent of government regulation should be minimal is too theological an argument to impress Dewey. In fact, Dewey looked forward to the day when the government would control, not merely many human activities, but even men's thoughts and wishes. He saw in the future a scientific advance that would enable politicians to manipulate men as we now manipulate physical things (*Problems of Men*, pp. 178, 179).

As a pragmatist, or instrumentalist, Dewey did not believe in fixed ethical principles any more than he believed in fixed truth of any sort. "We institute standards of justice, truth, esthetic quality, etc. . . . exactly as we set up a platinum bar as a standard measurer of lengths. The superiority of one conception of justice to another is of the same order as the superiority of the metric system" (*Logic, The Theory of Inquiry*, p. 216).

Dewey used an even better analogy. Moral standards are like the rules of grammar. They are both the result of custom. Language evolved from unintelligent babblings; then came grammar. But language continues to change and grammar changes with it. So too, the rules of morality change with changing customs, from which it may be inferred, though Dewey does not explicitly use the example, that cannibalism and rape would be moral wherever they occurred frequently enough.

In consonance with this, Dewey held that nothing is intrinsically good or bad; nothing is valuable in and of itself alone; all beliefs, all actions, and all values are instrumental. They are judged by their consequences. If they solve human problems, they are good instruments.

Unless the solution sought is itself an independent or intrinsic value, it is hard to see how it can confer value on the means. For example, chess can be considered as an instrument in cementing friendships. Yet this is hardly the reason why anyone plays chess. Usually its intrinsic merit is the motivation.

Dewey, in strange company with Aristotle, might have spurned this illustration on the ground that games are too trivial. As Aristotle said, recreation is for the sake of serious work. But Aristotle said this out of a theory of human nature that Dewey could not consistently use. If nothing is intrinsically valuable, there is no ground for distinguishing recreation from serious work.

In particular, Dewey could not accept Aristotle's view that knowledge is intrinsically valuable. He castigated such a view as a retreat to an ivory tower. Knowledge and going to college are instrumental. For a young man, they are instrumental in getting a job. For a young woman, they are instrumental in getting a young man. But the job and the marriage also are merely instrumental— to raising a family and sending the children to college. Chess, however, is instrumental in restricting social contacts, therefore in avoiding marriage and its expenses, and this saving is instrumental in buying a more handsome set of chessmen. Nowhere is there any intrinsic value. The choice therefore between marriage and chess is entirely irrational.

Dewey tried to escape this criticism by asserting that there are evil ideals. Without aesthetic enjoyment, mankind might become a race of economic monsters (*Reconstruction in Philosophy*, p. 127). But could Dewey consistently maintain that monsters are intrinsically bad?

In another place he relied on common opinion and declared that no honest person can think that murder is instrumental to anything good and that everybody resents acts of wanton cruelty (Dewey and Tufts, *Ethics*, pp. 251, 265, 292). Yet it is known that the Communists and other radicals use assassination as a political device (compare Hermann Raschhofer, *Political Assassination*, Tubingen [1964]); and some Latins enjoy the wanton cruelty of bullfights.

In his opposition to wanton cruelty, Dewey has inherited a Puritan ideal. In addition to the inconsistency of relying on Protestant ethics, there is the more formidable question as to how one decides between incompatible ideals: assassination, equal justice, minority rights, wanton cruelty, and kindness. If nothing is intrinsically valuable, how could Dewey choose?

In fact, how could Dewey choose to do anything? If there are no intrinsic values, if there is no final goal, like Aristotelian happiness, if man has no chief end, by which alone subordinate means become worthwhile, the ultimate ethical question arises in full force: Why continue living—why not commit suicide?

The value of life is not just one more point of detail, as if a group would discuss theft and honesty, brutality and kindness, and then discuss suicide. These particular details are subsidiary to the all-embracing question of the reason for living. Obviously a man can choose neither honesty nor theft, unless he has first chosen to continue living.

Many modern moralists, unlike Kant, refuse to face this question. F.C.S. Schiller, a pragmatist like Dewey, notes the logical possibility of a pessimism that holds life to be, not necessarily painful, but merely too dreary and boring to be worth the trouble. On the other hand, he offers no argument against this position.

This pessimistic view is not an odd affection of a few publicity seekers. Buddhism, with its millions, is a close approximation. Granted, the Buddhists do not approve of suicide—but not because they think life is worthwhile. Suicide is rejected because they think it is not effective enough. It does not extinguish life. Hence, they try to suppress all desire, try to make no choices, and thus attain the "extinction" of Nirvana.

The failure to give a rational refutation of pessimism is the final refutation of instrumentalistic ethics. To choose an action as a means to another *ad infinitum,* and to find value nowhere, resemble nothing so much as the frustration of Sisyphus.

## 5. Contemporary Ethics

One more contemporary view of ethics needs to be included, and it is the one that crowns the whole history of secular ethics with failure. The view (for it is not a theory but the absence of all theory) has a negative and a positive stage.

### a. P.H. Howell-Smith

Negatively, P.H. Howell-Smith in his *Ethics* writes, "Moral philosophy is a practical science; its aim is to answer questions in the form 'What shall I do?' But no general answer can be given to this type of question. The most a moral philosopher can do is to paint a picture of various types of life . . . and ask which type of life you really want to lead." Ethical choices are therefore personal preferences, and no one can question another's preference for murder and rape anymore than his preference for olives and onions.

## b. W.H.F. Barnes

The positive stage of this viewpoint is expressed by W.H.F. Barnes, A.J. Ayer, and C.L. Stevenson. Their point is that ethical propositions are emotional ejaculations. Barnes writes, "Many [and I do not see why he does not say "all"] controversies arising out of value judgments are settled by saying, 'I like it and you don't, and that is the end of the matter.' "

## c. A.J. Ayer

Ayer is more explicit: "If I say to someone, 'You acted wrongly in stealing that money,' I am not stating anything more than if I had simply said, 'You stole that money.' In adding that this action is wrong I am not making any further statement about it. I am simply evincing my moral disapproval of it. It is as if I had said, 'You stole that money' in a peculiar tone of horror . . . the tone . . . adds nothing to the literal meaning of the sentence."

## d. C.L. Stevenson

Stevenson goes beyond Ayer in that he emphasizes, not merely one's own approval or disapproval, but chiefly one's attempt to induce the same feeling in other people. When an individual says, "Stealing is wrong," he not only means that he does not like, it, but in addition he is trying to persuade someone else to dislike it also. It is similar to the ejaculation "onions taste horrible." This conveys no information about onions; it is merely an attempt to persuade another person to eat olives instead.

Suppose that the other person insists on liking and eating onions. Suppose that the other person insists on thievery and bullfights. What is to be done in such cases of moral disagreement? Here Stevenson frankly admits that there is no rational method for settling such a disagreement. The only method is eloquence and emotional persuasion.

It is true that persuasion, like bribery, sometimes works; but it does not support the conclusion that the action recommended is good or obligatory. It is not obligatory for the person persuaded, but, more to the point, it is not obligatory even for the first person. The only problem Stevenson has solved is the problem of getting other unprincipled people to do what the unprincipled persuader wants done. The real problem of ethics, however, is how to decide which action and which principles *ought* to be acknowledged. In the failure to solve this problem is where Stevenson, emotional ethics, and secularism all fail.

## II. Some Christian Principles

A satisfactory ethics needs principles for systematic consistency and details for practical application. Omitting the former produces chaos; omitting the latter removes all guidelines for choice and action.

## A. The Decalogue and its implications.

During the first century and a half of the Protestant Reformation, the Calvinists (Reformed, Presbyterian, and Puritan) distinguished themselves by their stress on ethics. They not only emphasized the Ten Commandments—one would naturally expect any form of Christian ethics to acknowledge the Ten Commandments as basic obligations—but they took the trouble to outline their implications. This work, initiated by Calvin in the *Institutes*, II, viii, is summarized in the *Westminster Larger Catechism*, from which several following quotations illustrate the detailed application of divine law to the moral situations of life.

Q. 93. What is the moral law?

A. The moral law is the declaration of the will of God to mankind, directing and binding every one to personal, perfect, and perpetual conformity and obedience thereunto, in the frame and disposition of the whole man, soul and body, and in performance of all those duties of holiness and righteousness which he oweth to God and man: promising life upon the fulfilling, and threatening death upon the breach of it.

Q. 99. What rules are to be observed for the right understanding of the ten commandments?

A. For the right understanding of the ten commandments, these rules are to be observed:—1. That the law is perfect, and bindeth every one to full conformity in the whole man unto righteousness thereof, and unto entire obedience for ever; so as to require the utmost perfection of every duty, and to forbid the least degree of every sin. 2. That it is spiritual, and so reacheth the understanding, will, affections, and all other powers of the soul; as well as words, works, and gestures. 3. That one and the same thing, in divers respects, is required or forbidden in several commandments. 4. That, where a duty is commanded, the contrary sin is forbidden; and, where a sin is forbidden, the contrary duty is commanded: so, where a promise is annexed, the contrary threatening is included; and, where a threatening is annexed, the contrary promise is included. 5. That what God forbids, is at no time to be done; what he commands is always our duty; and yet every particular duty is not to be done at all times. 6. That, under one sin or duty, all of the same kind are forbidden or commanded; together with all the causes, means, occasions, and appearances thereof, and provocations thereunto. 7. That what is forbidden or commanded to ourselves, we are bound, according to our places, to endeavor that it may be avoided or performed by others, according to the duty of their places. 8. That in what is commanded to others, we are bound, according to our places and callings, to be helpful to them; and to take heed of partaking with others in what is forbidden them.

Q. 134. Which is the sixth commandment?
A. The sixth commandment is, Thou shalt not kill.

Q. 135. What are the duties required in the sixth commandment?
A. The duties required in the sixth commandment are, all careful studies, and lawful endeavors, to preserve the life of ourselves and others, by resisting all thoughts and purposes, subduing all passions, and avoiding all occasions, temptations, and practices, which tend to the unjust taking away the life of any; by just defense thereof against violence; patient bearing of the hand of God, quietness of mind, cheerfulness of spirit; a sober use of meat, drink, physic, sleep, labor, and recreation; by charitable thoughts, love, compassion, meekness, gentleness, kindness; peaceable, mild, and courteous speeches and behavior: forbearing, readiness to be reconciled, patient bearing and forgiving of injuries, and requiting good for evil; comforting and succoring the distressed, and protecting and defending the innocent.

Q. 136. What are the sins forbidden in the sixth commandment?

A. The sins forbidden in the sixth commandment are, all taking away the life of ourselves, or of others, except in case of public justice, lawful war, or necessary defense; the neglecting or withdrawing the lawful or necessary means of preservation of life; sinful anger, hatred, envy, desire of revenge; all excessive passions, distracting cares; immoderate use of meat, drink, labor, and recreations; provoking words, oppression, quarreling, striking, wounding, and whatsoever else tends to the destruction of the life of any.

Q. 140. Which is the eighth commandment?
A. The eighth commandment is, Thou shalt not steal.

Q. 141. What are the duties required in the eighth commandment?
A. The duties required in the eighth commandment are, truth, faithfulness, and justice in contracts and commerce between man and man; rendering to every one his due; restitution of goods unlawfully detained from the right owners thereof; giving and lending freely, according to our abilities, and the necessities of others; moderation of our judgments, wills, and affections, concerning worldly goods; a provident care and study to get, keep, use, and dispose of those things which are necessary and convenient for the sustentation of our nature, and suitable to our condition; a lawful calling, and diligence in it; frugality, avoiding unnecessary lawsuits, and suretyship, and other like engagements; and an endeavor by all just and lawful means to procure, preserve, and further the wealth and outward estate of others, as well as our own.

Q. 142. What are the sins forbidden in the eighth commandment?
A. The sins forbidden in the eighth commandment, beside the neglect of the duties required, are theft, robbery, man-stealing, and receiving any thing that is stolen; fraudulent dealing; false weights and measures; removing landmarks; injustice and unfaithfulness in contracts between man and man, or in matters of trust; oppression; extortion; usury; bribery; vexatious lawsuits; unjust enclosures and depredation; engrossing commodities to enhance the price, unlawful callings, and all other unjust or sinful ways of taking or withholding from our neighbor what belongs to him, or of enriching ourselves; covetousness; inordinate prizing and affecting worldly goods; distrustful and distracting cares and studies in

getting, keeping, and using them; envying at the prosperity of others: as likewise idleness, prodigality, wasteful gaming, and all other ways whereby we do unduly prejudice our own outward estate: and defrauding ourselves of the due use and comfort of that estate which God hath given us.

In addition to official and therefore brief expositions of ethics, there are innumerable books, either on Christian ethics as a whole, or on particular problems, such as divorce, the family, alcoholism, etc., or on such Biblical sections as the ethics of the gospels and the ethics of the Old Testament. Some of these are Biblical and orthodox; others are liberal. In general they show how much detail can be derived by implication from the Biblical material.

## B. Christian presuppositions

If one of the purposes of ethics is to furnish concrete instruction applicable to everyday living, the superiority of Christianity over secular attempts is unmistakable. The Ten Commandments, however, rest on certain presuppositions that provide the more theoretical or theological basis for Biblical ethics.

### 1. Authority

The Ten Commandments derive their validity from Biblical authority. If the Bible is composed of myths, and superstitions—the product of ingenious human construction—no one would be obliged to obey its commands. Aside from the secular systems previously discussed, men could choose the Code of Hammurabi or could consider the claims of the Koran, the Vedas, and other sacred books. Christian morality, therefore, depends on Christian revelation.

Underlying the authority of the Bible is the authority of God who gave the Bible; and the God who gave the Bible is not just any kind of deity, but is One with definite characteristics.

### 2. Revelation

It is almost repetitious to insist that one of God's characteristics is the ability to speak. But the repetition is excusable because many contemporary theologians deny that God can speak. They may try to find some place for revelation in their theology, but it is a nonverbal revelation, something other than a communication of truth. Revelation in these theologies may be the mighty acts of God in history, or some mystic experience of encounter or confrontation.

This view of revelation is worthless. Without information divinely given man could not discern which historical events were mighty acts of God—the Exodus, perhaps; but why not also Caesar's crossing the Rubicon and Stalin's capture of Berlin? What is worse, after selecting a series of events, man would be at a loss to interpret them. Would there be any difference in value between Moses's crossing the Red Sea and Caesar's crossing the Rubicon? Do these events means that no one should eat pork, or that everyone should support civil rights, or that attendance at football games is acceptable worship? Attempts to draw practical implications from these historical events would only revert to the secular theories of developing ethics out of experience, which has been shown to be impossible.

Ethics requires definite information as to what is right and wrong, and such information can be revealed only by a living, communicating God.

## 3. Immutability

In the present decade several books have been published on theological ethics, presumably in opposition to irreligious secularism. The type of ethics depends on the type of theology. One such book defends the concept of the "New Morality," which in these days is offered as a substitute for the Ten Commandments. Dr. James Sellers declares that men need a new morality, a new ethics, and a new theology. In support of a changing ethics he approves Paul Ramsey's statement: "At the level of theory itself, any formulation of Christian social ethics is always in need of reformulation" (*Theological Ethics,* pp. ix, 39).

The notion that the principles of ethics (not merely their applications to changing social forms, but the basic principles themselves) must always be changing requires belief in a changing god and a changing revelation. Obviously this necessitates a rejection of the Ten Commandments and derivative Biblical precepts. Though Dr. Sellers is not too clear on the nature of God, he could not be clearer in his rejection of Scripture. He defines revelation as "something [that] has happened to us in our history which conditions all our thinking" (*ibid.*, p. 71); as for example, the death of one's mother. Concerning the Bible he says, "worse, in some places where it is not silent, it gives us advice that is manifestly bad if taken literally"; and "the Bible also illustrates its insights with outmoded or downright unacceptable examples of morality" (pp. 88, 92).

The notion of a changing morality presupposes belief in a changing god, and raises theological issues. If, on the other hand, men accept the Ten Commandments as permanent obligations, they must also accept the Biblical concept of an immutable God. Biblical morality and Biblical theology are inseparable.

The idea that the firm morality of the Bible must now be replaced with something loose is a practical danger of this present age. In opposition to Christ's specific instructions about divorce and remarriage, some denominations officially encourage their ministers to substitute their own permissive judgment; and individual ministers of various denominations approve of adultery if the two people "really love each other." All this "new morality"—actually as old as the Canaanites—stems from a rejection of the God of the Bible.

## 4. Sovereignty of God

Immutability, however, is not the only divine characteristic needed for a systematic Christian ethics. Sovereignty is even more important.

In the Platonic philosophy, the principles of ethics, though they differ in detail from those of Christianity, are sufficiently immutable. But god, the maker of heaven and earth, is not sovereign according to Plato; above the demiurge is an immutable World of Ideas to which even he must submit.

In modern times, the point at issue is exemplified in the philosophy of Leibniz. His famous phrase that this is the best of all possible worlds, a phrase Voltaire's *Candide* ridicules with brutal force, depends on the notion that various possible worlds exist in a sort of blueprint form independently of God. Because God is good, he naturally chose the best blueprint at the time of creation. Therefore the actual world is the best possible. This exactly follows Plato, who, in his *Euthyphro,* asserted that good is not good because God approves of it, but that God approves of it because it is antecedently and independently good.

The Jewish philosopher Philo, who lived at the time of Christ, though profoundly influenced by Plato, made an alteration that completely reversed Platonic and Leibnizian theology. This alteration consisted in making God supreme and in placing the World of Ideas in God's mind. Philo wrote, "God has been ranked according to the one and the unit; or rather, even the unit has been ranked according to the one God, for all number, like time, is younger than the cosmos." In this quotation, Philo subjects mathematics to the thinking activity of God. Similarly, God does not will the good because it is independently good, but on the contrary the good is good because God wills it.

To the same effect Calvin (*Institutes*, I, xiv, 1) wrote, "Augustine justly complains that it is an offense against God to inquire for any cause of things higher than his will." Later (III, xxii, 2) he says, "how exceedingly presumptuous it is only to inquire into the causes of the Divine will, which is in fact and is justly entitled to be the cause of everything that exists. For if it has any cause, then there must be something antecedent, on which it depends; which it is impious to suppose. For the will of God is the highest rule of justice; so that what he wills must be considered just, for this very reason, because he wills it."

The sovereignty of God is the key to the basic problem of ethics. Why is anything good, right, or obligatory? Neither utilitarianism, nor pragmatism, nor emotionalism can give a rational answer. Calvin has given the answer in very precise language: "the will of God is the highest rule of justice; so that what he wills must be considered just, for this very reason, because he wills it." God establishes moral norms by sovereign decree.

That this principle permeates the Bible can easily be seen. No devout Christian holds that anything external to God compelled or induced him to create a certain number of solar satellites rather than a different number. God could have created water with a different freezing point. Similarly, there was no external cause of his choice of detail in the Mosaic ritual. Could he not have willed the Tabernacle to have been hexagonal instead of rectangular? Similarly, could he not have imposed on man other commandments rather than the ten? Was it not merely his decision to have one Sabbath each week instead of two? Or could he not have created the world in five days and have substituted a different fourth commandment to fit a six-day week? Is it not due to God's will that man differs from the animals, and could not man have been made so that, as in their case, the sixth, seventh, and eighth commandments would not apply?

The omnipotence and sovereignty of God, as the controlling concept of Christianity, solve the problems of every sphere. The power of God is the answer to scientific objections against miracles; his will is the authority for civil government and the key to political science; and similarly his precepts constitute ethics. The good or the right is not the pleasure of the greatest number, to be determined by an impossible calculation; right or justice is what God commands, to be discovered by reading the written revelation. The sanctions are not Bentham's, nor is virtue its own reward; on the contrary, God enforces moral obligation by the joys of heaven and the pains of hell. Here is logical consistency unmatched by either the rationalist Leibniz or the emotionalist Stevenson; here is the practical detail absent in secularism; here are the sanctions Stalin and Hitler could not escape. Such is Christian ethics.

---

*Zondervan Pictorial Encyclopedia of the Bible*, Merrill C. Tenney, editor. Grand Rapids, Michigan: Zondervan Publishing House, 1975, pp. 385-404. Reprinted by permission.

# 16

# The Ethics of Abortion

Today many hospitals, institutions which are supposed to save life, permit and even encourage their doctors to kill innocent babies. They tear the babies limb from limb or sometimes the nurses have thrown the living babies into garbage cans.

Abortion is legal because the Supreme Court in Washington, D.C. said so. A majority of nine men, without any amending of the Constitution or any referendum of the population, but all by themselves, negated the legal right of innocent persons to live. Having rejected God, they wish to assume his prerogatives.

One argument abortionists frequently use to defend themselves against the charge of murder is the claim that the baby is not a human being. But if the baby in the womb is not human, what is it? Is it canine? Is it feline? I think that some babies born thirty or forty years ago have turned out to be asinine.

Another argument which abortionists use to defend their murder of innocent infants is that the government must not base its legislation on religious principles. Legislation should always be based on irreligious principles. No doubt you have all heard that the government should never enforce morality. This may be one reason why many abortionists oppose the death penalty for murder. This is consistent, for if murder be a capital offense, the abortionists, both doctors and mothers, are in great danger.

But if a government cannot enforce morality, rape would be as legal as murder. Nor could the government prohibit theft. Note carefully that the same Ten Commandments which condemn murder condemn theft also. When irreligious bureaucrats and secular judges prohibit the display of the Ten Commandments on the walls of a public school, they erase theft as well as murder from the list of crimes. Opposition to theft is just as religious as opposition to murder. Christianity condemns both murder and theft because both are condemned by God.

If atheism is to be the law of the land, there can be no laws at all to support morality, for there is no morality apart from the laws of God. I would like to make it clear that sociology, statistics, psychology, or any empirical science can never determine moral norms. Secular science at best can discover what people do; but it cannot discover what people ought to do. From observational premises no normative conclusion follows. Any attempt to define morality by observational science is a logical fallacy. Science can invent new ways of killing people, but science can never determine who should be killed. It cannot determine who should not be killed. It can only invent more effective ways of doing what somebody for some other reason wants to do.

The controversy between those who consider life sacred and those who kill babies is not a controversy between two systems of ethics, as if we had one system and the abortionists, secularists, and atheists had a different system. The point is that they cannot have any system of ethics at all. Scientific observation—what they sometimes call *reason* as opposed to what they misunderstand by *faith*—cannot establish any values whatever. Science often produces wonders but one thing it cannot do: It cannot establish the value of anything, even the value of itself. Repudiation of divine laws is destructive of all morality. Abortion is immoral.

Rejecting God, the abortionists try to justify their cruelty to babies, while at the same time condemning burglary, by an appeal to a social consensus. To this attempt to condemn theft while justifying murder, there is a single answer with two parts. First, no social consensus has been established. The Supreme Court alone, nine men out of two hundred million, legalized the killing of babies on its own arbitrary authority. This is the autocracy of evil dictators. Then, second, social consensus cannot determine what is right or wrong. The social consensus of the Spartans in antiquity and of some Indian tribes in North America condoned theft and even praised it. Before the Belgians took over the Congo a century or so ago, social consensus approved of cannibalism. The fact that various societies have considered theft and cannibalism to be right does not prove that theft and cannibalism are right—nor the murder of babies, either. One can perhaps with relative ease discover what groups of people think is right; but social consensus does not make anything right or wrong. So far as I can see, the only pertinent difference between the abortionists here and the cannibals in the Congo is that the abortionists do not eat the babies. They throw them in the garbage can.

What a waste of good meat in these times of famine. Of course the meat would have to be inspected by the USDA, but I can see no reason, on abortionist principles—or lack of principles—for prohibiting the eating of human flesh. A nice tender baby might taste better than a Cornish hen. Or if the mothers, for no good reason, do not want to eat their babies, they could at least send them to alleviate starvation in the Third World.

Of course babies are a little small, like Cornish hens. But if the Supreme Court can legalize the murder of infants, it can as easily legalize the murder of adults. Indeed some groups already propose the murder of the elderly. Abortion logically justifies the murder of anyone. Hence the Supreme Court could legalize the murder of all who support the right of life and so produce a unanimous social consensus.

If anyone thinks that this proposal is extreme, be it noted that Hitler's National Socialism and Stalin's International Socialism attempted just that. Hitler massacred the Jews and Stalin massacred the Ukrainians and hordes of others. And aside from historical example, rampant murder is well within the logical range of atheistic abortionism. There is a determined effort in this nation to reduce orthodox Christians to the status of second class citizens. Their recent interest in politics and law has been severely condemned. Even Barry Goldwater, supposedly a conservative of the conservatives, showed his anti-religious bigotry in denouncing the pro-life movement. In many public schools the secularist view is sustained by government imposition and the pro-life view is denied a hearing. Smut is legal, and even required reading, but the Ten Commandments are prohibited. The end of this, unless stopped, is the same persecution now practiced under Communism.

We must try to stop this atheistic program. And one place, a good place to start, is abortion.

---

*The Trinity Review,* May/June1982.

# 17
# Free Will

When a discussion grows excited, there are two possible explanations. Excitement may indicate the topic is of great importance. Now, in this series of articles on the Westminster Confession every chapter so far has seemed of great importance; and free will is also a matter of importance, though it can hardly be of such importance as the previous chapter on Christ the Mediator. In the second place, excited discussion frequently indicates that the debaters are not sure of themselves. When contenders have neglected essential distinctions and have proceeded beyond their resources, the discussion can go on endlessly and without conclusions. As this has often been the case with discussions on free will, it would be wise to see exactly what the Confession says.

"God hath endued the will of man with that natural liberty that is neither forced nor by any absolute necessity of nature determined to good or evil." Now, what does the Confession mean by natural liberty? Does a Presbyterian mean the same thing that a Romanist or an Arminian means, when they say that man is free? Are there various concepts of freedom?

Obviously there are various concepts of freedom, and most of them have little to do with the present topic. For example, we say today that American citizens are free men, but that the victims of communistic governments are not free. Freedom therefore has a political and an economic sense; but that is not what concerns us here.

More to the point is whether or not the will of man is free from his intellect. Theologians in the past have discussed this at length. But that the will is free from the intellect is not what the Confession means by natural liberty. Calvin, for example, asserted that "the intellect rules the will;" Charles Hodge said that man's "will was subject to his reason;" and Robert J. Breckenridge taught that our primary conception of will includes the notion of its being directed by intelligence. The theology behind all this may be a little intricate, and the matter is mentioned only to show that freedom from intellect is not what Presbyterians mean by the concept of freedom.

Then does freedom, free will, or natural liberty mean that man is free from sin? Or, more pertinently, does it mean that man is free not to sin? Perhaps an Arminian might claim that man has a free will in the sense that he can choose not to sin. But the Confession, in the same chapter, section iii, says, "Man by his fall into a state of sin hath wholly lost all ability of will to any spiritual good accompanying salvation; so as a natural man . . . is not able by his own strength to convert himself or to prepare himself thereunto." Some Arminians seem to say that a sinner can choose to prepare himself for conversion; but the Bible says that man is dead in sin and needs to be raised from the dead. A dead man cannot choose to be raised.

Freedom from sin, complete freedom, is attained only in heaven; but even in heaven a completely free and undetermined will cannot be found. It is equally impossible for the glorified saint to choose to sin as it was for the unregenerate to choose not to sin. As Augustine said, the condition of man in heaven is *non posse peccare:* not able to sin. Heaven would be a precarious place if its citizens had this sort of free will.

What then does the Confession mean by the natural liberty of the will? The remainder of the section quoted answers this question as well as two lines can. Man's will "is neither forced nor by any absolute necessity of nature determined." These words were written to repudiate those philosophies which explain human conduct in terms of physico-chemical law. Although the Westminster divines did not know twentieth century behaviorism, nor even Spinoza, they very probably knew Thomas Hobbes, and they certainly knew earlier materialistic theories. That man's conduct is determined by inanimate forces is what the Confession denies. Man is not a machine; his motions cannot be described by mathematical equations as the motions of the planets can. His hopes, plans, and activities are not controlled by physical conditions. He is not determined by any absolute necessity of nature.

But this does not mean that man is free from God. The Confession does not deny, but on the contrary explicitly affirms that God controls the will of man. To say that physics and chemistry do not explain conduct is not to rule out God's grace. Section iv states that by his grace alone God enables a man freely to will what is good; the Holy Spirit effectually calls elect sinners to faith in Christ (III vi); he makes them willing and able to believe (VII iii); Christ certainly and effectually applies salvation to his people (VIII viii); and similar expressions occur in later chapters.

Unless God "governs all creatures, actions, and things" (V i), or "all his creatures and all their actions" (Shorter Catechism 11), he would not be actually omnipotent, nor could we be sure his prophecies would infallibly come true. An interesting though obscure case of God's control over the will of men is found in Exodus 34:24. The men of Israel are commanded to appear before the Lord three times a year. As such an occasion would offer an excellent opportunity for an enemy attack, the Lord assures his people that their enemies will not desire to attack at those times. In II Samuel 17:14 Absalom chose the worse advice because the Lord had planned to defeat the better counsel in order to bring evil on Absalom. God also caused Rehoboam to adopt evil counsel (II Chronicles 10:15) in order to fulfil his promise to Jeroboam. Better known than these cases are the words of Paul in Philippians 2:12,13, "Work out your own salvation in fear and trembling, for it is God that worketh in you both to will and to do."

Man has a natural liberty not acknowledged by materialistic philosophy, but Christians should never construe that liberty to the detriment of God's omnipotence and grace.

---

*The Southern Presbyterian Journal,* December 22, 1954.

# 18

# Fruits of the Reformation in Philosophy and Ethics

That the Reformation caused tremendous changes in the spiritual and ecclesiastical conditions of Europe needs no emphasis. Its impact on politics is also indisputable. But its effect on philosophy and ethics no doubt requires some explanation.

During the early Middle Ages, philosophy (what there was of it) followed in general the principles of a Platonic Augustinianism. The spiritual realm was considered to be directly accessible to reason, while the sensible world neither provided the basis of knowledge nor contributed any great amount to its sum total. Philosophy in effect coalesced with theology.

In the thirteenth century Thomas Aquinas replaced Augustinian thought with that of Aristotle. Sensation became the basis of knowledge, and God's existence was proved by a tortuous argument from physical motion to an Unmoved Mover. Here is not the place to discuss the theological results of abandoning Augustine, but the philosophical result was an intricate scholasticism that led Jerome Zanchius to remark that "Thomas Aquinas [was] a man of some genius and much application, who, though in very many things a laborious trifler, was yet on some subjects a clear reasoner and judicious writer" (*Absolute Predestination,* chap. iv, pos. 8, par. 4, footnote).

Although there is no evidence that the scholastics ever seriously debated how many angels could dance on the point of a needle, Aquinas did indeed discuss whether an angel is in a place, whether an angel can be in several places at once, and whether several angels can be at the same time in the same place. These things, along with arguments on the passive and active intellect, prime matter, and whether only boys and no girls would have been born if Adam had not sinned, can easily produce the impression that Aquinas was sometimes a "laborious trifler."

Later scholastics, particularly Duns Scotus, increased the number of subtleties. Contrary to Augustinianism, the area common to philosophy and theology became less and less. William of Occam made the break complete: Nothing theological could be proved by philosophy—Christianity is based on revelation alone. If now Occam's philosophy can be shown to be skeptical, then there is a peculiar return to Augustinianism in which no knowledge is possible apart from revelation. Luther's philosophy was in effect this type of Occamism.

In a very real sense the Protestant Reformation may be said to have had no effect whatever on the subsequent history of philosophy. The main line—Descartes, Spinoza, Leibniz, the British empiricists, Kant, and Hegel—would presumably have developed essentially as it did, Reformation or none. Leibniz was a Lutheran and Berkeley a zealous Anglican, but the few necessary adjustments to Protestant or even Catholic thought do not seem to have had any really basic influence at all. Modern philosophy stems from the Renaissance, not from the Reformation.

Protestant thought on philosophic themes, on the other hand, was a complete reversal of scholasticism. Not only was the point of view of a spectator in an ivory tower condemned as useless, as trifling, and indeed as impious, but also the existence of God, instead of being a conclusion to an intricate Aristotelian argument, became the basis of all truth.

In the first chapter of the *Institutes,* Calvin, disdaining even to mention physical motion and an Unmoved Mover, begins with a question of greater Augustinian flavor: Does a man first know himself and then learn of God, or does he know God first and later learn about himself? Briefly Calvin's answer is: "No man can arrive at the true knowledge of himself, without having first contemplated the divine character, and then descended to the consideration of his own. . . . Though the knowledge of God and the knowledge of ourselves be intimately connected, the proper order of instruction requires us first to treat of the former, and then proceed to the discussion of the latter."

In opposition to Aristotelian empiricism, Calvin, far from basing this knowledge on experience, refers it to natural instinct. "Some sense of the Divinity," he says, "is inscribed on every heart. . . . All have by nature an innate persuasion of the divine existence, a persuasion inseparable from their very constitution. . . . We infer that this is a doctrine, not first to be learned in the schools, but which every man from his birth is self-taught" (I, iii, 1 and 3).

This Reformation theory of innate or *a priori* knowledge was not uniformly maintained in later centuries. Both deism and its Christian opponents introduced more and more natural theology. This should be regarded as a deterioration from the original position of Luther and Calvin.

Rejecting the ideal of one universal corrupt church, the Protestants were neither willing nor able to enforce philosophic uniformity. Jonathan Edwards was staunchly orthodox in theology, but he was peculiarly influenced by the British empiricists. Rudolf Bultmann thinks the New Testament anticipated [Martin] Heidegger and existentialism; but since Bultmann is not staunchly orthodox, he may be a poor example. At any rate, Protestant theologians have oscillated between Scottish common sense and Hegelian personalism. Today the Free University of Amsterdam is the center of a serious attempt to produce a comprehensive Christian philosophy. With Calvin's rejection of natural theology these men have brilliantly criticized non-Christian systems. Whether their constructive work will long endure remains to be seen.

The effect of the Reformation on ethics may be separated into theoretical and practical aspects. Consonant with the rejection of natural theology, the Reformation based its ethics on revelation and discarded natural law. This is pure theoretical gain. The theory of natural law commits a major logical blunder when it tries to deduce a normative conclusion from descriptive premises. No matter how carefully or how intricately one describes what men do, or what the provisions of nature are, or how natural inclinations function, it is a logical impossibility to conclude that this is or is not what men ought to do. The *is* never implies the *ought*. This criticism applies to all empirical theories. Both Thomism and utilitarianism insist that man is morally obligated to seek, not just his own good, but the common good. This principle, however, cannot be justified empirically.

When the Thomists argue that it is a natural law to seek what is good, because as a matter of fact everybody seeks what is good, they reduce the term good to the several objects of human desire. When they further state, "No one calls in doubt the need for doing good, avoiding evil, acquiring knowledge, dispelling ignorance . . ." ([Etienne] Gilson, *The Philosophy of St. Thomas Aquinas*, p. 329), they simply shut their eyes to beatniks, the Mafia, the tribes of the Congo, [Arthur] Schopenhauer, and [Friedrich] Nietzsche. Tautology or falsity is their fate.

The Reformation's ethical principles were the explicit commands in the Word of God. Of course this presupposes the existence of God—discussed above—and the possibility and truth of revelation. If revelation is false, then its ethical theory is false, too; but no one can accuse it of tautology.

The practical effect of the Reformation on ethics is more easily observed by the general public, and Jesuitical casuistry and Tetzel's scheme to raise money for St. Peter's provide the sharpest possible contrast with Puritan conscientiousness. The massacre of the Huguenots and the massacre of the Covenanters by the Catholic Stuarts are highlighted by the Presbyterians' refusal to take revenge when they came to power. Even in the days of John Knox, after the martyrdoms of the early Reformation, the Presbyterians in power in Scotland did not execute a single person for religious beliefs. Contrast this with the Spanish Inquisition and the Jesuit intrigues.

On a less gruesome plane, but not less an important point of ethics, the Jesuitical disregard and the Reformation regard for truth gives content to the discussion. It was no doubt the violation of oaths that led the Westminster divines to include in their summary of Reformation and Biblical doctrines the following paragraph:

"An oath is to be taken in the plain and common sense of the words, without equivocation or mental reservation. It cannot oblige to sin: but in anything not sinful, being taken, it binds to performance, although to a man's own hurt; nor is it to be violated, although made to heretics or infidels" (XXII.4).

We live today (so it is said, and, I regret, said with truth) in the post-Protestant era. The spiritual interests of the Reformation are no longer interesting. A materialistic attitude and a humanistic philosophy characterize our civilization. As Nietzsche said, "God is dead." It is an age of increased war and crime. Murder and rape occur in public, on the streets, in the subways, and New Yorkers refuse to get involved. Legislatures abolish capital punishment: and instead of punishing the criminal, the state rehabilitates him so that in seven years the murderer is paroled, sometimes to kill again.

Such are the results of liberalism, of banishing God and Christian ethics from the public schools, of denying the Bible, its miracles, and its salvation. Under these conditions a return to Luther and Calvin, a return to Protestantism, a return to the Bible would not be the worst fate imaginable.

*Christianity Today,* October 22, 1965.

# 19

# Good Works

Many people in the pews, and not merely liberal ministers in the pulpits, express a distaste for doctrine and theology. They want something practical. Well, who can deny that good works are practical?

Unfortunately for those who dislike theology and a detailed confessional statement, there cannot be much progress in good works unless it is known what works are good and what works are evil. And who can deny that a definition of good works is theological, doctrinal, and creedal? The popular disjunction between doctrine and practice, between theology and life, between knowing and doing, is a false one. The theory of practice must precede the practice of theory.

What then are good works? Are they those actions a benevolently intentioned gentleman may happen to enjoy? Is a substantial donation to an orphanage, hospital, or church a good work? Strange as it may seem to non-Christians, and even to uninstructed Christians, the answer is that these actions are not necessarily good. They may be good; but again they may not be. What then makes a work or action good?

Two requirements must be fulfilled before an act can properly be called good. The [Westminster] Confession says, "Good works are only such as God hath commanded in his holy word, and not such as, without the warrant thereof, are devised by men out of blind zeal, or upon any pretense of good intention."

The first part of this section teaches that unless we had the Bible, it would be impossible to know what is good and what is evil. To be sure, the heathen know that there is a distinction between right and wrong; and they regularly violate their consciences; but they do not know in particular what acts are right because their consciences are unenlightened. The Biblical revelation is essential to a knowledge of what works are good.

The second part of this same section teaches the same truth in a negative form. Without the warrant of the Bible an act done with good intentions is not a good work. Similarly, the blind zeal and arrogant authority of Romanism imposes practices, such as genuflections, crossing oneself, using holy water, kissing the big toe of St. Peter's image, which are not good works at all. Since they are beside the commandments of God, they are superstitious practices that God abominates. These are the things Paul had in mind in Colossians 2:18,23, where he speaks of the sins of voluntary humility and will worship.

Thus the first requirement for a good work is that it be commanded by God. But why was it said that a donation to an orphanage may not be a good work? Surely God commands us to take care of the widows and orphans in their affliction. This paradox is removed by considering the second requirement for a good work.

"Works done by unregenerate men, although, for the matter of them, they may be things which God commands, and of good use both to themselves and others; yet because they proceed not from a heart purified by faith, nor are done in a right manner according to the word, nor to a right end, the glory of God; they are therefore sinful and cannot please God, or make a man meet to receive grace from God. And yet their neglect of them is more sinful and displeasing unto God" (sec. vii).

Because a good work must proceed from a heart purified by faith, it follows that men's "ability to do good works is not at all of themselves, but wholly from the Spirit of Christ. And that they may be enabled thereunto . . . there is required an actual influence of the Holy Spirit to work in them to will and to do of his good pleasure" (sec. iii). Thus while good works are done voluntarily and not against our wishes and desires, they are not the result of a "free" will independent of God. God in his sovereign grace changes our desires and makes us willing.

In conclusion, for these articles must be extremely brief, no matter how great the totality of our good works, they do not merit pardon for sin or eternal life. Contrary to the modernist and Romanist theories of salvation by works, Calvinism teaches that when we have done all we can, we are still unprofitable servants. The Roman notion that some men can do actually more than God requires, and that the extra merits earned by these men avail for other less energetic sinners, is a Satanic delusion. Christ alone has satisfied the justice of his Father, and he has satisfied it perfectly. *Deo soli gratia.*

*The Southern Presbyterian Journal,* February 9, 1955.

# 20

# Greek Ethics

Greek ethics during the Pre-Socratic period did not exist in any systematic form. Heraclitus (c. 500 B.C.) condemned drunkenness on the ground that the cosmic principle is fire and therefore dry. Protagoras (c. 440 B.C.) and the other Sophists were relativists and concluded that whatever anyone thinks is just, is just for him. The mystery religions, over several centuries, imposed some irrational taboos (*e.g.*, do not eat beans) and engaged either in ascetic or licentious practices.

Plato (427-347) not only pursued ethical studies systematically, but made them essential to his whole philosophy. His early Socratic dialogues seek to define the several virtues: piety, justice, courage, and so on. So doing he concludes that virtue is knowledge and that no one does wrong knowingly. The reason is that no man wants to harm himself, and if he knows, really knows, that injustice and cowardice will harm him, he will avoid them.

In the period of the *Gorgias,* the *Phaedo,* and the *Republic,* Plato, under Pythagorean and Orphic influence, not only attacks hedonism, the theory that pleasure is the greatest good, but even adopts an asceticism in which pleasure is actually evil. This is combined with arguments for the immortality of the soul and an epistemological theory of suprasensible Ideas, among which the Idea of Good is supreme and even superior to God. On this broad and profound philosophy, Plato advocates a civil government in which philosopher-kings enforce a totalitarian control of art, education, and business so as to promote temperance, courage, justice, and wisdom, along with promiscuity and the abolition of the family.

Aristotle (384-322) made an even more detailed study of ethics than Plato, but the subject is more detached from his main system and is of less importance than it was for his famous teacher. Aristotle was just as totalitarian: The state is the supreme community that includes all others, and since communities are always organized for some good, the all inclusive state aims at the all inclusive good. The family, however, and other lesser communities, are natural and should not be abolished, but merely regulated. The good for man (Aristotle drops Plato's suprasensible Idea Good) is determined by nature, human nature. Since "all men by nature desire to know," as the *Metaphysics* says in its opening line, the highest good is the practice and enjoyment of contemplation and philosophy.

The moral virtues, as distinguished from the higher intellectual virtues, are such things as courage, liberality, temperance and so on. He defines these as the right amount (not too much, not too little) of feelings and action. Too much fear is cowardice; too little is foolhardiness; the right amount is courage. So too with liberality; but Aristotle reflects Greek custom when, so far as his means permit, he will keep up with and outdo "the Joneses."

He also investigates distributive and corrective justice, weakness and badness of will, the criteria of responsibility, and adds a long chapter on friendship. The whole, quite secular, is devoid of Plato's religious enthusiasm.

During their lifetimes Plato and Aristotle overshadowed two very minor schools that had been stimulated by Socrates. The Cynics stressed virtue, and Diogenes with his lamp searched for an honest man. The Cyrenaics on the contrary searched for the grossest pleasures of sense. Both schools refused to develop a full philosophy and were essentially anti-intellectual. They are mentioned only because they gave rise, respectively, to the Stoics and the Epicureans.

The Epicureans accepted hedonism; but unlike the Cyrenaics they defended their theory with a little logic and an extensive system of physics. Since pain is evil, and since religion causes the greatest crimes and worst pains, especially the fear of divine punishment in a life after death, one's first principle must be that nothing ever comes from nothing by divine power. The universe is a collection of atoms and all phenomena are explained by their bumping each other.

Rejecting the complete mechanism of Democritus, the Epicureans asserted that atoms occasionally swerve for no reason or cause at all. Otherwise men, whose bodies are composed of atoms, could not have free will. Aside from this swerving, the Epicureans explained physical phenomena mechanically in order to show that the gods have nothing to do with the world.

Unlike the Cyrenaics the Epicureans did not recommend gross sensual pleasures. Though good in themselves, intense pleasures produce pains, and therefore the calmer pleasures should be sought. Epicurus even gave a semi-recommendation of celibacy. More to his taste were good meals, dozing in the sun, while avoiding politics and family life. Unjust actions must also be avoided because, even if one escapes civil punishment, one cannot escape the fear of detection, and this fear or pain overbalances the pleasures derived from injustice.

Finally, since the atoms of our body disperse at death, since therefore no pain will be possible, even from the gods, the life of pleasure is best.

Stoicism, in opposition to hedonism, defined the rational life as a life of virtue. Besides ordinary personal virtues they insisted, against the Epicureans, on political and family responsibilities. It was necessary to insist that most men, maybe all men but Socrates, are totally evil. There are no degrees of evil: A man drowned in two feet of water is just as dead as if drowned in two hundred fathoms. One cannot grow from death to life or evil to wisdom. Moral regeneration must be complete and instantaneous.

A life of virtue and reason was defended on the ground that the substance of the universe itself is a rational fire or energy. Man is a spark of the divine fire and should therefore live according to reason. The Stoics were indeed materialists, or, better, like Heraclitus, hylozoists. They were not atomists. Nor did they allow irrational swerving or uncaused events in their universe. The divine Reason has intelligently planned all things with the result that there can be no free will. After the present cosmos finishes its history in a universal conflagration, things start over again on the exact same course.

Augustine, although he spoke kindly of the Stoic doctrines of fate, providence, and rational causation, deplored eternal recurrence as a pessimism without hope. Christians might also note that the Stoic emperor, Marcus Aurelius, was a cruel persecutor of the church. Then too Christianity sees a flaw in the virtue or wisdom that permits suicide when the going gets difficult.

---

*Baker's Dictionary of Christian Ethics*, Carl F.H. Henry, editor. Grand Rapids, Michigan: Baker Book House, 1973, pp. 276-277.

# 21

# Happiness

"Happiness" (*eudamonia,* from which we derive *eudaemonism*) is the term Aristotle used to designate the goal of life. It is an end in itself, never a means to anything else. "Honor, pleasure, intelligence, and all forms of virtue, we choose both for their own sakes, . . . and we also choose them for the sake of happiness. . . . But no one chooses happiness for the sake of honor or pleasure, nor as a means to anything else at all" (*Nicomachean Ethics,* I, vii, 1097b1-6).

Though the one term "happiness" seems to designate a single end, it acutally consists of several parts, all necessary. Two factors to be chosen voluntarily are virtuous and rational activity. The virtues are courage, temperance, liberality, and so on. Rational activity is a matter of studying physics, metaphysics, etc. The reason is that these are the natural functions of man as man. The purpose of a flute is to produce music; the purpose of a fish is to produce fish; the purpose of a shoemaker is to produce shoes; but the purpose of man as man is to live virtuously and rationally.

There are also some involuntary factors in happiness. A life of tragedy or disgrace (even unmerited) is not a happy life. Nor can a man be called happy if his children suffer tragedy. Therefore it is impossible to know whether a man is happy until after he is dead.

Augustine's ethics was also eudaemonism. The good life is one of happiness (*beatitudo, beatitas;* both terms coined by Cicero). All men desire happiness (*De Trinitate,* X, v, 7). "No one lives as he wishes unless he is happy" (*De Civitas Dei,* XIV, 25). Now Augustine would not disparage virtues such as courage and temperance; nor would he belittle rational thought. In fact, no one can be happy without knowledge of the truth. In this there is similarity to Aristotle. But Augustine replaces Aristotle's secularism with Christian content. God is truth and to know God is wisdom. Therefore the happiness Augustine recommends becomes blessedness or beatitude.

More explicitly: wisdom is not the knowledge of some heathen god, nor even of, say, Spinoza's first principle. To have wisdom is to have Christ. Christ is the truth; Christ is the wisdom of God.

One reason for making truth the aim of our endeavors is that if we love what can be lost, we cannot be happy. But God, Christ, and truth are immutable, and if we have this, our blessedness is permanent.

Eudaemonism therefore should not be confused with hedonism, as is sometimes ignorantly done; the two form a contrast.

---

*Baker's Dictionary of Christian Ethics,* Carl F.H. Henry, editor. Grand Rapids, Michigan: Baker Book House, 1973, pp. 281-282.

# 22

# Healthy, Sick, or Dead?

In these times when religious periodicals are so full of politics and so empty of Biblical exposition, the ignorance of the people is so great that every doctrine of the Westminster Confession needs vigorous proclamation. As we look at the doctrine of sin in Chapter VI, it is hard to avoid thinking that it needs even a more vigorous presentation than the others. This natural reaction may be exaggerated, but the chapter surely contains a wealth of material pertinent for our careless age.

Chapter IV had said that man was created righteous; the present chapter adds that our first parents sinned, and "by this sin they fell from their original righteousness, and communion with God, and so became dead in sin, and wholly defiled in all the faculties and parts of soul and body."

Roman Catholicism holds that man was not created positively righteous, but, rather, neutral; after his creation God gave him an extra gift of righteousness; and when Adam sinned, he lost the extra gift and fell back to the neutral state in which he was created. Thus man's present condition, according to Romanism, is not too bad. The Bible and the Confession say that man fell far below the estate in which he was created and is now wholly defiled in all his faculties and parts.

The modernists have a better opinion of themselves than even the Romanists have. If the race fell at all, it was an upward evolutionary fall; and man has been making rapid progress ever since. Herbert Spencer set the norm for much modernistic preaching in his prediction that the little evil remaining on earth would vanish in a short time. Books were written about moral man in an immoral society that needed only a good dose of socialism to become utopian. Ministers dilated on human perfectibility. And in the summer of 1914 a college president and Presbyterian elder had almost finished a book to prove there would be no more war. He had forgotten what Christ said. Now, forty years later, two world wars and the brutality of totalitarian governments have shaken the confidence of this type of muddle-headedness.

The neo-orthodox are now ready to admit that something is wrong with man. But do they agree with the Bible as to what this something is? Does their obscure mixture of a few Biblical phrases and a great deal of esoteric terminology mean that man is dead in sin, "utterly indisposed, disabled, and made opposite to all good, and wholly inclined to all evil"? One thing is clear: the neo-orthodox deny that the guilt of Adam's sin was imputed to his posterity. Adam was not our representative in his trial before God.

Indeed, Adam is only an unhistorical myth. And yet these men have had the effrontery to claim that they, rather than we, preserve the position of the Reformers. Let them read the Confession.

We too should read the Confession. And we should preach it with vigor. Not only have Romanists, modernists, and neo-orthodox departed from the teachings of the Bible, but there are also others, who in spite of professing to adhere to the Scripture, have diverged, sometimes widely, from the truth.

There was a Bible professor in a Christian college who taught that man was a sinner, man was in a bad way, man was sick in sin. Now, salvation, so the Bible professor explained it, is like medicine in the drug store; and the sick man ought to drag himself to the store and get the medicine, and be cured. There was also a convinced Presbyterian on this faculty, who taught in accordance with the Westminster Confession. So evident to the students was the contrast between these two theologies that the President disconnected the Presbyterian from his post.

The Bible and the Confession teach that man is not just sick in sin; he is dead in sin; and salvation rather than being compared with medicine is compared with a resurrection.

Another form of minimizing sin is the belief that sinless perfection is possible in this life. The Confession says, "This corruption of nature, during this life, doth remain in those that are regenerated; and although it be through Christ pardoned and mortified, yet both itself, and all the motions thereof, are truly and properly sin."

The error of the "holiness" groups is similar to the Romanist and modernist error in that it is a failure to recognize the exceeding sinfulness of sin. To them, sin seems rather superficial, and therefore it can be eradicated in this life. They sometimes restrict sin to "known sin." But if the aim of the Christian life is merely to avoid known sin, then the more ignorant of the law we are, the more righteous we would be.

Yet for all their sinless perfection, these are the people who hold that one can lose one's salvation and become unregenerate a second time. This shows that the Scriptural view of sin, so accurately summarized in the Confession, has far reaching implications. Its force is seen in the nature of salvation, the perseverance of the saints, the varieties of free will, the imputation of Christ's righteousness, and in fact throughout the whole system. Nor should we be satisfied with knowing only a part. We need the complete Confession.

---

*The Southern Presbyterian Journal,* November 17, 1954.

# 23

# Hedonism

Hedonism is the theory that pleasure is the good. Egoistic hedonism plausibly restricts pleasure to the pleasure of the individual. Utilitarianism defines the good as the greatest possible amount of pleasure for all sentient beings. Psychological hedonism, which Jeremy Bentham inconsistently incorporated in his utilitarianism, holds that as a matter of scientific fact, pleasure is man's only motive.

Plato mentions some Sophists who were hedonists; but the first school of hedonism were the Cyrenaics. They restricted pleasure to sense pleasures and tended to stress the most licentious. This form of hedonism has the advantage of providing a clear cut definition of pleasure.

The Epicureans, while they enjoyed eating and acknowledged the pleasure of sex, put more emphasis on peace of mind. Thus they would refrain from injustice because, even if one were not arrested by the police, there would always be that disquieting possibility. As for sex, Epicurus actually recommends celibacy. These moral advances over the Cyrenaics are purchased by the failure to give a clear cut definition of pleasure. True, the Epicureans defined pleasure negatively as the complete absence of pain. But as Plato had earlier noted, a broad definition of pleasure allows for such different types of life that, if one of them is good, another cannot be.

Bentham's utilitarianism suffered implicitly from the same defect; and Mill's explicitly. He distinguished between the pleasures of a man and those of a pig. But this is equivalent to denying that pleasure as pleasure is the good.

---

*Baker's Dictionary of Christian Ethics,* Carl F.H. Henry, editor. Grand Rapids, Michigan: Baker Book House, 1973, pp. 286-287.

# 24

# History of Ethics

Ethics, in its history from Plato to Jeremy Bentham, has been closely conjoined with politics. Political decisions require ethical judgments; an individual man cannot be separated from society; therefore there is no clear-cut distinction between ethics and politics, or between so-called personal ethics and social ethics.

To maintain some distinction, a degree of difference is inserted in the definition, making ethics a little more individual and politics a little more social.

Henry Sidgwick, the great ethical scholar of the nineteenth century, acknowledging the vagueness of ethics' boundaries, defined the subject as a rational procedure for determining what individual human beings "ought" to seek to realize by voluntary actions. Ethics could also be defined as the study and eventually the justification of criteria by which one human life can be identified as better or worse than another.

Although some of the main views can be described by a title (*e.g.,* hedonism, the theory that pleasure is the supreme good; altruism, the theory that not every natural impulse is selfish; instrumentalism and situationism, the theory that there are neither final ends nor fixed rules, and that each decision must be an individual aesthetic intuition), it is almost impossible to classify the historical views with exactitude, for there is too much room for cross classification.

If one should divide theories of ethics into teleological (those in which the value of an act is determined by some purpose) and ateleological, the only representative of the latter would be Kant;

and this makes an unbalanced classification. Then too, teleological systems are so various that their similarity (of being based on purpose) seems superficial.

For the Epicureans the purpose of a good act is the sense pleasure of the individual. For the Utilitarians it is the pleasure (maybe sense pleasure, maybe not) of the whole human race. For Aristotle the purpose of man, by nature, is happiness, and this is a combination of intellectual and moral activity in which pleasure plays but a small role. For contemporary existentialism the good life is anything one chooses, provided he does not choose to conform to his society.

Christianity, in detail, is not teleological. One does not determine a right from a wrong choice by calculating the probability of its achieving a purpose. Neither are its rules determined by formal logic alone, as Kant's categorical imperative is. The particular rules of morality are the commands of God. Yet these have a purpose in glorifying God and advancing man's blessedness. But no man has any knowledge of just how this is accomplished.

Since, too, philosophers frequently agree on ethics while disagreeing on metaphysics and epistemology, and vice versa, the best procedure is to study each view in its historical matrix.

---

*Baker's Dictionary of Christian Ethics,* Carl F.H. Henry, editor. Grand Rapids, Michigan: Baker Book House, 1973, pp. 220-221.

# 25

# Human Nature and Political Theory

Great literature portrays incredible variations in personality. Abraham and Jezebel in the Bible, Macbeth and Shylock in Shakespeare, and Thackeray's Becky Sharp are distinct individuals. Philosophers, on the other hand, focus on what is common in human nature. They study Man rather than men. But they provide diversity, not only in their disagreements one with another, but each in the application of his view of human nature to questions of politics, ethics, and religion.

## Plato

Plato, Aristotle, and the Stoics so well represent antiquity that other schools must be regarded as atypical. These three agreed that man is basically a rational being. The Sophists, to be sure, held that man was essentially emotional or at most volitional, so that his reasoning power, including the ability to make the worse appear the better argument, is but the slave of passion. In this they anticipated David Hume and other modern philosophers. Because the aim of life is to succeed in getting whatever you want, the Sophists generally considered a tyrannical dictator the happiest of men.

The reason behind this view of life was their skepticism. They believed that it was impossible to attain knowledge. Impossible because mathematics had stumbled upon irrational numbers. Impossible because physics, contemplating a world of constant change, could find nothing that would stand still long enough to be known. Impossible also because the Persian Wars had shown that morality is nothing but arbitrary conventionality. Therefore, concluded the Sophists, a man must choose his goals irrationally, and success is the only criterion of a good life. This makes the dictator or tyrant the best man.

For Plato, on the other hand, the aim of life is not determined by irrational desire but by a scientific knowledge of the Good. The physical world of flux is not the real world. The higher, more real, suprasensible World of Ideas consists of objects that do not change, and because they are immune to flux they can be known. Examples of Ideas are Equality in mathematics, Horse and Man in natural science, and Courage and Justice in ethics or morality. Above all is the Idea of the Good. These then are man's criteria for both private and public life.

Though the Idea Man is perfectly rational, men here below are not completely so. Men are three-fold beings. The highest human ability is of course rational and philosophical. Some men possess this ability in a superlative degre. Inferior to reason is man's principle of volition—his "spunk" or spirited element. This element is somewhat akin to reason, and together they make self-control possible. Spirited young men are the best candidates for mature philosophical study. The lowest human function is man's emotional or concupiscent nature.

Since human nature is thus three-fold, and since the State is composed of human beings, in each of which one or another of these three faculties is dominant, the State too is composed of three classes of people. Those persons whose desires control them do all sorts of harmful stupidities and may even become tyrants; but if they can be trained and restrained by wise rules they make useful businessmen and can provide the State with a satisfactory economic base. Those individuals who are spirited make good soldiers and become the Guardian army of the State—invincible because courageous, and incorruptible because they have no desire for money. But the only people who know enough to rule are the supremely rational philosopher-kings. In early life these persons approved themselves as good soldiers; they were then chosen for further training; and eventually learned enough to govern by the knowledge of the Good.

The virtue proper to the lowest function of the soul and to the lowest class in the State is temperance; that proper to the middle class is courage; and wisdom characterizes the highest function in the individual and the philosopher-king in the State. Justice is defined as the harmonious arrangement among the three—each keeping to its own place.

This scheme is essentially a form of communism or totalitarian paternalism in which the family is abolished as divisive of social unity, religion is a civic duty, and business is rigidly regulated. The two upper classes have no private property, They own the State. In the lower class the richest man may have no more than four times the poorest. If the poorest gets two thousand dollars a year, the president of Athenian Motors is allowed only eight.

Philosopher-kings can be trusted to remain paternalistic instead of turning into tyrants because they have eradicated their desire for wealth by their knowledge of the Good and their understanding of psychology. Everybody admits that he desires what is good for him. No one wants to harm himself. The reason many people do is that they are ignorant of the Good. If they knew that cigarettes injure the heart and cause lung cancer, they would stop smoking. If they knew money is morally corrupting, they would not be capitalists. Education and knowledge therefore are the cure for all ills. Those who are incapable of learning are better off if, instead of being left to their own desires, they are controlled by philosophers who know the Good.

Plato also provides supernatural sanctions for morality. After death the soul of an evil man is punished. In some places this punishment is described in the mythological terms of being reborn as an animal: The glutton becomes a pig, the tyrant a lion. In other dialogues the punishment is rebirth as a bad man again. Though there is this variation in Plato's writings, it is beyond doubt that the home of the eternal soul is heaven—the World of Ideas—that the body is a tomb, and that incarnation or reincarnation is a punishment.

## Aristotle

Aristotle rejected the World of Ideas; aside from an unintelligible reference to the active intellect there is no hint that a man survives death; and knowledge all by itself does not ensure a moral life. Nevertheless, Aristotle as well as Plato insists that man is essentially rational.

Since there is no world of Ideas, man is not born with any innate tendency toward the Good that an incorporeal existence in heaven might have given him. In strictly naturalistic fashion man is born morally neutral. Therefore morality is a matter of developing good habits. The process is similar to that of learning to play a musical instrument. Knowledge is admittedly essential, but practice is also indispensable. When a person makes a moral mistake, he must practice longer to erase the effect of this mistake. Eventually, in accordance with a fairly detailed explanation of how to practice, a man may become an excellent moral musician.

This practice of virtue cannot take place in isolation. Courage and liberality require other persons. The processes of nature, psychological as fully as biological, produce persons by means of family organization. Therefore, since the family is natural, the State should not abolish it for a communism of wives. Thus Aristotle does not accept Plato's theory of politics. The subsidiary societies or organizations must be integrated into the State, not abolished.

The State too is a natural development, having grown out of the primitive family; for man is not only a rational animal, he is also a political animal. Naturally, a rational animal must be political.

Accordingly Aristotle opens his book on *Politics* with this paragraph: "Every state is a community of some kind [a community is the condition of having some purposes or things in common; *e.g.* a business community], and every community is established with a view to some goal [children, money, amusement]; for men always act in order to obtain that which they think good as Plato said; but if all communities aim at some good, the state or political community, which is the highest of all, and which embraces all the rest, aims in a greater degree than any other at the highest good."

This paragraph shows that while Aristotle was not a communist, he was just as totalitarian as Plato. The State, he says, embraces all other societies, not only in the sense of regulating their financial activities, but in controlling their purposes. The State not only aims at good in a greater degree than other organizations, it aims at the highest good. Thus the sphere of governmental activity is all-embracing. There could be no "freedom of religion." There could be no church, either like the medieval church that was independent of criminal law, or like the Scottish Presbyterian church that, willing to obey criminal and civil law in purely human matters, insisted that Christ alone, not Pope or King, was the head of the church in its essentially spiritual functions.

Of course neither Plato nor Aristotle ever imagined an organization such as a Christian church. Religion for them was rational, cultural, and natural; therefore the State, as was also the case with art and sport, was the judge of the allowable details.

## The Stoics

The Stoics, whose school was influential from 300 B.C. to A.D. 300, also believed that man is rational; and virtue is an expression of reason. Indeed this school above all others gained a reputation for practical, actual, and high morality.

Unlike Plato and Aristotle, the Stoics were essentially pantheistic. Following Heraclitus they taught that the universe was made of fire and that this fire is a rational, living force. Each man has or even is a divine spark. Hence, as Epictetus says, nature never gives us any but good inclinations. Surprisingly, however, most men are wicked. In fact, very wicked. Just how a spark of divinity, acting under the all encompassing laws of causation, the rational, inviolable causation of the universal Reason, could choose evil and become depraved is a puzzle the Stoics never solved.

Aside from that, they of all the Greeks were the first to emphasize the role of motive in morality. The others centered their attention on external action. Aristotle in particular held that a man could not be moral when idle or asleep. He was courageous or liberal only when actually doing the things required. These actions, too, are possible only when the physical conditions are right. A poor man cannot be generous, simply because he has no money. The Stoics, however, make morality more internal. It is the action of the will, rather than the action of the hands that counts. Therefore a paralytic can be courageous and a poor man generous. Virtue does not depend on external circumstances, but on an inward disposition.

This interiority of virtue leads the Stoics to view the laws of the State more as conventional than as natural. No doubt society is natural, but the particular constitutions of cities and nations are arbitrary. Here the Stoics hit upon a distinction that the earlier Greeks had not discovered: the distinction between society and the State. In the golden age of vigorous cities, the state seemed to be the producer of society, and Plato thought that families and other organizations endangered the unity of the nation. But now conditions had changed. Even in Aristotle's time the city-states were in decay. Soon the Romans were to enslave them all. Participation in government was no longer a possibility for these erstwhile citizens.

With such external conditions plus the idea of a universal Reason, the Stoics claimed to the "citizens" of the world. They were not "politans," but "cosmo-politans."

This universal outlook, however, did not lead them to anarchy or insurrection. Quite the contrary, they were deliberate conservatives, not only in politics, but also in religion (the Stoic emperor was one of the most vigorous persecutors of the new Christian religion), and in the home. Unlike the Epicureans, who avoided all three in their search for pleasure, the Stoics accepted family obligations as natural and, if called upon, would faithfully execute the office of magistrate. Faithfully, but perhaps also pessimistically. For while some depraved men will be converted to Stoicism and become wise and virtuous, the steadily increasing degradation of Roman society evinced little hope of many conversions. The empire was corrupt and collapsing; and if a Stoic concluded that the situation was intolerable, it was a virtue, or at least not a vice, to commit suicide.

## Christianity

Christianity disagreed. This new religion, though actually very old with its Hebrew foundation, had a totally different world-view. No doubt it stressed virtue, but not Stoic virtue; no doubt it classified man as rational, but for reasons Plato would have repudiated; no doubt it asserted the existence of God, but he was neither Aristotle's Unmoved Mover nor a member of the pagan pantheon.

The basis of all the differences between the Hebrew-Christian or Biblical world-view and all other systems is the nature of God. Unlike the Homeric or Roman gods he is omnipotent; unlike the Unmoved Mover he is omniscient and intervenes in the affairs of men—the Incarnation being the most important instance; and unlike Plato's Demiurge, Jehovah is not subject to a higher and independent World of Ideas. All this can be summarized by saying that God is sovereign.

A Biblical implication is that God has created the world. Even time and space are not eternal principles: They are, if Augustine has understood it correctly, *a priori* forms of the created mind. Such ideas the pagans never had.

Another consequence is that man is rational: not because he is a spark of a pantheistic divinity, but because God created him in his own image and likeness. God has knowledge and wisdom, Christ is the *Logos* or Reason, and God made man similar.

Since God is sovereign, the "World of Ideas" must be the

result of God's thinking. In the moral sphere (to contradict Plato) the Good is Good because God chooses it. That is to say, God legislates and imposes laws on mankind. Adam, however, broke the law and rebelled against God. If the position of moral law in Christianity differs so fundamentally from the inferiority of the Demiurge to the Ideas, so too rebellion against God cannot be reduced to Aristotle's child who makes mistakes as he practices his scales.

The result of Adam's sin is the total depravity of the human race. Instead of loving and obeying God, men naturally hate God. Instead of always acting rationally, they often act irrationally.

Augustine supplies a pointed illustration. As a boy he went out with some others one night and stole some pears. It was lots of fun. It was not fun because the pears were good to eat; they were hard and bitter. Nor was he motivated by hunger: He could have eaten better pears at home. The motivation was simply the fun of stealing with the gang. W.T. Jones (*A History of Western Philosophy*, Vol. 1, p. 346) chides Augustine for taking so seriously "the pranks and escapades which are the normal products of youthful exuberance." Professor Jones misses the point. Augustine deliberately chose the story of the pears because the act itself was as trivial a one as he could think of. Its triviality, however, and the worthlessness of the pears all the more emphasized the point that the motive was the love of evil for the sake of evil.

Such motivation is normal for youths and for adults as well. Therefore civil government, though it be an evil in that it restricts men's liberty, is a necessary evil because men at liberty are dangerous. The Old Testament too says that God ordained civil government for the good of sinful men. The New Testament specifically upholds the government's power of taxation and of waging war and executing criminals.

But there is one tremendous difference between Christian and pagan politics. The pagan theories are totalitarian. The State is supreme. But King Ahab in the Old Testament was condemned by God for stealing private property. The King did not make the law, nor could he change it. Theft and murder are condemned by the laws of God. Therefore in Christian theory there are some things that a State ought not to do.

This is, of course, consistent with the view that all men are totally depraved. Government is necessary because anarchy with evil men is intolerable. But the rulers also are evil and need to be restrained. Power always tends to corrupt, and absolute power corrupts absolutely.

Civil government is not God's only method of restraining sin. The Bible is largely, one might even say exclusively, the proclamation of salvation in Christ. When a man hears this Gospel, the Holy Ghost may regenerate him and give him faith in Christ. This removes him from the city of this world and makes him a citizen of the City of God. Once again, then, Augustine describes how these two cities, of different origins and different destinies, are yet intermixed upon the surface of the earth. But they can never be spiritually or intellectually unified; for unification would require either the massacre of all Christians (which God will not allow), or the conversion of all humanity (which God has not decreed). Again the conclusion is that Christianity condemns all totalitarian governments.

## Hobbes

Since the views of Augustine were largely accepted until A.D. 1275, when Aquinas turned back the clock to Aristotle, it is permissible to proceed directly to modern times for something new. In contrast with the prevailing opinion that the State was a development of nature, Thomas Hobbes (1588-1679) proposed a social contract theory: Individual men deliberately make a contract among themselves and organize a government. This idea may be called new, for its nearest antecedent is a short paragraph insufficiently developed by Callicles in Plato's *Gorgias.*

Hobbes believed that politics could be deduced from a metaphysical materialism and psychological behaviorism. Neither an exposition of his metaphysics nor a discussion of his fallacies is necessary here. One can begin simply by stating Hobbes's view of human nature. Briefly, every man has a natural right to preserve his life; all men are practically equal; and the basic motivations are competition, diffidence, and glory. Implications follow.

Since a man has no more necessary aim than to preserve his own life, it follows, Hobbes says, that he has a natural right to any weapons, property, or means necessary thereto. Obviously this includes the right to kill anyone who threatens him. Obviously, again, this state of affairs is a war of each against all. Further, all men are practically equal. What one man lacks in physical strength, he may compensate for in stealth or better weapons. The war therefore is a war no one can win. The state of nature is intolerable and suicidal.

Only one solution is possible. Men must assemble and transfer all their rights to a king, an absolute monarch, for only an all powerful king can end the war of each against all. Because religion in Europe had been a cause of division and war during the preceding hundred years, Hobbes made the King the legislator, the judge, and the executive in all religious questions. Neither Pope, Bible, nor individual conscience could be superior to the sovereign. In thus eradicating all divisions and ensuring the peace that every man needs for his self-preservation, the King, himself a man, is not motivated by any altruistic sentiment: he protects the lives of his subjects for his own wealth and glory.

## Rousseau

Rousseau is sometimes pictured as a romanticist whose ideas are directly antithetical to those of Hobbes. This is not quite accurate. In fact it is hard to make an accurate statement of Rousseau's view of human nature, for it seems that he occupies a confused transitional position.

First, as to romanticism, Rousseau is far removed from Goethe's position that the good life is one of the unrestrained, infinite variety of sensual experiences. Rousseau's good man is a law-abiding citizen. Nor did he ever say to Mephistopheles:

Lead him on thy downward course,
Then stand abashed when thou perforce must own
A good man in the direful grasp of ill
His consciousness of right retaineth still.

Second, as to Hobbes, Rousseau was not his antithesis in the sense of describing man as naturally unselfish. To be sure, he does not paint man so black as did Hobbes; nor does he speak of a war of each against all. Still, in the "state of nature" there were enemies and inimical actions. "Before civilization had fashioned our customs . . . our morals were rustic, but natural; and the way a man met a man disclosed his character immediately. Essentially human nature was no better . . . ," but now we are subjugated to a deceitful etiquette and we cannot distinguish a friend from an enemy before it is too late.

The important difference between Rousseau and his predecessors, whether Augustine, Hobbes, or even the French Enlightenment, is that he makes man less rational and more emotional. In this he seems to have been the initiator of an irrationalistic view that came to clearest expression toward the end of the nineteenth century.

Consider his strictures on a scientific education. Education, he says, does not make people better, but worse; in fact, the difficulty of getting an education is nature's way of warning us against the evils of civilization. The errors of science are a thousand times more dangerous than the truth is useful. Actually, the only truth science discovers is that there is an infinite number of ways of going wrong. "The impious writings of Leucippus and Diagoras perished with them: The art of immortalizing the extravagances of the human mind had not yet been invented. But because of the printing press . . . the dangerous dreams of men like Hobbes and Spinoza will endure forever."

"O Virtue! Sublime knowledge of simple souls, must one go to so much trouble to know thee? Are not thy principles engraved on every heart? And to learn thy laws, is it not sufficient to re-enter oneself and listen to the voice of conscience when passions are silent?"[1]

But though learning the laws of virtue may require no more than listening to the voice of conscience, enforcing those laws so as to produce a happy society requires a particular form of government. It is impossible to return to a "state of nature." There never really was such a state; and there is no historical solution to the

---

1. Christian Gauss remarks: "If Rousseau did not always practice virtue, he at least always talked about it." *Selections from the Works of J.J. Rousseau.* Princeton: Princeton University Press, 1920, p. 27.

puzzle of how government and civilization began. "Man is born free; and everywhere he is in chains. . . . How did this change come about? I do not know. What can make it legitimate? That question I think I can answer."

Rousseau's answer is very much like Hobbes's. Everyone must surrender all his rights, not to a king to be sure, but to the whole community. No one retains any rights, for this would be divisive; and all individuals become cogs in the governmental machinery. Parents are not permitted to educate their children; priests may not appeal to the Pope nor Huguenots to the Bible against the State; and all must conform to a governmentally imposed religion on pain of exile or execution.

Rousseau sugar-coats this prescription with enticing words concerning the General Will that always acts for the good of the people. The State cannot have any interest contrary to that of the individual: "The sovereign is always what it should be."

Now, the selfish, personal motivation of Hobbes's king to preserve his own property is plausibly dependable; but Rousseau's optimism is utterly naive.

## Marx

Karl Marx undeniably has exerted tremendous influence on twentieth century society; but it can hardly be said to have resulted from the comprehensiveness or profundity of his philosophy. He left so many gaps in his system that his disciples have been able to develop it in several different directions. Even dialectical materialism, now the orthodox Communist position, seems to have been repudiated by Marx in his more mature writings.

There is no doubt, however, as to his materialism. Like his predecessor Ludwig Feuerbach, he vehemently repudiated Hegel and every form of idealism. Like Feuerbach too he ignored the epistemological difficulties of materialism. Unlike the more recent behaviorists he does not try to explain mind or knowledge by the motions of particles. He just jumps from atoms to man in society. Marx has no noble savage in the distant past, nor brutal savage, either. There is no fixed human nature. Man is a product of society. His ideas, his actions, his mind, his "essence" are created by the methods of manufacture and distribution in use at the time.

For all of Marx's insistence on the real living individual, as opposed to Hegel's abstract Man, the individual is no more than a blood corpuscle in a larger stream of life. Society, not man, is the unit. Therefore private property is immoral.

Two problems arise here. Marx was and Communists are unsparing in their denunciations of the immorality of capitalism. At the same time they accept a relativistic theory of morals that provides no basis for condemnation of anything. More characteristically they reduce moral norms, so-called, to class demands; and these are to be settled by violent action rather than by rational argument.

Rationality itself has a precarious position in Marxism. The laws of nature or real being are not the laws of thought. Logic is merely an adaptation that material man makes to the world. The function of mind is to act, not to understand. Like Friedrich Nietzsche and his disciple Sigmund Freud, Marx makes man basically irrational. But if so, "logical" argument, the result of irrational urges, counts for nothing in establishing the truth or value of Communism. Only violence counts.

The present years have been years of violence throughout the world. In fact this century is the most violent in all history. Large scale disturbances occur in the United States. Do these activists have any precise view of human nature? Do they have a consistent theory of politics? It hardly seems so. If one may judge from appearances—in the absence of scholarly publications—the hippies most closely resembled the ancient, irresponsible Cyrenaics who after some decades faded away into more sober Epicureanism. Neither school was interested in politics. The present day militants seem bent on destruction and offer no blueprint of a better society. Presumably they are more opposed to logical system than even Marx was. If any theory can be imposed on them, it is probably anarchy. Here Hobbes was right: No society will tolerate anarchy. Anarchy made emperors of Napoleon and Caesar.

That all these theories but one favor totalitarianism is a fact that deserves to be pondered. The United States was founded on the principle that individuals transfer some but not all of their rights to the government. Rights not explicitly so transferred were retained by the people. Although Locke in England and Jefferson here were rather Deists than Christian, their theories came from the Christian principles of the Scottish Covenanters. It was these people, Samuel Rutherford, Richard Cameron, and Donald Cargill, in their struggle against the persecutions by the British Crown, who invented the division of powers (legislative, judicial, and executive) and advocated republicanism. With the Puritans in New England and the Presbyterians in Pennsylvania and the Carolinas, such influence determined the form of our Constitution. Only if man, and the State as well, are regarded as subject to God can an argument against totalitarianism be logically complete.

---

Unpublished essay, c. 1970.

# 26

# Humanism

Humanism in America is the result of two related factors, unitarianism and modernism. The latter was the more extensive in its influence and the more philosophical in its principles, though the less consistent in its earlier forms.

[Friedrich] Schleiermacher (1768-1834) initiated modernism by replacing written revelation with religious experience, and thus replacing theology with psychology. Our knowledge of God is the result of analyzing experience, precisely the experience of the feeling of dependence. In this way, Schleiermacher believed, the essential doctrines and values of Christianity could be defended against secular scientism, and only the unessential husks of religion would be discarded.

Early modernism was inconsistent because it retained too much Christian content that could not be obtained by psychological analysis. Humanism is the result of a consistent application of Schleiermacher's principles by which everything Christian is repudiated.

This is most fundamentally seen in the argument about God. The nineteenth century modernists almost without exception believed in God. In Hegelian fashion they may have doubted his personality, but they believed in God.

However, the logic of the matter soon showed that psychological analysis of feelings, in addition to losing the God of Abraham, Isaac, and Jacob, never arrived at anything that could clearly be called God. The more consistent thinkers then asked, Why should the term God be retained when none of its common historical meaning remains?

What can be retained is a set of values, of which the integration of personality is not only one, but, as many humanists say, the highest. They use this as an argument against Christianity. Christianity used to be successful in integrating personality, they contend, but recent experience has shown it less successful. Buddhism and secularism are equally successful. Therefore Christianity is not essential.

This argument, however, leaves Christianity unscathed because Christians do not admit that integration, in this life at least, is the highest good. Furthermore the argument injures humanism because humanists admit that Christianity in some cases produces integration. Now, if integration is the highest good, Christianity in these cases is better than humanism, and humanism has no claim on these people for acceptance. But a philosophy that is "true" or useful only part time and has no logical claim on some people, is not true and cannot make a universal demand.

Other values that humanism discovers in experience are truth, friendship, and beauty. On these humanism bases its ethics, or religion, if one wishes to retain the term.

This is also another point at which the Christianity of verbal revelation, and even secular philosophy, can easily attack the modernist-humanist line of thought. The reason is that experience can justify nothing. Nietzsche is more convincing than any humanist when he asserts that falsehood is usually a greater value than truth. It is even more difficult to justify beauty—if the word has any definite meaning at all. And friendship, developed into some socialistic or communistic political theory, has no empirical argument in its favor. The most that empiricism can say (and more skeptical considerations would dispute even this) is that such and such is the case: *e.g.,* truth seemed useful to John Doe's purposes on a given date; or, Little Lord Fauntleroy thinks the Sistine Madonna is beautiful. But to say that Mr. X on one occasion thought that Y was a value, or that many X's so thought, is far from proving that Y is a value.

Ethics requires normative principles that never follow from descriptive premises. Therefore humanism cannot prove that humanism itself is of any value.

---

*Baker's Dictionary of Christian Ethics*, Carl F.H. Henry, editor. Grand Rapids, Michigan: Baker Book House, 1973, pp. 302-303.

# 27
# Idealistic Ethics

Idealistic ethics specifically designates the ethics of [G.W.F.] Hegel, his Kantian predecessors, and immediate disciples; the inclusion of [Bishop] Berkeley, [G.W.] Leibniz, and Plato (all idealists in virtue of the term's elasticity) would leave no common ethics to be discussed.

Hegelian ethics develops out of [Immanuel] Kant's attempt to escape Spinozistic mechanism. Kant agreed that all bodily motions, including the motions of the human body, are mathematically determined by the inviolable laws of causation. But morality, to which Kant was fervently attached, presupposes God, freedom, and immortality. To harmonize these two themes Kant postulated two worlds: the sensory world of space, time, and causality, and the noumenal world of things in themselves, free transcendental egos, and God. This solution encounters both epistemological and ethical difficulties.

Johann Gottlieb Fichte (1762-1814) admitted that there is no logical flaw in scientific mechanism. But though mechanism cannot be disproved, it is morally unacceptable. No philosophy can demonstrate its own principles, and in these matters one is faced with an ultimate choice. Whether a man chooses Spinozism or freedom depends on what kind of a man he is. Fichte chose morality and freedom.

The moral self, now accepted as the fundamental principle of philosophy, also removes the epistemological difficulties of an unknowable world. Kant had analyzed knowledge into two components; the *forms* of the mind, such as space, time, and causality, which it imposes on experience, and the *contents* that are *given to* the mind by experience. *Das Gegebenes,* the data, required an unknowable source. If, however, we commence with the moral self, the objects of nature become constructions of my consciousness. I *give* them to myself, and no unknowable source is needed.

This idealism avoids the great absurdity of materialism. The latter denies fundamental reality to mind, as for example the twentieth century behaviorists deny even the existence of consciousness; but knowledge can begin only with some sort of *Cogito* [I think]. Philosophy and experience both start with the self. But if this is the starting point, the objects of nature are derivative. Having so deduced them, a philosopher cannot then reverse himself and profess to explain the self as a result of nature.

The moral self also solves the problem of solipsism. The moral self has obligations. But neither Humean images nor Kantian phenomena have. Therefore the self is not a phenomenon. Furthermore, no obligations are due to images or phenomena. Obligations can exist only among persons. Therefore solipsism is impossible and I am a member of a world of free spirits.

If these free spirits were totally independent, the world would be a chaos. Beyond the plurality is a single, all inclusive Absolute Self.

Fichte's Absolute Self is by no means the personal God of Christianity. Fichte opposed Christianity: Its people are hedonistic (since they desire heaven) and therefore immoral; and what is worse, its God is also hedonistic because he created the world for his own pleasure. Such a God is the devil.

Therefore Fichte concludes, "It is not doubtful . . . that there is a moral world order . . . that every good action succeeds and every evil fails, that for those who love only the good, all things must work for the best. . . . It can as little remain uncertain . . . that the concept of God as a particular substance is impossible and contradictory."

Hegel, in conformity with his triadic method, divides the general subject into abstract right, morality, and social ethics. Although abstract right is supposed to concern externalities, like property, and morality concerns inner motivation, the former includes a theory of the person that lays the foundation for early twentieth century personalism.

A person is a consciousness that knows itself, as animals do not, and therefore has rights. Things have no rights. Therefore property is justified. The exercise of property rights may be possible only in a State, but the right itself is inherent in the individual. This means that not merely property is justified, but private property.

How far Hegel would have approved of latter developments may be hard to decide. Even communism can argue that the State does not abolish private property but merely distributes it—the food one actually eats must be private.

A consideration of crime and punishment brings morality into focus. Crime reveals an opposition between the will of one individual and the universal will. But since the latter is the essence of the former, a criminal will does not conform to what it ought to be. Thus it violates its own personality. It negates its own right. Punishment is the negation of the negation. Morality consists in the conformity of the individual will to the universal.

But morality is a one-sided abstraction that must be completed by social ethics. Freedom, the rational goal of man in history, is the individual's subjection to the State. The State is the individual's true self, and if, as is sometimes the case, an individual must be sacrificed to or for the State, it is a sacrifice of the individual to his own higher self.

Hegel went into many details about marriage and the family, agriculture and industry, the judicial system including the police, the forms of government, and world history—none of which can be included here.

Hegel's influence on [Karl] Marx must also be omitted to allow space for a disciple who was more orthodox and more interested in ethics. Thomas Hill Green (1836-1882), an English idealist, was very much interested in refuting utilitarianism. Empiricism had resulted in skepticism; evolution had reduced morality to a vestigial fear inherited from animal ancestors; and physics explained all phenomena mechanically. Green gave the idealist reply.

To begin with, knowledge cannot be explained empirically or mechanically. Natural change does not know itself. Knowledge of change is not a part of the changing process, for, if it were, it could not know any process as a whole but would be confined to the moment.

Since, therefore, man is free, rather than a natural product, morality is possible. Green is not concerned with an indeterminism that asserts unmotivated willing; he wishes to maintain the existence of moral motives that are not natural phenomena. This rules out animal wants. Such appetites do not lead to distinctively human action. Morality requires a self-conscious subject and the idea of self-satisfaction or self-realization.

Such a man and such a morality cannot exist in the world that materialistic science pictures. The universe must be conceived as personal. We can conceive of such a world, a world that is an object to a single mind, and a connected whole, only because we are conscious objects to ourselves. The irreducibility of this self-objectifying consciousness to mechanistic science compels us to regard this our consciousness as the presence in us of the mind for which the world exists.

This divine mind or god is not merely a Being who has made us; he is a Being in whom we live and have our being. We are one in principle with him. He is all that human spirit is capable of becoming.

Therefore morality consists in self-realization. It cannot consist in utilitarian pleasure. Our aim must be a state of self-conscious life that is intrinsically desirable, the full realization of our capabilities.

---

*Baker's Dictionary of Christian Ethics*, Carl F.H. Henry, editor. Grand Rapids, Michigan: Baker Book House, 1973, pp. 310-312.

# 28

# Immanuel Kant

Kant (1724-1804) stood in awe of the starry heavens above and the moral law within. But the mechanism of the one seems to conflict with the freedom of the other.

Since empiricism results in skepticism, as Hume so clearly showed, knowledge is possible, Kant held, only because sensory content is molded or formed by a priori categories. One of these categories is causality. Therefore whatever we see, whatever occurs in time, must be causally determined. Scientific law is inviolable and human bodies are as mechanical as the starry heavens.

However, morality, obligation, or duty is as irrefragable a fact as any scientific law. Moral imperatives are also categorical. To explain:

Moral law is a priori and cannot be deduced from experience. An empirical morality would be hedonistic. But if pleasure were the end of action, the end would justify any efficient means. Yet means as much as and even more than ends are subject to moral praise or blame. Further, if doing right depends on calculating future consequences, only the most intelligent would have a chance of being moral. Even they would have little chance; and surely morality ought to be within the reach of all. Therefore moral laws must not be degraded into the hypothetical imperatives of prudence, calculation, or science. They cannot be empirical. Moral laws are categorical imperatives.

The test of a moral law is necessity and universality. Suppose someone, in order to avoid embarrassment, considers making a promise with the intention of breaking it. This is wrong because it involves a logical contradiction in our will. If all broke their promises, there could be no promises because promises depend on the universal principle that they are made to be kept. The contradiction is that this man recognizes the *universality* of the principle (since he makes a promise) and yet intends to make an *exception*. Moral law therefore is categorical, a priori, universal, and necessary.

The fundamental law of morality is "Act in conformity with that maxim and that maxim only which you can at the same time will to be a universal law." Particular duties, like telling the truth, are special applications of this fundamental law.

The motive of a moral act must be reverence for law. The only thing that can be absolutely good is a good will. Other things, money and even health, may sometimes be bad. A will is good if it is motivated by reverence for law. A will motivated by pleasure, by a desire to produce some result, or by anything other than reverence for law is not a good will, even if the act is objectively moral.

This system of morality requires the transcendental presuppositions of God, immortality, and freedom. Though desire for happiness is immoral, a good world must find them combined; and only God can guarantee the coincidence of virtue and happiness. Next, moral progress to the goal of perfection is an infinite process; therefore man must be immortal. But the most serious problem for morality is freedom.

The category of causality, an a priori form of the mind, compels us to construct out of chaotic sensations a world in which every temporal event is the effect of a cause. Not only bodily motions but desires, inclinations, psychological events also are subject to mechanical law. In such a world freedom is impossible.

But the categorical imperative of morality is an undeniable, a priori fact. And from this fact freedom can be deduced. Here then is the problem: Are not mechanism and freedom contradictory? The very possibility of knowledge requires mechanism. The very possibility of morality requires freedom. Must not Kant discard one or the other?

Kant's solution lies in the existence of two worlds. The mechanical world is the world of phenomena, the world of space and time, the world we "see," or, rather, the world we construct by imposing our forms of peception on sensory stimuli. In this world there is no freedom.

However, there must be another world. Since what we perceive are phenomena or appearances, since the sensory stimuli must come from somewhere other than our minds—only the forms come from the mind—there must be a world of noumena, a world of things-in-themselves, of things as they do not appear. To these things the category of causality cannot apply, for the categories are imposed only on appearances. This implies, to be sure, that we cannot know things as they are in themselves, for knowledge is a composite of form and content. The things-in-themselves have no form.

God may also be a resident of the noumenal world; though there is some doubt here. Kant had said that God, or at least the idea of God, is necessary to morality. On the other hand, he also said that God is not a constitutive idea (an existent component of the universe), but a regulative idea. That is, God is a rule of conduct. At any rate, God cannot be known; and someone has quipped, We cannot know there is a God, but we must live as if there were one.

Another resident of the noumenal world is more closely connected with ethics, namely, ourselves. Hume had described the empirical self, not as a soul-entity, but as merely a collection of images. Kant insisted that a collection requires a collector. Therefore behind the empirical self stands a self-in-itself, a transcendental self, a noumenon. Unknowable, of course.

Now, if freedom and mechanism were both attributed to one world, we would be enmeshed in contradiction. But no contradiction arises if the empirical self in the world of space and time is mechanically determined, and the noumenal self is free.

But though this is not a formal contradiction, a difficulty in application arises. A particular act of theft, i.e., the visible, temporal motions of surreptitiously putting your friend's credit card in your pocket, is a mechanical necessity of the causal world. It is inevitable; it cannot be otherwise; it is devoid of freedom. This, however, is only the appearance or phenomenon of theft. The theft-in-itself, the noumenal theft, could occur only in the noumenal world where we are free. Hence the theft-in-itself could have been avoided, but the appearance of the theft could not have been avoided.

Kant sagely concludes: "While therefore it is true that we cannot comprehend the practical unconditioned necessity of the moral impulse, it is also true that we can comprehend its incomprehensibility; and this is all that can fairly be demanded of a philosophy that seeks to reach the principles which determine the limits of human reason" (*Fundamental Principles of the Metaphysic of Morals,* Chap. III, end).

---

*Baker's Dictionary of Christian Ethics,* Carl F.H. Henry, editor. Grand Rapids, Michigan: Baker Book House, 1973, pp. 365-367.

# 29
# John Dewey

Dewey's (1859-1952) philosophy, unlike that of Aristotle and Augustine, is basically ethical because all research, logical as well as physical, has for him the purpose of solving life's problems. Knowledge for knowledge's sake is anathema to Dewey.

Since there are both efficient and awkward ways of solving life's problems, and since problems change from time to time and place to place, Dewey concludes that there are no fixed norms for human action. "We institute standards of justice, truth, esthetic quality, etc. . . . exactly as we set up a platinum bar as a standard measurer of lengths. . . . The superiority of one conception of justice to another is of the same order as the superiority of the metric system . . ." (*Logic, the Theory of Inquiry,* New York: Holt, Rinehart, & Winston, p. 216). Another and better illustration is that the rules of morality, like the rules of grammar, are the unforeseen and unintended results of custom. There are no antecedent ideal standards. (See *Human Nature and Conduct,* New York: Modern Library, I, Section 5.)

Scientific method can determine what customs at a given time and place are best. We should neither distrust the capacity of experience to develop ideals and norms, as Christians do in their belief in divine law; nor unthinkingly enjoy pleasures irrespective of the method used to produce them, though this is a better attitude than theism. Values are fugitive. A method is needed to discriminate among them on the basis of their conditions and consequences. The reason for enjoying a value is often (to have a conclusive argument Dewey should have said *always*) that the object is a means to or a result of something else.

Nothing is valuable in itself. A genuine good differs from a spurious good because of its consequences. Nor are the consequences good in themselves. They too are good only as a means to something further. Nothing carries its own credentials; everything is instrumental; there is no final, intrinsic value on which the value of other things depends. Science can establish norms, or at least show which customs are best, because the problem is not one of intellectual certainty as rationalists and Christians think, but of security. Chemistry improves the food supply; and so science, by studying the conditions by which values are made more secure, solves the problems of ethics.

Again, science is the solution because not all enjoyments are *de jure*, rather than *de facto*, values. "Enjoyments that issue from conduct directed by insight into relations have meaning and a validity due to the way in which they are experienced. Such enjoyments are not to be repented of; they generate no aftertaste of bitterness" (*Quest for Certainty*, Minton, Balch, 1929, p. 267). For example, heating and lighting, speed of transportation and communication, have been achieved, not by lauding their desirability, but by studying their conditions: "Knowledge of relations having been obtained, ability to produce followed, and enjoyment ensued as a matter of course" (*Quest for Certainty*, New York: Putnam, p. 269).

The examples of heating, lighting, and communication concretize Dewey's view that there are no intrinsic values. But if there are no intrinsic values, why should one engage in arduous scientific investigations to make heating and lighting more secure? If Dewey answers, "to obtain something further," the question repeats itself: Why should one arduously develop them as means to something further, which itself has no intrinsic value? The moral question is not, as Dewey says, how to make values more secure, but, rather, how to select which values to secure.

Dewey admits that there are wrong ideals. Without aesthetic enjoyment mankind might become a race of economic monsters (*Reconstruction in Philosophy*, New York: Holt, 1920, p. 127). But why not choose economic monstrosity? If *de jure* value is conferred by a scientific study of complicated means, not only economic monstrosity but nearly any other imaginable purpose is justified.

Dewey also gives the examples of murder and wanton cruelty (*Ethics,* with Tufts, pp. 251, 265, 292). But it is significant that Dewey with communistic massacres and Spanish bullfights before him nowhere gives a scientific proof that these are evil.

There is a reason why Dewey dare not try to prove that murder is bad. To do so would result in a fixed rule, a hierarchy of values, and intrinsic qualities. Therefore Dewey makes all moral judgments aesthetic determinations in single cases. Each contemplated case of murder must be decided singly and individually. Hence in some cases murder may have beneficial results.

The final criticism is then that scientific technique cannot select any goal. It can be used for opposite purposes. Scientific methods of communication are efficient for preaching the gospel and equally efficient for totalitarian subjugation of the Hungarians, Czechs, and Vietnamese. And this means that Dewey has not solved the problem of morality.

---

*Baker's Dictionary of Christian Ethics,* Carl F.H. Henry, editor. Grand Rapids, Michigan: Baker Book House, 1973, pp. 179-181.

# 30
# Kant and Old Testament Ethics

In current literature, and specifically in college textbooks, we meet frequent distortions of Christianity. One such is the subject of the present discussion. Two quotations from two textbooks by two well known American Professors set forth the distortion in question and furnish this article with an appropriate point of departure.

"Perhaps the best way to introduce [Immanuel] Kant is to conceive him as the last and most logical of the long line of Hebrew prophets and Christian Apostles."[1]

---

1. T.V. Smith, in *Readings in Ethics,* by Clark and Smith, p. 223.

Consider also a second quotation. "Either then there is some way of defining a good end—an end which justifies the means—or else there must be a moral excellence that belongs to certain types of act irrespective of what they may lead to, if indeed they lead to aught in common. . . . The second interpretation is in the spirit of the Decalogue. . . . This world, we might call it the Old Testament world, is then exactly the kind of world in which morality as Kant defines morality could and would exist."[2]

That some have had doubts as to the truth of the view given in the quotations is attested by the following footnote of the second writer. "This image of the Old Testament world is not of course supposed to be that of the ancient Hebrews. Rather does it represent this world as reflected in the thought of a modern Christian community."[3]

Now whatever the force of this last admission may be, the two quotations strongly suggest a fundamental similarity between the ethics of Kant and of the Old Testament. Because of the footnote, however, this discussion needs to distinguish between the Testaments themselves and what that vague entity, a modern Christian community, might happen to think of those ancient documents. But both authors imply, and the second distinctly asserts, that common opinion makes Kant's strict morality essentially that of the Hebrew-Christian religion.

This opinion, permit me to repeat, seems to be a definitely mistaken one. And why those who express such an opinion without some qualification like that in the second author, are mistaken, admits of an easy psychological explanation. The modern Christian community is simply not Christian. The views of the intelligentsia artistically if sometimes flippantly expressed in dilettante magazines err through a profound unfamiliarity with the contents of the Old and New Testaments. The modern educated community is largely pagan, so largely in fact that the condition usually escapes notice. Owing to an educational system originated to preserve religious freedom, the victims of public

---

2. E.A. Singer, in *Modern Thinkers*, pp. 132, 137.

3. *Ibid.*, p. 137.

instruction have been kept not so much free as ignorant. By means of a deliberate silence through the schools, a silence relieved occasionally only by a slur or a sarcasm, the great majority of college graduates go through life either with distorted views of the contents of Christiantiy or none at all—alternatives which in reality amount to the same thing. When asked in class the most authentic sources for the examination of early Christian thought, the instructor named certain twenty-seven books; the student then asked again if the Epistles of Paul had been included in the list. Yet this particular student (a Roman Catholic) knew more than another student who thought Christianity taught mainly that the universe was created in six periods of twenty-four hours. Aside from scholars who are both trained in research and have made this particular research, the educated people of the United States are not in general capable of deciding whether Kant is fundamentally similar to the Old Testament or not. Nor does their inability arise from any meagre acquaintance with Kant. If they were presented with the pamphlets of [Martin] Luther and [John] Eck, the *Institutes* of [John] Calvin or the Tridentine symbols, these writings would appear not so much untrue as unintelligible. In matters of religions these people are as advanced as high school pupils who think *hors d'oeuvres* means "out of work." It may, therefore, seem appropriate to show that any similarity between Kant's ethics and the Hebrew-Christian system is accidental and superficial.

There are two main views respecting the intent of the Old Testament which we must consider. One is that of the Jewish people both of Christ's day and, so far as I am informed, of to-day as well. The second is the Christian view. We anticipate little difficulty in showing that the Pharisees of the first century were not in harmony with the categorical imperative. For them, no one will deny, morality was the means of winning God's favor, of improving oneself until acceptable by God, in short of achieving salvation. Omniscient Jehovah knows and balances each fault against each good deed and if by observing the multitudinous regulations of the Pharisees, a man's good deeds exceed his evil ones, God accepts him as worthy of heaven. Far from any suggestion that man should do his duty regardless of consequences, purely from the motive of vindicating an abstract formal duty, the Pharisees act deliberately for reward. Whether the reward be crudely or more intellectually conceived does not alter the matter. Any reward as a motive of action is inconsistent with Kant's theory.

Sometimes articles are written to show how primitive the Hebrews, or more strictly the Old Testament is in making fear of punishment so prominent in moral exhortation. Kant, whose position is sounder, higher, more ethical, would never, or ought never, to avoid evil through fear of punishment. With perhaps the exception of some obvious exaggerations, this attack on the Old Testament is far more accurate historically than the view we are here opposing. There is no need to make this article appear scholarly by quoting the penalties attached to infractions of the Mosaic code. Occasionally, through the lack of historical perspective, as in the case of eye for eye and tooth for tooth, these laws are understood more as vicious savagery than as an alleviation of the customary eye for an insult and a life for an eye; nevertheless the penalties, both civil and religious, are enunciated very explicitly. Likewise there are numerous promises to those who will honor father and mother, who will pay the tithe or who have the faith of Abraham. Nor, in this respect at least, can there be drawn any antithesis between the Law and the Prophets. The Prophets protest against violating the law by means of evasive technicalities, they inveigh against a self-complacency in obeying parts of the law and not other more important parts, but they never annul the rewards and punishments, nor preach duty for duty's sake. Amos in particular is singled out as having attained to high ethical standards of social justice. But his very first verses give warning of punishment in a tone indiscernible from the thunder of Mount Sinai. These facts, it seems reasonable to conclude, suffice to show that both the writers of the Old Testament and the Pharisees of Christ's day do not agree with any system which removed reward and punishment as motives toward morality.

But, it is maintained, Jesus attacked the Pharisaic interpretation of the Old Testament. He objects to their praying on the street corners to be seen of men, adding pointedly—they have their reward. Does his attack therefore apply to the point in question?

Did he add some new spiritual principle abrogating the reward and punishment morality? No one can object to referring to the Sermon on the Mount as an important piece of evidence. Some members of the modern Christian community have placed this sermon, especially its specifically moral injunctions, in a position more systematically basic than sound scholarship would show it deserved. By making Jesus principally if not solely an ethical preacher, they have reversed the relation that obtains in the New Testament between ethics and theology. Yet on an ethical question, the Sermon on the Mount demands appeal. Its opening words are: "Blessed are the poor in spirit, for theirs is the kingdom of heaven." Blessing and reward begin the Sermon; rains, floods, winds, and destruction end it. Can then anyone seriously maintain that Jesus preaches a categorical imperative in the Kantian sense? "For if ye love them which love you, what reward have ye? Take heed that ye do not your righteousness before men, otherwise ye have no reward of your Father. Let not thy left hand know what thy right hand doeth, and thy Father shall recompense thee." Not less than three times in the sixth chapter of Matthew is the reward mentioned. In other discourses punishment is as clearly stated as reward. "Depart from me ye cursed into everlasting fire prepared for the devil and his angels. And these shall go away into everlasting punishment but the righteous into life eternal."

We have no intention of minimizing the differences between the Pharisees and Jesus. They held thoroughly inconsistent views respecting the sense of the Old Testament. They differed radically on the effective power of human morality with God, but neither obscured, it is quite permissible to say both emphasized reward and punishment. If Jesus objected to the Pharisees, it was not because they wanted a reward but because of the measly reward they wanted. Perhaps then it was the Apostles who changed Jesus's teaching in a Kantian direction.

Peter on the day of Pentecost testified and exhorted with many words, "Save yourselves from this untoward generation." At the Beautiful Gate he declares, "Repent so that there may come seasons of refreshing." Paul in 2 Thessalonians 1 asserts, "It is a righteous thing with God to recompense tribulation to them that trouble you." Or should we proceed to quote the Apocalypse?

Indeed Christianity must be a strange thing to draw upon itself the attacks of those who consider heaven and hell a barbarous philosophy and at the same time to be understood as teaching duty for duty's sake.

This confusion results from assuming that modern communities are Christian. Scholarly opinion is still in process of recuperating from the effects of nineteenth century criticism. Historical investigations are showing that certain popular conceptions of the God of the early Christians derive more from Kant than from the early Christians. The God of the New Testament strikes Ananias and Sapphira dead for fraud. He is indeed a God who so loved the world that he gave his only begotten Son, but he is also a God who reveals his wrath from heaven against all ungodliness of men who suppress the truth in unrighteousness. At the present moment there are two classes of scholars who have seen something of the Christian genius. First are those who definitely and consciously oppose it. Among others we may cite the example of George Santayana in *Winds of Doctrine*. This distinguished gentleman has some peculiar notions about Christianity; he thinks for example, that the universe was created for the glory of man (*Winds of Doctrine*, p. 45, and *Genteel Tradition at Bay*, p. 42) but for all of that he sees clearly that modernism is not Christian. He judges modernists to be in a state of "fundamental apostasy from Christianity," "worship(ing) nothing and acknowledge(ing) authority in nothing save in their own spirit." He accuses the modernist who thinks he is Christian of "an inexplicable ignorance of history, of theology and of the world," and of substituting a theory which "steals empirical reality away from the last judgment, from hell and from heaven." Santayana may have some queer views on the nature of Christianity, but the views of our modern Christian community are still queerer.

The second class of scholars who grasp the essence of Christianity is that small group which definitely and consciously accepts it. More and more is it being seen that the absolute anti-Christian radicals and the ultra-conservative Evangelicals are historically accurate, while the third class, the "modernists," are befogged in a cloud of subjective mysticism. This is a mere modern sentiment; the communities, to which the influence of Kant has finally seeped, insistently argue that the term *Christian* has noble connotations and therefore, refined and cultured as they know themselves to be, they must naturally be Christian. In order to discover what Christian thought is, therefore, it is no longer necessary to study the New Testament or make erudite investigations into ancient centuries; one needs only to express his own fine ideals and Christianity is thereby defined. Mysticism saves one so much trouble, you know.

This attitude, however, comes from Kant through [Albrecht] Ritschl. These are the men who in separating scientific truth from value judgments, have led, consistently or inconsistently, to the discarding of historical in favor of psychological investigation in religious matters. These men attempted to enclose intellect and religion in separate pigeon-holes so that neither should disturb the other. Yet such a separation is a complete reversal of the Christian world-view. Now, while this modern development may be much nearer the truth and the Testaments largely nonsense, as is usually assumed without much research, this is just one more reason for not confounding Kant's morality with that of the Old Testament.

The Hebrew-Christian system is more likely to cut the knot than follow the subtle wisdom of Kant. If we have no reason to believe there is a God, why should we act as though there were one? The early Christians were more empirically minded than the modern development would lead one to believe. John in his first epistle insists on the testimony of ears, eyes and hands. Paul in his defense before King Agrippa requests consideration of evidence, "for this thing was not done in a corner." The Christian preacher demands faith to be sure, but the faith he demands is a belief based on evidence. Those who reject Christianity act unwisely in refusing to engage in archaeological argument to demonstrate the mythical character of the Testaments. Such a demonstration would be far more convincing and presumably more scholarly than the actual publications of the day.

There still remains the question whether Kant and his followers, now shown to be at variance with Christianity, have provided a philosophically more acceptable ethic. It is doubtful. Any ethic to prove acceptable must, at least in my opinion, provide room for one principle among others, which Kant would be sure to deny, *viz.* each individual should always seek his own personal good. Such a principle is usually designated egoistic, and egoism usually carries unpleasant connotations. Yet when unnecessary implications are avoided and misunderstandings removed, it is my opinion that even apart from any discussion of Christianity, only some form of egoism can withstand criticism. A universalism, like [Jeremy] Bentham's for instance finds embarrassment in considering the possible incompatibility of an individual's good with the good of the community. Kant, representing a different system, is forced to resort to elements discordant with the rest of his philosophy when he considers the possible conflict between an individual's good and the same individual's duty. It is true Kant attempts to harmonize duty and good by providing a *Deus ex machina* to reward duty, but he makes hope of that reward immoral.

Christ, on the other hand, did not think it immoral to seek one's own good. If you judge that Hebrews xii.2, "who for the joy that was set before him endured the cross," does not warrant any conclusion as to the nature of Christ's motives in undertaking the work of redemption, still we think we can insist that both Christ and the Apostles made abundant use of hope and fear in appealing for converts. So if anyone reproach Christianity as being egoistic and based on fear, partially, ask the objector if fear and self-interest are or are not worthy motives for preferring orange juice to carbolic acid for breakfast. The Bible appeals directly to fear and self-interest; it teaches that absolute destruction awaits him who rejects Christ; and it also teaches that although the Christian may have temporary tribulation, he ultimately loses nothing but gains everything in accepting Christ. Now this is what egoism means, and Kant would have none of it. Unfortunately, however, egoism is sometimes regarded as countenancing sharp practices and shady morality. Yet it requires but little reflection to conclude that sharp practices do not pay in the long run. Honesty and all other forms of virtue are the best policy. Egoism when correctly understood cannot in the least sanction violation of conscience. In this relation no better reference can be made than to a paragraph from the good Bishop Butler. "Conscience and self-love, if we understand our true happiness, always lead us the same way. Duty and interest are perfectly coincident; for the most part in this world, but entirely and in every instance in the future and the whole."

If we follow Bishop Butler and many others who have held that egoism does not counsel shady actions, that virtue is the best policy precisely because it is an indispensable means to our end, we are ready to consider the position assigned in this scheme to the good of others, for egoism in general and Christianity in particular have been attacked as selfish.

This is not quite the same problem as that usually raised about the compatibility of the good of all people. An egoist, Christian or not, will find quite a little difficulty in proving that the good of one individual harmonizes with the good of all other individuals. As a matter of fact the Christian might well conclude that had Judas done what was best for him, it would be too bad for us. Apparently, then, the good of some people is incompatible with the good of others. But whether we do accept this conclusion or not, that the good of two people may under given conditions conflict, it does not follow that egoism teaches selfishness. And yet Christianity has been assailed as selfish. That one must save his own soul first, and only afterwards turn his attention to others, and that his helping others reacts again to benefit himself, Hastings Rashdall for example frankly considers "nauseous." To me, however, the attempt to help others before attending to one's own condition is a case of the blind leading the blind. Nor have I been able to find anything disgusting in regarding one's own development as a motive in missionary activity. We sing about stars in our crown, we speak of souls for our hire. If, then, I may be an instrument of effectual calling in God's hands, and if such instrumentality brings a blessing, I can see no good reason for denying that that blessing may properly be a part of the evangelistic motive.

Now, to bring this discussion to an end and perhaps to a conclusion as well, we should say that if portions of the modern Christian community regard Kant as the last of the prophets, a polite acquaintance with the Bible would remedy their misapprehension. And second, when our opponents claim that Christianity is a selfish soul-saving, egoistic religion, we should advise Christians not to be apologetic in the colloquial sense of the word but to be apologetic in the technical sense, and, with the aid of oranges and carbolic acid, follow the examples of Christ and the Apostles in holding out to them the hope of heaven and the fear of hell as legitimate motives for availing themselves of Christ's gracious redemption.

---

*The Evangelical Quarterly,* July 1935.

# 31

# The Law of God

A certain denomination, of which I am not a member, sponsored a Christmas service in which part of the worship was (what word shall I use) performed by a troupe of ballet dancers. When I remarked, upon being pressed for an opinion, that ballet was a bit incongruous with divine worship, one of their ministers replied that any exercise that stimulates love of humanity is appropriate in church. Then I tried to tell him of the Puritan principle and of the law of God from which we should not turn aside, either to the right hand or to the left. And, since this minister expatiated on love versus law, I quoted, "If ye love me, keep my commandments." But he concluded the conversation, politely enough, by saying that my viewpoint appeared legalistic to him.

The extreme modernists who introduce dancing into the worship service have strange allies in some fundamentalists who also reject the law of God. With all their insistence on the infallibility of the Scripture and on the necessity of Christ's death on the cross for our redemption—may God bless them abundantly, they are really Christians—this segment of fundamentalism denies that the Ten Commandments are binding in this age of the world's history. We are not under law but under grace, they say; we are free from the law and need pay no attention to it. To do so would be legalism.

Now, the three chapters of Romans where our freedom from the law of sin and death is most emphasized are far from disparaging the law. In addition to the strong insistence on the necessity of a righteous life (Romans 6:2, 6, 12, 15; 8:1, 4, 13), Paul asserts that the law is holy and good (Romans 7:12), spiritual (7:14), a delight to the godly man (7:22), and the rule of service (7:25). In most cases where the English translation speaks of being *free* from the law, the Greek more accurately says *justified* from the law. That is, we are free from the penalty of the law. It does not mean that we are free to disobey God's commands.

This is not legalism. Legalism, or justification by works, is the unscriptural teaching that man can merit heaven by his own efforts. And it is very strange that modernists, who have rejected the gracious sacrifice of Christ, should accuse anyone of being legalistic. But the meanings of words often get twisted these days, both in religion and in politics.

In opposition to legalism the Scriptures base our redemption solely on the merits of Christ. Yet, as we are redeemed from sin, as we come to Christ in repentance, as we are born to newness of life, we are under the same obligation to keep his laws. "If ye love me, keep my commandments."

The [Westminster] Confession of Faith sums up the whole matter very succinctly. After distinguishing the moral law from the ritual and the national laws, it says, (sections v, vi),

"The moral law doth forever bind all, as well justified persons as others, to the obedience thereof; and that not only in regard of the matter contained in it, but also in respect of the authority of God, the Creator, who gave it. Neither doth Christ in the gospel any way dissolve, but much strengthen this obligation.

"Although true believers be not under the law as a covenant of works, to be thereby justified or condemned; yet is it of great use to them, as well as to others; in that, as a rule of life, informing them of the will of God and their duty, it directs and binds them to walk accordingly; discovering also the sinful pollutions of their nature, hearts, and lives; so as, examining themselves thereby, they may come to further conviction of, humiliation for, and hatred against sin; together with a clearer sight of the need they have of Christ and the perfection of his obedience."

---

*The Southern Presbyterian Journal,* January 12, 1955.

# 32
# Legalism

Legalism, in the history of theology, is the theory that a man by doing good works or obeying the law earns and merits his salvation. Pelagius argued that since man has free will, he is able to keep God's commandments perfectly. The Pharisees, who denied free will, gave greater scope to grace, in that if a man's sins and merits were in balance, God would graciously remove one's sin.

The evangelical doctrine is justification by faith alone, and that faith itself is a gift of God. The merits are all Christ's.

The Apostle Paul considers the objection that justification by faith alone removes all need for good works and allows the regenerate man to continue in sin. His reply is that redemption is salvation from sin and that justification irresistibly issues in sanctification.

In the present century the term legalism has been given a new meaning. Situation ethics despises rules and laws. Anyone who conscientiously obeys God's commandments is regarded as legalistic. Therefore Joseph Fletcher approves the breaking of every one of the Ten Commandments. He thus transfers the evil connotation of legalism to the historical morality of Protestantism.

---

*Baker's Dictionary of Christian Ethics,* Carl F.H. Henry, editor. Grand Rapids, Michigan: Baker Book House, 1973, p. 385.

# 33
# Modal Spheres and Morality

In Volume II of his four great volumes on *A New Critique of Theoretical Thought,* Herman Dooyeweerd begins with a discussion of cosmic time. This important part of his system leads directly into his discussion of the modal spheres, which I propose to examine in this paper. In the *Gordon Review* of September 1956

I offered several objections to the theory of cosmic time. The first few were generally philosophical, but the last was pointedly religious because it uncovered the implications of cosmic time for the inspiration of Scripture. It would be better to repeat here the entire context, but the time allows only a brief quotation as a basis of discussion.

"In this eschatological aspect of time," says Dooyeweerd, "faith grasps the 'eschaton' and in general that which is or happens beyond the limits of cosmic time. In this special sense are to be understood the 'days of creation,' the initial words of the book of Genesis, the order in which regeneration *precedes* conversion etc. . . . I cannot agree with some modern theologians, who identify the eschatological aspect of time with the historical and reject the supra-temporal central sphere of human existence and of divine revelation."

This quotation shows that Dooyeweerd assigns the first chapters of Genesis and eschatological passages, such as prophecies of Christ's return, to a place beyond the limits of cosmic time, beyond the cosmic temporal order, and beyond historical time. How Dooyeweerd distinguishes between an eschatological passage and a non-eschatological passage, I do not know. May I ask, Is the account of Christ's crucifixion eschatological? If it is, the crucifixion did not occur in historical time. Surely the return of Christ must be considered eschatological. Then on Dooyeweerd's principles it too cannot occur in any historical sequence. Even with his restricted example of the days of creation as supra-temporal, one is justified in wondering whether the temptation of Eve and the fall of Adam are historical. If not, and if the fall is existentialized, Romans 5:12-21 forces the question as to whether we should in consistency existentialize Christ himself.

Further, in opposing some theologians who reject the "supra-temporal central sphere of human existence," does Dooyeweerd imply the eternity of man and make salvation a deification? Surely he seems to deny that man is forever a temporal creature.

Like the theory of cosmic time Dooyeweerd's theory of fifteen law spheres also impinges on the subject of Scriptural inspiration. Once again I shall not repeat the criticisms of this confused theory that I published in an earlier work. I shall only add a discussion of its bearing on the Scripture; and in doing so I shall refer more to some of his disciples than to Dooyeweerd himself.

The theory of law spheres is a sort of classification of sciences. The basic science is arithmetic. It is basic because everything can be counted. Plants as well as atoms can be numbered. The higher biotic sphere is subject to all the laws of arithmetic, but not all numerable quantities are subject to the laws of plant life. Each higher sphere of the fifteen exemplifies the laws of the spheres below it, but none of the lower spheres exemplifies the higher laws.

Above the sphere of plant life, and here I omit several steps, there come the spheres of economics, ethics, and at the very top the sphere of faith. Although Dooyeweerd allows this to be any faith, Buddhist or even communist perhaps, the present aim is to see what happens in the case of Christian faith. The problem is this: If the laws of the higher spheres do not apply to the lower spheres, can the Christian faith provide any principles for ethics or economics? Since the formal principle of the Reformation is the plenary and verbal inspiration of the Bible, the question more simply put is: Does the Bible supply us with normative principles in economics and ethics? The initial impression is that the theory of law spheres does not allow the Bible to speak on such matters.

This initial impression is strengthened by material published by some of Dooyeweerd's disciples in this country and Canada. There is a booklet entitled *Understanding the Scriptures* by A.H. DeGraaff and C.G. Seerveld. Almost at the beginning (page two in fact), Dr. DeGraaff says, "You distort the Scriptures when you read them as a collection of objective statements about God and man. . . . They do not contain any rational, general, theological statements about God and his creation. . . . It is not the purpose of the Bible to inform us about the nature of God's being or his attributes" (p. 9). He also adds, "The Scriptures are neither rational nor irrational in character" (p. 18).

In my opinion all of these statements except the last are false, and the last is nonsense. The assertion that the Scriptures contain no rational, general, theological statements about God and his creation is clearly false because the Scriptures say that God is righteous and man is sinful. To say that the Scriptures are neither rational nor irrational is nonsense. Everyone knows that the statement, Today is Friday, is rational. Similarly, Wellington defeated Napoleon. These statements can be understood, easily understood. On the other hand, the profound pronouncement, Onts skom bubbits, is irrational. There is nothing in it to be understood. It has no meaning. For that matter the assertion, Two equals three, is not merely false: It is irrational because the predicate is the logical contrary of the subject. Therefore it cannot be understood. It has no meaning. But what example can be given of a sentence that is neither rational nor irrational, a sentence that has a meaning and equally has no meaning, a sentence that cannot be understood and at the same time can be understood? Looking for one in a book, such as the Bible, is like going to the zoo to find an animal that is neither vertebrate nor invertebrate.

More obviously connected with the theory of law spheres is Dr. DeGraaff's view of ethics. He writes, "Nor does it—the Bible —contain moral applications that tell us how to live the good life —virtues that we share with the humanist" (p. 21). The additional words after the dash cause confusion. It is true that a Christian does not share any virtue with a humanist because a humanist just cannot have any Christian virtue. But it is false to say that the Bible gives no moral rules. Dr. DeGraaff objects to teaching boys and girls in Vacation Bible School moral lessons about purity, chastity, and Victorian, middle-class American standards. Instead of warning them against the prevalent loose view of sex, we should tell them about irresponsbile de-foresting, yellow smog, dirty water— and we should tell them these things in "a non-moralistic manner" (p. 26). Apparently dirty water is worse than a dirty mind.

In answer to many objections from Christians Dr. DeGraaff repeats, "The Bible does not teach us how to be good and how to avoid being bad" (p. 29). So says Dr. DeGraaff. But the Bible says, "All Scripture . . . is profitable . . . for correction, for instruction in righteousness, that the man of God may be . . . completely furnished to every good work." The Bible also says, "Thy word have I hid in my heart that I might not sin against thee."

But Dr. DeGraaff plunges on. Speaking of the Ten Commandments (which he strangely says are not commandments at all), he says, "None of them can be literally followed or applied today, for we live in a different period of history in a different culture" (p. 35).

Imagine! It is impossible to follow or apply the commandment, Thou shalt not steal, because we live in a different culture. Thou shalt not commit adultery cannot be literally obeyed today because God commanded it in 1500 B.C. This line of thought is incredible. But check the references: page 35, *Understanding the Scriptures*, DeGraaff and Seerveld, Association for the Advancement of Christian Scholarship, Toronto, Canada. Since none of the Ten Commandments can be literally applied today, Dr. DeGraaff suggests that for them we substitute agitation against police brutality (p. 36). Love your neighbor's wife, but hate the police.

There is a further implication. If God's command against adultery is inapplicable in our different culture, why should we suppose that God's covenant with Abraham is applicable? Dr. De Graaff seems to retain some respect for the covenant. Yet how can the Mosaic command against adultery be culturally conditioned in 1500 B.C., while a religious covenant some 500 years earlier escaped such cultural conditioning? A rational thinker, might, in consistency, reject both. A consistent Christian accepts both. But it takes some explaining to accept the one and reject the other.

In order that no one may suppose Dr. DeGraaff to be an anomaly among the disciples of Dooyeweerd and that these criticisms are not relevant to the whole movement, the same ideas are to be noted in the writings of Dr. Calvin Seerveld. In the same volume with Dr. DeGraaff, Dr. Seerveld has an interesting section on the exegesis of Numbers 22-24. He uses this passage to distinguish three methods of understanding the Scriptures.

The first method is that of evangelical fundamentalists. Dr. Seerveld has collected phrases from Alexander Maclaren, W.B. Riley, Clarence Edward Macartney, and others who note that (1) Balaam had a strong passion for earthly honor; (2) he wanted the best of two incompatible worlds; and (3) he beat his ass unmercifully. From these points the fundamentalist concludes that we should not put earthly honor first among our choices; that we should seek righteousness first of all; and that we should not be cruel to dumb animals. Dr. Seerveld continues his list with a number of such applications and moral lessons.

The second method is beside the present purpose. The third method Dr. Seerveld assigns to the "remnants of staunch orthodox churches," and he cites Hengstenberg and Calvin. This method specializes in doctrine, rather than in ethical application. It notes that Numbers 23:19 is a clear statement of God's immutability. This divine dependability extends to the covenant with Abraham, which therefore applies to the Israelites whom Balak wanted Balaam to curse. In the account the fulfillment of the covenant is prophesied in the words, "There shall come forth a star out of Jacob." And there is considerably more in the passage.

Dr. Seerveld disapproves of these methods. He challenges their hidden *aprioris;* he suggests that they miss the richness of Scripture, and mislead fledgling readers who use them (p. 67). As for the fundamentalist method of moral application, Dr. Seerveld says, "Balaam's invitation from Balak is not remotely within my experience as a Christian school teacher because my twentieth century situation and the ancient parallel made abstractly ideal jibe of sorts only after a dozen qualifications. . . . [T]he binding force is lost" (p. 68). Thus "the world-upsidedown changing message of Numbers 22-24 is reduced to a mess of moralistic pottage" (p. 69).

The method of the Reformers, the orthodox Calvinistic method, is equally bad. This "Scholastic reading of the Scriptures is always after truths that can be theoretically formulated and held to be universally valid, consistent Bible teaching against all attack (p. 74). This Reformed method is bad, says Dr. Seerveld, because "it removes the reader half a step from the convicting comfort and humbling facing God's love and anger brings, removes the reader half a step away from existential confrontation with the living Word of God and asks him to comprehend these realities for codified propositional dogmas" (p. 75).

But is the Reformation method, the method of studying and learning what the Bible says, such a bad method? Is it not rather commendable? Let it be noted that the Apostle Peter at the beginning of his second epistle says, "Grace to you and peace be multiplied by the knowledge of God" (II Peter 1:2). At the end of the same epistle he repeats, "Grow in grace and knowledge" (3:18).

The Apostle John also emphasized doctrine and propositions. Without mentioning existentialism or irrational confrontations, John, in fact, Jesus himself says, "If any one guards my doctrine, he shall not see death, ever" (8:51). Another verse that makes Christianity depend on an understanding of and an assent to propositions is, "If you believed Moses, you would believe me, for he wrote of me; but if you do not believe his writings, how can you believe my words!" (5:47). Jesus also said, "The words that I have spoken to you are spirit and life" (6:63). (Compare my short volume, *The Johannine Logos*.)

The Reformation use of the Bible, like the evangelical-fundamentalist method, also "is interested in the practical lessons we can learn from it." The Westminster divines would have rejected Dr. Seerveld's charge of reducing the Bible to a "mess of moralistic pottage." Their careful and very detailed exposition of the Ten Commandments in the Larger Catechism shows how greatly they valued morality.

But Dr. Seerveld in his remarks on Numbers says, "To make Balaam a warning model for the reader is to distort the nature of biblical narrative and ignore the historical solidity of God's disclosure. Scripture never gives biographic snatches to serve as ethical models" (p. 68).

In contrast with Dr. Seerveld's view of the Bible stands the practice of the Apostle Peter. Speaking of the false teachers who introduced heresies instead of accepting orthodox propositions, and who lived in contempt of Dr. Seerveld's moralistic pottage, the Apostle writes, "having forsaken the right way they went astray, having followed the way of Balaam, son of Beor, who loved the hire of wrong-doing" etc. (II Peter 2:15 ff.). Here the Apostle most assuredly uses "biographic snatches to serve as ethical models." If a modern exegete condemns the Apostle's use of the Bible, then it seems to me that the modern exegete has gone astray—not the Apostle.

---

Unpublished essay, c. 1973.

# 34

# Natural Law and Revelation

The Fourth of July is an appropriate time to consider the basic problems of politics.

In the Declaration of Independence the American people accused the British government of abuses, usurpations, despotism and tyranny. The King had exceeded his just powers. He had forbidden his governors to execute important laws until his assent had been obtained; he had repeatedly dissolved duly elected legislatures; he had made the judiciary dependent on his will; he had erected a harassing bureaucracy; he had made the military superior to the civil power; he had imposed taxes without the consent of the people; he had deprived them of trial by jury and transported them beyond the seas to be tried for pretended offenses.

Evidently the colonists thought that there were some things a government had no right to do.

So also when the Constitution brought into being the United States of America, a Bill of Rights had to be written into it. Congress shall make no law respecting an establishment of religion. . . . The right of the people to be secure in their persons, houses, papers, and effects, against unreasonable searches and seizures, shall not be violated. . . . The powers not delegated to the United States by the Constitution, nor prohibited by it to the States, are reserved to the States respectively, or to the people.

Liberty today more than ever needs to be defended from totalitarian encroachments. Not only is there the brutality of reducing a populace to the level of abject slavery, with a controlled church to applaud its atheistic rulers; but also in western lands the burdens and budgets, the regulations and controls, become constantly more onerous. The tenth article of the Bill of Rights is almost a dead letter.

Can limitations on governments, can the protection of minorities from majority action, can individual rights and liberties be rationally maintained? Or does democracy mean mob rule?

Some of the colonists, Thomas Jefferson, for example, were deists. Jefferson regarded Jesus simply as a a good moral teacher. Nonetheless he founded individual rights on a sort of theology. After referring to the laws of nature and of nature's God, Jefferson wrote, "We hold these truths to be self-evident: that all men . . . are endowed by their Creator with certain unalienable rights."

The Thomistic philosophy of the Roman Catholic church also bases its (all too totalitarian) political theory on the idea of natural law. [Jacques] Maritain has said, "There is, by the very virtue of human nature, an order or a disposition which human reason can discover. . . . The unwritten law, or Natural Law, is nothing more than that." And if Maritain has not, others add that this unwritten law is the minimum religious premise because it means that the universe is not indifferent to man's individual life.

Thus the law of nature is considered superior to the statutes of a state; it is a norm for legislation; and a state is under theoretical obligation to confine its legislation within the limits prescribed by nature.

In this discussion the important point is whether or not human reason can discover in nature an order of morality that sets the norm for statutory law. Are Jefferson's unalienable rights self-evident? The argument does not center on individual rights as such, nor on the existence of a Creator, nor on the Creator's authority to judge the nations. The point at issue is whether or not these propositions can be proved by an observation of nature. Perhaps they can be obtained only by special revelation.

It is instructive to note that political theorists who were untouched by the Christian revelation, almost without exception, advocate totalitarianism. If Plato was a communist, Aristotle was a fascist. Private parental education is forbidden because education has as its aim the production of citizens for the good of the state. The number of children a family may have is controlled by the government, and surplus children are to be fed to the wolves. And everybody must profess the state religion. [Jean Jacques] Rousseau is equally totalitarian: "There is therefore a purely civil profession of faith of which the Sovereign should fix the articles. . . . If anyone, after publicly recognizing these dogmas, behaves as if he does not believe them, let him be punished by death."

If individual liberties were as evident as Jefferson said, would not Rousseau have recognized them? If they could be learned by observing nature, would Aristotle have missed them? And in any case, would there not be a fairly widespread agreement on what in detail these laws are? Jefferson thought that all men are created equal; Aristotle believed that some are born to be slaves. Aquinas argued that all things to which man has a natural inclination are naturally apprehended by reason as being good; but Duns Scotus replied that this leaves no method for determining whether an inclination is natural or unnatural.

[David] Hume and [John Stuart] Mill also, in their criticisms of the argument for God's existence, throw doubt on the theory. In those passages where they emphasize the injustices in the world, and Mill in particular does this vigorously, they show clearly the difficulty, or rather the impossibility, of discovering by human reason any perfect justice in nature.

Although Hume and Mill are in bad repute among devout Christians, their attack on natural theology may prove to be a blessing in disguise. At least, their insistence on observable injustice and misery is a recognition, however unintentional, of the existence of sin in the world. Too often philosophers with optimistic blindness ignore or minimize sin.

Now, one of the theoretical deficiencies of natural theology and natural ethics is its assumption that human reason has not been depraved or distorted by sin and remains a competent and unbiased observer. An orthodox Christian has no wish to deny that God at creation wrote the basic moral law on man's heart. Even yet this conscience acts after a fashion. For example, experiences of guilt occur, though they may occur too infrequently; self-commendation also occurs—with greater regularity; and both are often improperly assigned. Natural political law and personal moral law can therefore be barely discerned, if at all.

Thus, Caesar, Napoleon, and Stalin can take pride in their crimes. Looking carefully on nature and seeing it red in tooth and claw, they can conclude that the universe is indifferent to the fate of any individual and that it is the law of nature for the brutal to rule the meek. There are natural inclinations for domination and a will to power. And if Aquinas says otherwise, he can't see straight and reasons like a bourgeois gentilhomme.

If now one turns from nature and reads special revelation, ambiguity and confusion are replaced with clearly stated principles. In such contrast to the heathen nations surrounding Israel—such a contrast as to be unintelligible to Jezebel—Ahab could not legally expropriate Naboth's vineyard. Here for one instance there is the divine sanction on private property, and therefore the rights of individuals, and a limitation of government. In another instance Daniel defied the religious laws of Nebuchadnezzar. And Peter said, "We must obey God rather than men."

These brief considerations indicate that the theory of natural law is not a satisfactory theoretical defense of minority and individual rights. Human reason, that is, ordinary observation of nature, leads more easily to totalitarianism than to anything else other than anarchy. But an acceptance of God's word justifies a limited government.

Unfortunately this is a theoretical justification only; it is not a civil guarantee. It does not, it actually has not prevented tyrannies in history. What is needed to protect our unalienable rights is a popular acceptance of biblical principle. Only in so far as a determined and vocal segment of the populace forces power hungry politicians to curtail their ambitions, only in so far as the will of the people can reduce budgets, relax controls, and eliminate pork barrels, only so can the twentieth century trend to Communism be slowed down.

> Long may our land be bright
> With freedom's holy light;
> Protect us by thy might,
> Great God, our King.

---

*Christianity Today,* July 24, 1957.

# 35

# Oaths

Oaths as a moral problem and the conscientious refusal to swear (Quakers and some others) result from an unqualified application of Christ's command, "Swear not at all." However, this passage in the Sermon on the Mount is connected with commands concerning legitimate vows. Since in the same passage the sixth and seventh commandments are not abrogated, but extended to cover Jewish evasions, so too here Christ's command must not be interpreted as repealing Old Testament oaths and vows. He was extending, or, better, applying the Old Testament to the practice of repeatedly swearing on trivial occasions. Christ's accepting the oath at his trial confirms this interpretation.

The Old Testament, in the places referred to, approves of oaths or vows seriously made. See also Genesis 24:2ff.; Exodus 13:19; Joshua 9:18-20. Not only so, God himself swears (Isaiah 45:23; Hebrews 6:13, 16, etc.).

There are also examples of sinful oaths: Saul's in I Samuel 14:24; Herod's in Matthew 14:7; Peter's denial; and the oath of Paul's enemies in Acts 23:12.

Better known among Protestants for making and keeping solemn oaths and vows are the Reformed Presbyterians, whose constancy under Claverhouse's massacres earned the Cameronians the name of Covenanters.

---

*Baker's Dictionary of Christian Ethics*, Carl F.H. Henry, editor. Grand Rapids, Michigan: Baker Book House, 1973, p. 465.

# 36

# The Puritans and Situation Ethics

In spite of the deplorable decline in the morals of our nation, it may be that this year in which America celebrates its two hundredth birthday some public figure will make a polite reference to the Puritans. They deserve more than a polite mention. It is they who maintained the high morals of an earlier era and established the intellectual foundations of our colleges and universities.

Samuel E. Morrison, in a book called *The Puritan Pronaos* —the entry to the temple is the meaning of the word—says, "The story of the intellectual life of New England in the 17th century is not merely that of a people bravely and successfully endeavoring to keep up the standards of civilization in a new world. It is one of the principal approaches to the social and intellectual history of the United States." The Puritans, however, do not constitute the total American heritage in religious and intellectual affairs. One must assign a good measure of credit to the Presbyterians of Pennsylvania and the Carolinas. These people too had a sturdy religion and high academic standards. Though there were some differences between the Presbyterians and the Puritans, nevertheless, the differences were minor and their basic Calvinistic religion was the same.

## Misrepresenting the Puritans

Of these two groups the Puritans have been the more maligned and dishonestly caricatured. Even the gentle Longfellow, and perhaps because he was gentle, felt it necessary to say, "The stern old puritanical character rises above the common level of life; it has a breezy air about its summits; but they are bleak and forbidding."

Calvinism has always seemed bleak and forbidding to gentle opponents, while the less gentle use stronger terms. Within the field of ethics the main reason for opposition to Calvinism is the seriousness with which it views the Ten Commandments. Calvin's

*Institutes* and the Westminster catechisms broke with Romish laxity by devoting important sections to their exposition. The Scottish Presbyterians and the English Puritans both endeavored to obey the law of God. Sir Walter Scott, despite his antipathy toward the Covenanters, tellingly describes their devotion to truth under the most heart-rending temptations to lie, in *The Heart of Midlothian.* Similarly the English Puritans were moral giants, and men of lesser stature still feel uncomfortable in their presence. Macaulay, who ought to have known better, for he wrote one paragraph acknowledging the virtues and importance of Puritanism, allowed himself to make the jibe, now become familiar, "The Puritans hated bear-baiting, not because it gave pain to the bear, but because it gave pleasure to the spectator." Certainly the Puritans condemned people for taking pleasure in the wanton and deliberate infliction of pain on animals. The man who can enjoy torturing animals will soon develop a pleasure in torturing human beings. Is Puritanism to be condemned because it would condemn Hitler for torturing Jews? But it is false to say that the Puritans condemned pleasure as such. Yet Macaulay's jibe has been more irresponsibly developed by a later writer.

Ernest Boyd, in *Portraits Real and Imaginary* (p. 109), is more imaginary than real when he wrote of the Puritans, "Pleasure is the enemy, not evil, and so the joys of mind and body are under suspicion." This is caricature because the Puritans were not enemies of or insusceptible to pleasure. They enjoyed even the physical pleasures of food and drink. Apparently Professor Boyd had never heard of Thanksgiving dinner. Instead of confining themselves to the drabness of black clothes as cartoons regularly represent them, they actually wore bright colors. Those who condemn them on the ground that they hated beauty and art not only failed to make allowances for the necessity of wresting a dependable living from an uncultivated wilderness, but also fail in their own appreciation of the Puritan sense of art and proportion in their architecture and household utensils. But credulity and animosity are extreme when Boyd, in the quotation just made, accuses them of disparaging and avoiding the joys of mind. Does he not know that the Puritan community enjoyed a higher degree of literacy than any other American colony?

Two authors, J. Truslow Adams, in *The Evolution of the Massachusetts Public School System;* and Harlan Updegraff, in *The Origin of the Moving School in Massachusetts,* two other authors whose moral standards of truth do not attain to the Puritan ideal, complain that in the town of Natick in 1698 only one child in seventy could read. But what J. Truslow Adams fails to say is that Natick was an Indian town without a single white inhabitant.

The New England populace was well educated and its scholars were not far below the best in Europe. They founded Harvard in 1636, only 16 years after landing. It is true, however, that they were unwilling to assign to pleasure, especially physical pleasure, a value higher than their philosophy allowed it. Pleasure can be deceitful. It can be evil and it would seem that modern detractors of the Puritans are less realistic in their appraisals. But it was the evil, not the pleasure as such, that they fought against. And if Puritans attacked bear-baiting and bull fights it is because they believed that pleasure in wanton cruelty is evil.

Ralph Barton Perry, Professor of Philosophy at Harvard from 1902 to 1946, has a well-written section on "The Puritan as the Moral Athlete," in *Puritanism and Democracy* (pp. 245-268). Now let us first understand one thing. Perry is no advocate of Puritanism. He firmly rejects their ideals. Furthermore, he seriously misunderstands Puritan theology and this results in an appreciable measure of distortion. Nevertheless, he sees more clearly than many the moral strength of Puritanism and turns back on careless critics their inconsistent objections.

Perry begins by describing a school boy he knew who wanted to become the best high hurdler in the world. This decision was grim, unconquerable, irresistible. He abstained from tobacco and candy. His vacations were taken, his friends were made, and his hours of sleep arranged by schedule. He weighed himself daily and clipped fractions of seconds from his record. Finally, he gathered assurance that he was one of the elect.

Perry then transfers this picture to the moral athleticism of the Puritans. Jonathan Edwards, for example, determined to achieve complete self-mastery and control. He deliberately undertook moral exercises, weighed himself regularly, and kept his spiritual record. Cotton Mather was even more methodical and business-like than Edwards. He actively sought ways of moral improvement.

The objection to this moral athleticism is the one also directed against Perry's school boy athlete, namely, he exaggerated the importance of the activity and turned play into hard work. Instead of remaining a college amateur, he wanted to become a professional. This obvious objection, however, is superficial, and those who use the objection are inconsistent. They are inconsistent because, although they do not want to be professional moralists, they want to be professional in some other field. One may be a professional politician aiming at the Presidency, and for the purpose he chooses his friends and arranges his hours of sleep according to schedule.

Another may be a professional businessman, exhausted and ulcerated because business is all important. So too the artist, who is perhaps the most contemptuous critic of the Puritan. He objects strongly to moral discipline but devotes himself with infinite patience to the mastery of his own technique. The point is that a professional cannot consistently object to professionalism.

Perry then gives reasons for rejecting Puritanism. Some of these are objections to the Puritan technique. In some matters of method and detail, their decisions were faulty. They were not professional and efficient enough. This objection, however, is an objection to Puritans. The Puritans themselves would have agreed, in fact did agree, that they never achieved perfection either in method or in achievement. But while this is an objection to Puritans, it is not an objection to Puritanism. Perry's basic objection is, and consistently must be, an objection to their theology, their concept of God, and their high regard of moral excellence.

In what line Perry wanted to be professional I do not care to say. On what supreme principle he wished to organize all his life's activities may be difficult to discover. But it is quite clear that Perry's god could not command his allegiance. "God," he said, "and conscience, like the Supreme Court, take no cognizance of the greater part of life" (p. 264). Clearly this sort of finite god, ignorant of the greater part of our life, is little better than another human being to whom we should, no doubt, pay some attention, but who, after all, is of minor importance.

Yet for all his rejection of the Puritan God and conscience, Perry, with commendable candor and honesty can say,

> The Puritan sailed his ship in the open seas. Despite his cult of moral vigor, he was not a moral introvert. He did not confine himself within his moral gymnasium but used his strength out-of-doors, in the world. . . . In the wars . . . he assumed the role of statesman and soldier . . . such men as William the Silent, Admiral Coligny, John Knox, Oliver Cromwell . . . and our New England ancestors. The Puritans imprinted on English and American institutions a quality of manly courage, self-reliance and sobriety. We are still drawing [—now this is not written by a man who agrees with the Puritans, but he was candid enough to say—] we are still drawing upon the reserves of spiritual vigor which they accumulated.

## Contemporary Impuritans

We need very much to replenish those reserves today. That this country needs to replenish its moral resources seems too obvious to need saying, but so few people seem to care that it cannot be said enough. The list of American deficiencies can begin with riots, the looting, the arson, and the murders in Detroit, Newark, and many, too many, other cities. These riots did not just happen spontaneously. They were prepared. Remember the plot uncovered in Philadelphia to put cyanide in the soldiers', policemen's and firemen's coffee. But while these riots were prepared by Communists and pro-Communists like Stokely Carmichael, Rap Brown, and Martin Luther King, of sainted memory, there has been a much longer preparation of indifference to mounting crime. The government officials whose responsibility it is to protect life and property are dilatory, because for years the increase of violent crime has been encouraged by liberal theories of penology, a perverted judicial development that has hamstrung the police and prosecutors, and a general sympathy with the criminal instead of his victim.

In addition to the increase of unorganized crime, there is also the tremendous power of the Mafia. Not only does it deal in prostitution, narcotics, and gambling, but more recently it has infiltrated legitimate businesses to confiscate their assets, all of which entails the bribery and intimidation of government officials and a few murders when necessary.

Narcotics were just mentioned. Below the level of heroin there is LSD, glue, marijuana, alcohol, tobacco, barbiturates, sleeping pills, and tranquilizers. The halls of scholarship also, where claims to seek truth are proudly made, are tainted with moral and intellectual decay. Professor Carl Van Doren, a few years ago, shamed us all on television by being able to answer a stupendous array of questions on all sorts of topics. Haled into court, he denied under oath that he had been coached. He was then convicted of perjury. After his conviction, the students at Columbia voted to have him returned to the faculty. They shared their professor's devotion to truth.

The central cause of this widespread moral collapse, so it seems to me, is located in the decline of Puritan religion. This returns us to the main theme of religious rather than civil history. When the seminaries and churches declare that God is dead, or when, less extreme, they substitute for the Puritan God of the Ten Commandments a different concept of god, inconsistent with the Ten Commandments, it logically and factually follows that morality is changed too. A man's view of morality depends on his view of God or whatever his first principle may be. Different types of theology produce different types of morality.

## Joseph Fletcher

In order to avoid the inaccuracies and vagueness of a general description of contemporary Protestant theology, I choose the single and well-known case of Dr. Joseph Fletcher, Professor of Social Ethics in the Episcopal Theological School at Cambridge, Massachusetts. Certainly he is representative of a great many contemporary theologians and churchmen, but for the sake of clarity and definiteness, I shall confine myself to his precise formulations.

To make very clear the contrast between Professor Fletcher and the Puritans, let us note first that he attacks the Ten

Commandments one by one right down the line. He advocates disobedience to every one and approves of profanity, murder, adultery, theft, false witness and covetousness. To be sure he does not advocate these actions for every day of the week. His position is that on occasion, in certain circumstances, we should commit murder, adultery, and perjury.

Professor Fletcher supports his attack on the Ten Commandments, first by a general argument and second, by particular examples. The general argument is motivated by a distaste for a divine law and a view of life that disparages system, or as I would put it, disparages logical systematization. He contrasts system and method; the former, system, "indicating that which is most opposed to life, freedom, and variety, and the other, that which without they cannot exist."

It is not clear that this distinction between system and method can be sustained. A logical, methodical procedure must be systematic. If, on the other hand, a method is not logical and not systematic, the kind of freedom and variety it produces is what I do not want. I see no advantage in relinquishing the logical rationality of Calvinism for irrational lawlessness. However, Fletcher goes on to say, "Any ethical system is unchristian. . . . Jesus had no ethics, if . . . ethics [is] a system . . . intelligble to all men." On a later page a subtitle reads, "Principles, Yes, but not Rules." This subtitle seems to indicate that Fletcher is not so unsystematic and unprincipled as the previous quotation suggests. However, under this subtitle he very pointedly says that "even the most revered principles may be thrown aside" in certain situations. Therefore, one is justified in asserting that Fletcher repudiates all inviolable principles. There is no divine law and every one of the Ten Commandments ought to be broken.

In addition to his idea of a life of lawless variety, Fletcher supports his attack on the Ten Commandments with a list of horrible examples. His procedure is to state a law, then describe a situation in which obedience to the law results in disaster. Some of these laws, however, are not chosen from the Ten Commandments but are merely civil laws. Such examples are irrelevant because a Christian is not obliged to defend the rectitude of every civil law. An evil law or a foolish law can, of course, produce unfortunate results, but these cannot be used as arguments against Puritanism.

Let us therefore consider a relevant attack on one of the Ten Commandments. It's perhaps the best known example in his book. Fletcher's defense of adultery is a story of a German woman, captured at the end of World War II and sent to prison in the Ukraine. Her children were scattered. Shortly her husband returned from his prison camp in England and collected the children, but the wife was still absent. Somehow she heard of her husband's return, but release from the Ukrainian prison camp was allowed only for serious illness or pregnancy. Accordingly, she became pregnant by one of the other prisoners and returned to her family. Therefore, concludes Fletcher, it is sometimes moral to commit adultery.

In reply to this specific case used as an argument, there are two things to be said: First, no such heart-rending story justifies Fletcher's apparent approval of suburban clubs for daily wife-swapping. Nor can he on this basis assert, as he does assert, that "whether any form of sex, (hetero, homo or auto) is good or evil depends on whether love is served. . . . All situationists would agree . . . that they can do what they want as long as they don't do it in the street and frighten the horses." I insist that the story of the German woman does not justify the inviolable law and universal principle of not frightening horses.

There is a second and more cogent reply to Fletcher's story. The force of Fletcher's story depends on the assumption that adultery is a legitimate price for returning home. This is precisely the proposition that needs to be proved. And Fletcher gives no reason whatever for this assumption. The general idea seems to be that the wife loved her husband, and this love justifies any kind of conduct that returns her to him. One may question whether a wife who really loved her husband would commit adultery for any reason. One could also question whether a devoted husband would want his wife to commit adultery, and, if committed, whether he could accept such a sacrifice. These are aspects of the situation Fletcher never mentions. His horrible examples beg the question and assume the point at issue.

The Puritans would have asked a still more basic question. Regardless of how much the woman loved her husband, did she love God? The Puritans would insist that no specious assertion of love can possibly justify disobedience to God. Christ said, "If ye love me, keep my commandments." The Ten Commandments are not civil laws poorly written or stupidly conceived. They are divine commands.

But what about the broken family? Here the Puritans would point out that by the rules of the prison camp, the woman would be released if she fell seriously ill. Adultery was not the only possibility. Further, even Communist rules are sometimes changed, and one could pray for less severe restrictions. There is also the possibility of a personal appeal to the Soviet authorities, and God might cause the officials to favor her. Hence, there are several possibilities of release that Fletcher ignores in his attempt to justify adultery. But if these possibilities do not eventuate, the Puritans would still insist that man must obey God.

Fletcher advocates adultery not so much because of horrible examples, but rather because he acknowledges a different god. Theology is the crux of the matter, for ethics depends on theology. Instead of a God who gives moral laws, Fletcher acknowledges a god who commands nothing but love. Now, one can wax eloquent and plausible about love. One can even sound devout and Christian, but if we are logical and rational, we must analyze the position to see exactly what it means.

It is not clear that Fletcher knows what he means by love. He quotes Tillich that the law of love is the ultimate law because it is the negation of law. But his paradoxical statement contains no positive information. Fletcher tells us also that "Christian love is not desire . . . it is an attitude." But this statement too is negative and devoid of specific information. Later he says that love and justice are the same. "Justice," he says, "is Christian love using its head, calculating its duties." But Fletcher does not tell us what justice is or how we are to use our heads. Beyond this, Fletcher makes several other statements about love. But even if some of them should happen to be true, none of them shows how love can justify any action, even any good action, let alone disobedience to God.

The point I wish to make is not merely that love all by itself does not justify murder, theft, and perjury. The important point is that love all by itself does not justify any action. Morality cannot be based on love alone because love alone gives no guidance whatever. As a quotation a moment ago showed, the Scriptures may require us to love God but how we are to love God is spelled out in detail: "If ye love me, keep my commandments." Without the specific and detailed instruction of the commandments we could never know how to express our love for God.

Now this is an appropriate place, and it will surely contribute to a fuller understanding of the matter, to show that very little Christianity remains in Fletcher's construction. The quotation from John's Gospel, already twice made, disposes of Fletcher's contention that Jesus had no ethics if ethics is a system of values and rules intelligible to all men. In another place he agrees with Judas in condemning the waste of costly ointment on Jesus. But then he adds that the story must be wrong because Jesus never said, "The poor always ye have with you." But if the Gospels are so untrustworthy that we cannot accept this statement as genuine, how do we know that the recorded remark about loving one's neighbor is genuine? This type of textual criticism, ignoring all the established criteria, eliminates indefinite amounts of Christianity's contents.

The fact is, Fletcher has trouble even with the command to love. When he rejects "all revealed norms or laws but the one commandment to love God *in* the neighbor," he misquotes the commandment he refers to and omits the one on which it depends, namely, "Thou shalt love the Lord thy God with all thy heart, and with all thy soul, and with all thy mind."

Now a man doesn't have to be a Christian. A man may adopt any principles he pleases if he can rationally defend them. But what kind of a Christian is it that accepts a garbled second commandment while rejecting the first from the same authority?

Again Fletcher says, "Christian situation ethics"—he calls it Christian—"Christian situation ethics . . . denies that there are any unwritten, immutable laws of heaven, agreeing with [Rudolph] Bultmann that all such notions are idolatrous and a demonic pretension." This quotation needs analysis on three points: First, Christian situation ethics; second, unwritten laws; and third, idolatrous demonic pretensions.

The present subdivision of this lecture aims to show that there is no such thing as Christian situation ethics. Situation ethics is anti-Christian. Second, Christian ethics does not inculcate unwritten laws. The Ten Commandments are written. Why Fletcher threw in this irrelevant word can only be guessed. One may guess that in the absence of a rational defense of this principle, this word prepares the way for his invidious question-begging accusation of idolatrous demonic pretensions. Does love dictate such name calling?

It is no doubt too intricate for a lecture of this sort to examine some of Fletcher's attempts to use the Pauline epistles. Such an analysis would interest those who had the time to study it; and were this done, one could see in greater detail how much Fletcher deviates from Christianity. But even without this additional material what has already been said is sufficient to show that "Christian situation ethics" is not Christian.

## Utilitarian Calculation

The final section of this lecture must now attempt to do justice to a part of Fletcher's theory not yet mentioned. Above, it was said that love, all by itself, gives us no information as to what we ought to do. Fletcher actually admits this and tries to supply the deficiency. In fact, he says, "Love can calculate. Otherwise it is like the bride who wanted to ignore all the recipes and simply let her love for her husband guide her when baking a cake." Now this is excellent, and I could not have said it better. Because Fletcher wants to provide love with a recipe, or a method, one might infer that my remarks on the uselessness of love, all by itself, were beside the point, and that they leave Fletcher untouched.

There were, however, two reasons for noting the uselessness of love. One reason is that some other religious writers do not provide love with a recipe or method so that this facet of our religious situation should be somewhere turned to the light. The second reason is that a recipe seems inconsistent with Fletcher's attack on rules, laws, and systems. His attempt to substitute the word *method,* and even worse the word *recipe,* for system does not remove the inconsistency. Nevertheless, if Fletcher's methodical calculation succeeds, the inconsistency can be forgotten. On the other hand, if Fletcher cannot carry through his method, then he faces the full force of the objection to love all by itself.

I now wish to show that Fletcher's method of calculation is a failure. To make love workable and to give the bride a recipe for cake, Fletcher professes to accept the use of the utilitarianism of Jeremy Bentham. "The love ethic," he says, "takes over from Bentham and Mill the strategic principle of the greatest good of the greatest number." There is, however, one important difference between Bentham and Fletcher. Original utilitarianism aimed to produce the greatest amount of pleasure. In choosing between two lines of action, one should determine which gives the most people the most pleasure. At this early point, Fletcher shies away from the notion of hedonism. Pleasure seems too ignoble. Therefore, he explicitly substitutes love for pleasure.

Now the proposal to seek pleasure for one's self and to give other people pleasure is intelligible. It is as intelligible as my inviting you to have a dish of ice cream with me. But while I understand how to increase your pleasure, I am at a loss as to how to increase your love. Utilitarianism is not a method for achieving the greatest amount of love for the greatest number of people. If the vacuity of choosing your actions on the basis of increasing other people's love does not fully register at first, and if you want some further technical details, why we can have either public or private discussion. But if it doesn't fully register at first, it can also be shown that the utilitarian method of determining, producing, and distributing pleasure is impracticable. If then the method will not work for pleasure, and I've tried to show that in other publications, if this method will not work for pleasure, all the less can it calculate love.

Bentham's method of calculation presupposes the identification of units of pleasure. Whether we wish to count pebbles or pints, we must be able to identify a single pebble and a single pint. We may then discover that a quart of ice cream is exactly twice a pint. But is the pleasure of eating a quart of ice cream exactly twice the pleasure of eating a pint? Does a movie give one and a half times the pleasure of a television show? What is the unit of pleasure? We can count pints of ice cream, but do we count pints of pleasure, or perhaps inches or ounces of pleasure? Without distinct numerable units, a calculation is impossible. If now this objection is one unit of impossibility for utilitarianism, the next objection is three or four units of impossibility.

The method requires us not only to count the units of present pleasure, but, in order to select the course of action, utilitarianism requires us to predict the amounts of future pleasure this action will produce. For example, should a college student take a job on a newspaper as a war correspondent, or should he become a professor? Both choices would produce some pleasure. The professor's life will be more calm but will have fewer hardships. The war correspondent will face hardships but his pleasures will be more intense. Which life gives the greater sum total? Can you count it up?

Remember also that thirty years from now your views on what is pleasurable will have changed. Does this moral arithmetic help you decide? Worse yet, the principle of the greatest good for the greatest number requires you to count not only your own future pleasures but the future pleasures of every member of the human race. It's the greatest good of the greatest number. But can anyone, in order to chose between two actions, seriously claim to predict which one will give the greatest amount of pleasure to a Chinese peasant ten years from now? Yet, unless such calculations can be completed, the greatest good of the greatest number is a meaningless formula.

The usual utilitarian defense against this objection is to rely on some vague general guesses and estimates. But such sloppy arithmetic is insufficient for any confidence in purely personal matters, let alone in questions of universal scope.

A particular case puts this objection in emphatic form. This is the case of Hitler's massacre of the Jews. The principle of the greatest good for the greatest number is precisely what Hitler needed to justify his brutality. He murdered five million Jews to make ninety million Germans happy—really more than ninety million, for Hitler and utilitarianism looked forward to a thousand year Reich. If anyone should suggest that Hitler wanted only Germans to be happy and was less solicitous about pleasure on a universal scale, we may turn from national socialism to international socialism. Not only is utilitarianism a support for Hitler, it is even a better defense for Lenin and Stalin. It is, indeed, standard liberal left-wing policy.

When Lenin lost interest in the proletariat because he perceived that the working classes would not support a revolution, and transferred his hopes to criminal conspirators, the theory was that these latter were the avant-garde whose massacres would usher in better days for all mankind.

Hence, the Ukrainians and later the Tibetans and all the officers of the Polish army must be liquidated for the greatest good of the greatest number. The calculation may have been a little rough and sloppy, but anyone with a sense of the future can see that the sum of pleasure will soon be sufficiently great to overbalance a few temporary pains.

The conclusion is obvious. Utilitarianism does not preserve Fletcher's love from moral vacuity. The bride has no recipe for baking a cake. Nobody has any reason for doing anything. Everyone is free to follow his own individual, irresponsible, irrational preferences. Fletcher prefers occasional idolatry, occasional profanity, occasional murder, not so very occasional adultery, occasional theft, and occasional perjury.

## The Toronto School

Situation ethics and the rejection of the Ten Commandments have more recently insinuated their way into supposedly Calvinistic camps. This is the work of certain disciples of Herman Dooyeweerd of the Free University of Amsterdam. These disciples of Professor Dooyeweerd, located chiefly in Toronto, Canada, have established multiple organizations for the vigorous propagation of their views. To what extent Professor Dooyeweerd approves of his disciples' views is not now under consideration. The point under discussion is the ethical stance of members of the Association for the Advancement of Christian Scholarship and the other related organizations they have founded.

Attention must now be centered on their rejection of the Scriptures, with which rejection Dooyeweerd agrees, and the implications relative to the Ten Commandments, with which the Professor in Amsterdam may or may not agree.

In a small book entitled *Understanding the Scriptures*, A.H.

DeGraaff, on page two, begins by saying, "You distort the Scriptures when you read them as a collection of objective statements about God and man. They do not contain any rational, general, theological statements about God and his creation. It is not the purpose of the Bible to inform us about the nature of God's being or his attributes" (p. 9). He also adds, "The Scriptures are neither rational nor irrational in character" (p. 18).

All these statements are patently false. The first three are false because the Scriptures say that God is righteous and man is sinful. In saying this the Bible informs us about the nature of God's being and attributes. The last of the four statements is nonsense. To say that the Scriptures are neither rational nor irrational is like saying that the number two is neither odd nor even, or like saying that man is neither mortal nor immortal. To search the Bible for even one statement that is neither rational nor irrational is like going to the zoo to find an animal that is neither vertebrate nor invertebrate.

More directly concerning morality, Dr. DeGraaff writes, "Nor does it—the Bible—contain moral applications that tell us how to live the good life—virtues that we share with the humanist" (p. 21). It is true that a Christian does not share any virtue with a humanist because a humanist just cannot have any Christian virtue. But it is false to say that the Bible gives no moral rules. Dr. DeGraaff objects to teaching boys and girls in Vacation Bible School moral lessons about purity, chastity, and Victorian, middle-class American standards. Instead of warning them against the prevalent loose views of sex, we should tell them about irresponsibile deforesting, yellow smog, dirty water—and we should tell them these things in "a non-moralistic manner" (p. 26). Apparently dirty water is worse than a dirty mind.

In answer to many objections from Christians Dr. DeGraaff repeats, "The Bible does not teach us how to be good and how to avoid being bad" (p. 29). So says Dr. DeGraaff. But the Bible says, "All Scripture . . . is profitable . . . for correction, for instruction in righteousness, that the man of God may be . . . completely furnished to every good work." The Bible also says, "Thy word have I hid in my heart that I might not sin against thee."

But Dr. DeGraaff plunges on. Speaking of the Ten Commandments (which he strangely says are not commandments at all) he says, "None of them can be literally followed or applied today, for we live in a different period of history in a different culture" (p. 35).

Imagine! It is impossible to follow or apply the commandment, Thou shalt not steal, because we live in a different culture. Thou shalt not commit adultery canot be literally obeyed today because God commanded it in 1500 B.C. This line of thought is incredible. But check the reference: page 35, *Understanding the Scriptures,* DeGraaff and Seerveld, Association for the Advancement of Christian Scholarship, Toronto, Canada. Since none of the Ten Commandments can be literally applied today, Dr. DeGraaff suggests that for them we substitute agitation against police brutality (p. 36). Love your neighbor's wife, but hate the police.

There is a further implication. If God's command against adultery is inapplicable in our different culture, why should we suppose that God's covenant with Abraham is applicable? Dr. DeGraaff seems to retain some respect for the covenant. Yet how can the Mosaic command against adultery be culturally conditioned in 1500 B.C., while a religious covenant some 500 years earlier escapes such cultural conditioning? A rational thinker might in consistency reject both. A consistent Christian accepts both. But it takes some explaining to accept the one and reject the other.

In order that no one may suppose Dr. DeGraaff to be an anomaly among the disciples of Dooyeweerd and that these criticisms are not relevant to the whole movement, the same ideas are to be noted in the writings of Dr. Calvin Seerveld. In the same volume with Dr. DeGraaff, Dr. Seerveld has an interesting section on the exegesis of Numbers 22-24. He uses this passage to distinguish three methods of understanding the Scriptures.

The first method is that of evangelical fundamentalists. Dr. Seerveld has collected phrases from Alexander Maclaren, W.B. Riley, Clarence Edward Macartney, and others who note that (1) Balaam has a strong passion for earthly honor; (2) he wanted the best of two incompatible worlds; and (3) he beat his ass unmercifully. From these points the fundamentalist concludes that we should not put earthly honor first among our choices, that we should seek righteousness first of all, and that we should not be cruel to dumb animals. Dr. Seerveld continues his list with a number of such applications and moral lessons.

The second method is beside the present purpose. The third method Dr. Seerveld assigns to the "remnants of staunch orthodox churches," and he cites Hengstenberg and Calvin. This method specializes in doctrine, rather than in ethical application. It notes that Numbers 23:19 is a clear statement of God's immutability. And there is considerably more in the passage.

Dr. Seerveld disapproves of these methods. He challenges their hidden aprioris; he suggests that they miss the richness of Scripture, and mislead fledgling readers who use them (p. 67). As for the fundamentalist method of moral application, Dr. Seerveld says, "Balaam's invitation from Balak is not remotely within my experience as a Christian school teacher because my twentieth century situation and the ancient parallel made abstractly ideal jibe of sorts only after a dozen qualifications . . . . the binding force is lost" (p. 68). Thus "the world-upsidedown changing message of Numbers 22-24 is reduced to a mess of moralistic pottage" (p. 69).

The method of the Reformers, the orthodox Calvinistic method, is equally bad. This "Scholastic reading of the Scriptures is always after truths that can be theoretically formulated and held to be universally valid, consistent Bible teaching against all attack" (p. 74). This Reformed method is bad, says Dr. Seerveld, because "it removes the reader half a step from the convicting comfort and humbling facing God's love and anger brings, removes the reader half a step away from existential confrontation with the living Word of God and asks him to comprehend these realities in codified propositional dogmas" (p. 75).

But is the Reformation method, the method of studying and learning what the Bible says, such a bad method? Is it not rather commendable? Let it be noted that the Apostle Peter at the beginning of his second epistle says, "Grace to you and peace be multiplied by the knowledge of God" (3:18). The Apostle John also emphasizes doctrine and propositions. Without mentioning existentialism or irrational confrontations, John, in fact Jesus himself says, "If any one guards my doctrine, he shall not see death, ever" (8:51). Another verse that makes Christianity depend on an understanding of and an assent to propositions is, "If you believed Moses, you would believe me, for he wrote of me; but if you do not believe his writings, how can you believe my words?" (5:47). Jesus also said, "The words that I have spoken to you are spirit and life" (6:63).

The Reformation use of the Bible, like the evangelical-fundamentalist method, also "is interested in the practical lessons we can learn from it." The Westminster divines would have rejected Dr. Seerveld's charge of reducing the Bible to a "mess of moralistic pottage." Their careful and very detailed exposition of the Ten Commandments in the Larger Catechism shows how greatly they valued morality.

But Dr. Seerveld in his remarks on Numbers says, "To make Balaam a warning model for the reader is to distort the nature of biblical narrative and ignore the historical solidity of God's disclosure. Scripture never gives biographic snatches to serve as ethical models" (p. 68).

In contrast with Dr. Seerveld's view of the Bible stands the practice of the Apostle Peter. Speaking of the false teachers who introduced heresies instead of accepting orthodox propositions, and who lived in contempt of Dr. Seerveld's moralistic pottage, the Apostle writes, "having forsaken the right way they went astray, having followed the way of Balaam, son of Beor, who loved the hire of wrong-doing" (II Peter 2:15ff.). Here the Apostle most assuredly uses "biographic snatches to serve as ethical models." If a modern exegete condemns the Apostle's use of the Bible, then the modern exegete must have gone astray—not the Apostle.

## Conclusion

Now, for a short conclusion let it be noted, as was indicated four paragraphs back, that the Scriptures stress doctrine, information, and knowledge. Second, let it be noted that this information and knowledge includes rational statements about the nature and attributes of God. Third, let it finally be noted that the Bible teaches morality. While the outside world flounders in moral perplexity and considers the murder of unborn children as desirable, while the apostate churches organize congregations for homosexuals and make contributions of fifty-thousand dollars to a prostitutes' union, we who believe the Bible can rely on the Ten Commandments. In contrast with a great amount of contemporary counseling, let us emphasize the exposition of those commandments as it is found in the Westminster Larger Catechism. The Puritans lived by the Ten Commandments. Our choice today, then, is between the colonial Puritans and the contemporary impuritans.

---

*The Trinity Review,* January/February 1989 [1976].

# 37

# Responsibility

Responsibility and morality are inseparable. The one cannot exist without the other. A mechanistic or behavioristic philosophy has no place for either. Other philosophers differ among themselves concerning the basis or nature of obligation.

Plato found responsibility in a suprasensory, supratemporal World of Ideas; Aristotle, in the nature of man; Kant, in the force of logic. Fichte made obligation an original datum. Christianity, of course, bases responsibility on the imposition of the Creator's commands.

Ethical writers usually spend more time on the extent of responsibility. Probably there is universal agreement that a man is not responsible for involuntary actions: If a man is knocked down by an auto, he is not responsible for falling. Trivial? Not so trivial when a man is knocked down by insanity, sets fire to his house and kills his children.

The Stoics put great stress on volition; but it was Aristotle who best enumerated the details. He examines actions done through fear. What, then, about actions done under the "compulsion" of pleasure? How about drunkenness? Some actions are done in ignorance. There are various kinds of ignorance. A man may be ignorant of who he himself is (he thinks he is Napoleon or Christ); he may not know what he is doing ("Father, forgive them, for they know not what they do"); he may not know the person on whom his act terminates (mistaking a friend for an enemy); he may not know the instrument (the gun that "wasn't loaded"); he may not know the manner of his doing the act (he intends to shake your hand cordially and nearly breaks your joints). Ignorance in any one of these particulars relieves one of responsibility. Aristotle continues with other details.

The Bible does not give any systematic account of these matters, but both in the Mosaic Law (*e.g.*, the cites of refuge) and in the New Testament examples occur. I Timothy 1:13 says, "I was before a blasphemer, and a persecutor, and injurious, but I obtained mercy because I did it ignorantly in unbelief." In addition to particular cases, general statements occur in Luke 12:45-48 and John 15:22; but particularly in Romans 1:32, "Knowing the ordinance of God, that they who do such things are worthy of death, not only do the same, but approve of those that do them."

This last reference meets the objection that the heathen are not responsible because they have never heard the gospel. They are responsible because they know the law. "When the Gentiles, who do not have the [Mosaic] law, act lawfully by nature, they are, without the [Mosaic] law, a law to [or, for] themselves: They show the work of the law written in their hearts" (Romans 2:14-15). Thus responsibility is both established and limited by knowledge.

Theologians and popular preachers who do not care to emphasize knowledge sometimes try to base responsibility on free will. But, aside from the fact that the Scripture does not so teach, a will free from and independent of knowledge, of one's own character, and of God furnishes a poor foundation for morality.

---

*Baker's Dictionary of Christian Ethics,* Carl F.H. Henry, editor. Grand Rapids, Michigan: Baker Book House, 1973.

# 38

# Sanctification

"He died that we might be forgiven,
He died to make us good."

In this third stanza of *There Is a Green Hill Far Away*, the
doctrines of justification and sanctification are conjoined. Naturally, the limitations of hymnology do not permit an explanation
of the conjunction: It would seem that forgiveness and being made
good are two results, otherwise unrelated, to Christ's death. But
the [Westminster] Confession of Faith, Chapter XIII, and still nore
explicitly Paul, in Romans VI and elsewhere, make sanctification
the purpose or aim of the preceding stages of salvation. It is true,
but not sufficient to say, we are justified *and* we are also being
sanctified; it is downright false to say, we are justified by faith
alone *but* of course we must now do some good works; to express
the relation with a minimum of adequacy we must drop the *and*
and the *but* and use the conjunction *therefore:* We have been
acquitted and pardoned of sin apart from any human merit,
*therefore* we must do good works. Or, to quote Romans 6:14, "Sin
shall not have dominion over you [sanctification], *for* ye are not
under the law but under grace" [justification]. "He died to make
us good."

Such is the Scriptural answer to the objection that justification by faith alone is an immoral doctrine. It is sanctification that
unmasks the caricature quoted in a previous article, "Free from
the law, O blessed condition; I can sin as I please and still have
remission." Paul's argument is clear: "Shall we continue in sin
that grace may abound? Not at all; how shall we that are dead to
sin live any longer therein? . . . Our old man is crucified with
Christ in order that the body of sin might be destroyed, in order
that henceforth we should not serve sin. . . . Sin shall not have
dominion over you."

Because Paul said, "Sin shall not have dominion over you,"
and because of other expressions, certain groups of people who

were not privileged to be guided by the Westminster Confession in their study of the Scriptures have concluded that it is possible to achieve sinless perfection during our earthly life. I know one man who boasted that he had not sinned for twenty-six years. And the fact of the matter is that compared with other Christians he was a very good man. Compared with God's law, however, he was, I am sure, imperfect. It is only through a feeble appreciation of God's righteousness and holiness coupled with an ignorance of the definition of sin that one can imagine that one is sinless. Job was able to hold his own against his irritating friends. He was sure he had not committed any particular sin of which his plagues were the punishment. But when his friends left him and God appeared to him, Job said, "Behold, I am vile. What shall I answer Thee? I will lay my hand upon my mouth."

Sin is any want of conformity unto or transgression of the law of God. To define sin as selfishness or to restrict sin to known sins is inadequate. Sin is defined in terms of the law of God. And no mere man since the fall is able perfectly in this life to keep God's commandments—even for a day. Only Christ was sinless.

---

*The Southern Presbyterian Journal*, December 15, 1954.

# 39
# Situation Ethics

Situation ethics, though popularly and correctly associated with the name of Joseph Fletcher, has a background in [Friedrich] Nietzsche and [John] Dewey.

Nietzsche's evolutionary logic, repudiating Kantian *a priori* forms and making our learning processes nothing more than practical expedients for handling things, is the extreme of nominalism in the thesis that there are no identical cases in nature. Observed similarities are due to the coarseness and inadequacies of our perceptive organs. The use of moral rules therefore, treating different cases as if they were alike, falsifies the situation. Intelligence should evaluate each case uniquely.

Dewey invites the same inference. He constantly stresses the concrete (*i.e.,* the individual) situation. For example, since the rationalistic theory affords no guidance and by its futile attempt to construct an hierarchical scheme of values or duties confesses its inability to judge the concrete, the implication seems to be that general rules should be replaced by an intuition of the individual situation (*Quest for Certainty,* New York, Putnam, 1960, pp. 265ff.).

If perchance Dewey would not word it just that way, there is no doubt whatever that Fletcher fulminates against moral rules and universal laws. He urges us to break every one of the Ten Commandments and insists that "Any ethical system is unchristian. . . . Jesus had no ethics, if . . . ethics [is] a system of values and rules intelligible to all men."

The attack on system is sustained: "System is that which is most opposed to life, freedom, and variety." Later on he says, "Christian situation ethics . . . denies that there are . . . any unwritten laws of heaven, agreeing with [Rudolph] Bultmann that all such notions are idolatrous and a demonic pretension." (Why did he say *unwritten* laws? It is the written Commandments he does not like.)

Apparently in an effort to avoid complete anarchy Fletcher inserts a subhead: "Principles, Yes, But Rules, No." What follows is pretty much a play on words, but the pretense cannot be maintained, for two pages later he returns to his first love, "In situation ethics even the most revered principles [!] may be thrown aside if they conflict in any concrete case with love" (pp. 31-33).

Presumably he does not mean to throw aside his own revered principle, but clearly he has no sympathy with the universal laws of the Ten Commandments.

Love is what Fletcher wished to substitute for system, commandments, or rules intelligible to all men. On the page before the Table of Contents he quotes [Paul] Tillich: "The law of love is the ultimate law because it is the negation of law; it is absolute because it concerns everything concrete." In his own words he says, "Christian ethics posits faith in God and reasons out what obedience to his commandment to love requires in any situation." Again, "the ruling norm of Christian decision is love: nothing else."

Ignoring his own prescription here, Fletcher never "reasons out" what love requires. To be sure, he asserts that love dictates abortion on the ground that no unwanted and unintended baby should be allowed to live. He approves of bachelor mothers; and very clearly states, "Whether any form of sex—hetero, homo, or auto—is good depends on whether love is served." But there is no reasoning to support these assertions. Could not love for babies prohibit abortion? Could not love for God abominate homosexuality?

Fletcher indeed has some apprehension that love furnishes no guidance in the concrete situations of life. Accordingly he appends a method or system to remove the deficiency. Even so he never makes use of the method in solving any concrete problem. The method is simply the utilitarian calculus applied to love: "Love can calculate."

But if [Jeremy] Bentham could not calculate pleasures, Fletcher has no easier problem. First, he does not make it clear whether an adulterer should try to maximize his own feelings of love, or those of his paramour, or those of his paramour and his wife, or perchance of the whole human race. Since in one place he uses the phrase "on the whole," the last possibility is probably the correct interpretation. But how does a man measure the feeling of both women? Second, the measuring is impossible because there are no identifiable units of pleasure or love to make counting possible. Third, if there were units, there is no way to total them for a single individual and a total for the whole human race is so impossible as to be ridiculous.

Finally, Fletcher rejects the Scriptures. He denounces Paul's "obscure and contradictory" views of the justice of God—"a confused wrangle in which Paul did not provide a cogent answer to the questions he raised." Fletcher seriously misinterprets Galatians 5:1 and Matthew 5:27-32; and, of course, discards the Ten Commandments. How then can he appeal to the Bible for the one phrase, "Thou shalt love"? A person who believes all the Bible can consistently appeal to any verse, as Jesus did in John 10:35; but a person who does not must give reasons for accepting one verse rather than another. Fletcher gives no reason. To all intents he treats it as if it were a verbally inspired revelation to himself alone. Strange that Fletcher is inerrantly inspired and the Scripture is not.

---

*Baker's Dictionary of Christian Ethics,* Carl F.H. Henry, editor. Grand Rapids, Michigan: Baker Book House, 1973, pp. 623-624.

# 40

# Thomas Aquinas

Thomas Aquinas (1225-74) as a dutiful disciple of Aristotle introduces his ethics by an empirical distinction between animals and men. Unlike inanimate objects that cannot determine their actions, animals have inclinations determined interiorly. The inclinations, however, are completely natural, and the animal cannot avoid desiring what he desires. But as one ascends the scale from inanimate, to animate, to men and angels, the nearer to God a being is, the more freedom it has—the more it is determined by itself.

Of course, man shares sensitivity with the animals, but in addition man has intellect and will. Sensitivity apprehends what is pleasant and what is useful to self-preservation, but only reason grasps the universal good. By reason man can know the end and the means to it, and so can determine his own inclination.

The main object of the will according to Aquinas, is the good as such: to desire it is a natural necessity for the will. But not all the acts of will are necessitated. Just as the intellect necessarily accepts the first principles of knowledge and cannot deny what follows from them, but does not necessarily accept contingent truths whose denial does not contradict first principles, so too the will necessarily wills the universal good but may or may not will certain particular goods. But goods that are necessarily connected with beatitude, the will wills necessarily, provided the intellect knows the connection. Clearly, an object must be known, before it can be willed. This explains why the fool does not even will God, since he does not know the necessary connection between God and beatitude.

The intellect is superior to the will in the sense that it apprehends universal truth. The object of the will, the general good, and the objects of the will, the particular goods, are included among the objects of the intellect, truth and being, and so the intellect is superior. However, if we consider the good as universal and the intellect as a a special power of the soul, the will is superior, both because every item of knowledge is good and because the will sets the intellect in motion.

This defense of free will makes morality possible, for we could not deserve blame or earn merits if our actions were all unavoidable.

The will and the intellect develop habits. Man is not a pure substance, not a theoretical construction of intellect and will, but is affected by his own actions. Habit is a quality that modifies man's substance and is therefore either good or bad. (God, of course, has no habits because he is in no way potential.) The habit of grasping first principles is virtually innate (though habituations and innateness are mutually exclusive). Virtues are not innate but are developed by repeated actions.

Virtues are good habits, in that they conform to man's nature. Vice is a habit that leads in the opposite direction. To distinguish between them we must bear in mind man's natural end—beatitude or God. Some acts are in accord with reason and lead to God. Others are the reverse and are irrational. Some, like picking up a wisp of straw, lead nowhere and are morally indifferent. Thomas then continues by describing moral virtues and intellectual virtues, much as Aristotle had done.

Ethics must consider law as well as good. Law is an obligation founded on reason. Different types of law should be distinguished. The eternal law of God rules the whole universe; but as it is inscribed on human nature, it becomes the legitimate tendencies of our nature or natural law. The first law of all nature is self-preservation. The second law of sensitive beings is reproduction. The third law of rational beings is to live rationally. This includes living in communities (the family and the state) in order to achieve the good more effectively by cooperation.

There is also human law. A gap opens between the universal principles of natural law and the infinite complexity of particular actions. On these matters peoples and states disagree. Kings should deduce civil law from natural law; and if they do, a just man will conform to it with perfect spontaneity, as if the civil law did not exist. But unjust decrees are not law and need not be obeyed. It may be prudent to obey some unjust laws in order to modify them. But if a decree infringes on the rights of God, it should never be obeyed.

---

*Baker's Dictionary of Christian Ethics*, Carl F.H. Henry, editor. Grand Rapids, Michigan: Baker Book House, 1973, pp. 32-33.

# 41
# The Trouble with Humanism

"Religion ceased to be a significant factor . . . between the First and Second World Wars." Humanism raises this self-confident shout of victory in "Religions of the Future," an essay by Tolbert H. McCarroll, editor of *The Humanist* (Nov./Dec. 1966, p. 190).

As an organized philosophical movement, humanism functions in the International Humanist and Ethical Union, the American Humanist Association, and other regional bodies. C.H. Schonk says that "humanism is . . . to a rather high extent the concern of the intelligentizia [sic]" (*International Humanism,* April 1966, p. 27), and he hopes that the view will spread among ordinary men. Evangelical Christians can assure him that it has already done so, for in unorganized form humanism now permeates labor unions, political parties, and even large Protestant denominations where some say God is dead.

## What Is Humanism?

If religion lost its significance between the two world wars, the precise date may have been 1933. In that year thirty or more distinguished ministers and professors (E. Burdette Backus, Harry Elmer Barnes, A. J. Carlson, John Dewey, John Herman Randall, Roy Wood Sellars, and others) published *A Humanist Manifesto.* On July 13, 1963, the American Humanist Association cautiously disavowed the economic pronouncement of Article XIV but by silence apparently approved the remainder.

This distinguished company of humanists said in 1933, "First, religious humanists regard the universe as self-existing and not created." That is to say, humanism is atheism. And later in the manifesto: "Fifth, humanism asserts that the nature of the universe depicted by modern science makes unacceptable any supernatural or cosmic guarantees of human values." Or, in other words, neither God, whose existence is excluded, nor the universe cares about man.

To this day, these ideas and the import of the other articles of the manifesto continue to be repeated in *The Humanist* with pietistic insipidity. For example: "Essential to our survival is the ability to distinguish those who search their condition in joyous affirmation from those who would forsake and annul life. . . . The enforcement of conscientious life is humanism. . . . The major task for humanism is persuading people to join the human race" (*The Humanist,* Mar./Apr. 1966, p. 46).

The number of vague generalities in the humanist publications is astounding. Some humanists themselves recognize the meaninglessness of their hazy formulas: "If one merely put down what all humanists hold in common, the result would not be very inspiring" (*International Humanism,* April 1966, p. 1). Is it not pedantic as well as uninspiring to say that "the humanist makes a judicial reassessment of human beliefs and practices in the light of modern knowledge and discards whatever is found groundless"? Is there not a tinge of self-contradiction in the next sentence: "He accepts reasoned findings but keeps his mind open" (*ibid.,* p. 12)? In the matter of definiteness and clarity, the contrast between humanist generalities and the precisely formulated supernaturalism of the Westminster Confession is amazing.

The unifying principle so conspicuously absent from humanism's platitudinous affirmations is provided, however, by its

thoroughly definite negations. Humanists know what they are
against. They hate God. They "take counsel together, against the
Lord, and against his anointed, saying, Let us break their bands
asunder, and cast away their cords from us" (Psalm 2: 2, 3).

## What Humanism Is Not

Despite humanism's inability to agree on any definite affirmations, one should not be blind to its negative force. Nor to its
unorganized prevalence. When people neglect Bible reading, they
are advancing humanism. When they no longer "say grace" at
meals, when golf or fishing is their Sunday occupation and civil
rights their sacrament, they are practicing atheists.

So victorious has been the humanist advance that McCarroll
can even tar Eugene Carson Blake with defeatism ("Dr. Blake has
good reason to fear"—*The Humanist,* Nov./Dec. 1966) when
Blake asserts that "humanism . . . is nonetheless the greatest threat
to man's morality or even to his survival or salvation."

It is somewhat amusing, of course, that Blake should thus
express his fear of humanism. While under his control a large
denomination was directed away from the Bible to the so-called
Confession of 1967 and to new ordination vows that commit the
clergy to a very small fraction of what the present standards
require. As far back as 1924 those who shortly gained control of
that denomination had denied the infallibility of the Scripture
and, in the Auburn Affirmation, had denied that the Virgin Birth,
the Atonement, and the Resurrection are essential to Christianity.
Since that date supernaturalism has steadily evaporated in Dr.
Blake's organization.

## Humanistic Ethics

Humanism is not all platitude and propaganda. Nor is it all
completely negative. The more competent representatives offer
some positive views on ethics. Their ethics, of course, is not
Christian.

Thomas S. Szasz argues for abortion. "Such an operation
should be available in the same way, as, say, an operation for the
beautification of a nose: the only requirement should be the
woman's desire to have the operation" (*The Humanist,* Sept./Oct.

1966, p. 148; compare *loc cit.*, Nov./Dec. 1966, p. 206, col. 3). This proposal is neither negative nor vague.

In general, humanism advocates promiscuity in sex. Says Gerald A. Ehrenreich, "Nor . . . is sexual behavior immoral in itself—in or out of marriage, with oneself or with someone else. . . . Judging sexual behavior in moralistic terms . . . results in laws which arbitrarily impose the moral views of one group on others. This is unfortunate" (*loc. cit.*, Sept./Oct. 1966, pp. 153ff.).

Also sufficiently definite, but not commanding complete agreement, are the socialistic proposals advanced by various humanists. Although they frequently criticize the Communists for doctrinaire fanaticism, their social and economic views hardly coincide with those of Barry Goldwater.

These ethical pronouncements help to rescue humanism from total vacuity. At the same time, however, they raise the philosophical problem of the identification or justification of alleged values. It is not enough to advocate freer sex and abortion; one must explain why these are good, right, or obligatory. Very few humanists attempt to justify their ethical principles.

Two notable exceptions deserve mention. Erich Fromm (*loc. cit.*, July/Aug. 1966, p. 121) employs a subtitle, "The Validity of Human Values." Having rejected divine revelation as the ground of moral distinctions, he relies on "an examination of the conditions of the existence of man, an analysis of the intrinsic contradictions in human existence, and an analysis of how they can be solved." Some lines later he adds that "humanism must have a strict hierarchy of values." Unfortunately this does not take us very far. It merely repeats the problem. Although Fromm has some kind words for Zen Buddhism, Spinoza, Goethe, and Marx, the question he so courageously faced remains unanswered.

Herbert Feigl, a man of no mean ability, also faces this question (*International Humanism*, April 1966, p. 11). But like many others, he does not direct his ability in this direction. He merely says, "Does life have meaning without a transcendent creed? Of course it does." And that is actually where he leaves the matter.

## A Christian Question

The Bible teaches that man was created for God's glory. It was God who gave man a purpose, and therefore man's good is to fulfil that purpose. But if nature is indifferent to man's desires, comfort, or well-being, as atheistic naturalism teaches, can man have any purpose at all? Men may have purposes, but logical positivism cannot maintain a teleological unity of the human race. This philosophy repudiates every objective system of morals or values to which all men are answerable.

Yet the unity of the human race is a pet theme of the humanists. They urge us to join the human race. Their goal is to become human. A Christian, with the doctrine of creation, has an adequate base for biological and teleological unity; and with the doctrine of the fall he has an adequate reason to deny the spiritual unity of mankind. But the humanists assert spiritual unity without reason, contradict generic purpose both by their positivism and by their atheism, and by evolution cast doubt even on the biological unity of the race.

If, now, neither a purposing God nor an indifferent nature imposes a purpose on all men, if "humanists believe that mankind has only itself to rely upon" (*Living with Uncertainty,* promotional folder of the American Humanist Association), and if, further, morality is relative and constantly changing, then it is hard to see what obligation anyone has to accept humanistic ideas. Each person must select his own purpose. One man will choose the life of a playboy; another will desire to be a miserly recluse; and, to put the question most pointedly, how can a humanist insist that anyone should choose to live rather than to commit suicide?

The question of suicide must be insisted upon, no matter how distasteful it is to humanists. An exponent of ethical culture once engaged in public debate with a Calvinist. The Calvinist was asked: If you were persuaded that theism was false, how would you live? Perhaps the humanist expected a sheepish avowal of orgiastic desires. More probably he expected a respectable choice based on common notions of prudence. On this second possibility the ethical culturist would have claimed victory, for if rules of prudence allow choices of action, then theism is unnecessary for ethics.

But the actual answer given was, "I would shoot myself and

save a lot of trouble." At this the humanist threw up his hands in despair, as well he might, because he could not justify the value of life itself. Obviously, if life is not worth living, discussion of the relative merits of a playboy versus a hermit is irrelevant.

When, in answer to the question, "Does life have meaning without a transcendent creed?" Feigl merely asseverates, "Of course it does," we cannot accept his optimism without verification. Indeed, verification is one of the main points in Feigl's naturalism. Not only is the (temporarily) true distinguished from the (temporarily) false by verification, but the identification of meaningful statements as opposed to sentences that hold no meaning depends on verifiability. With his strong insistence on scientific procedure, verification becomes a matter of sensory observation. "If and only if assertion and denial of a sentence imply a difference capable of observational (experiential, operational, or experimental) test, does the sentence have factual meaning" ("Logical Empiricism," reprinted in *Living Schools of Philosophy,* ed. by Dagobert D. Runes, p. 334).

Among factually meaningless sentences Feigl classes all expressions of "praise or blame, appeals, suggestions, requests and commands" (*ibid.,* p. 334). He would therefore be compelled to agree that the suggestion to join the human race is meaningless. So also with every moral command. Such sentences cannot be tested by observation or empirical validation. "An ethical imperative like the Golden Rule . . . having its accent in the emotive appeal, could not possibly be deduced from a knowledge of facts only; it is neither true nor false. . . . The question raised (and sometimes answered negatively) by metaphysicians, 'Is the satisfying of human interests morally valuable?' is therefore not a factual question at all. . . . The term 'valuable' (in the non-instrumental sense) is used purely as an emotive device."

Now Feigl, as well as other humanists, does not refrain from emotional devices. He writes, "A completely grown-up mankind . . . will acknowledge no other procedure than the experimental and no other standards than those prescribed by human nature" (*ibid.,* pp. 354 ff.). Not only is this sentence with its context emotional and pejorative, but even if we choose to live rather than commit suicide, there is no experimental procedure that verifies the superiority of a "scientific" or positivistic life. Nor can the ideals of Jesus, St. Francis, Newton, or Einstein be considered superior to or more practical than those of Stalin. Certainly Stalin meets every empirical test of success.

## A Christian Conclusion

In view of the logical flaw at the basis of logical empiricism, in view of the relativity of humanistic moral standards, and in view of the insipid pietism of its emotional exhortations, the best thing for the Christian churches to do is to recover their full-fledged supernaturalism. The God who by creation imposed purpose on the human race has infallibly revealed to the prophets that the chief end of man is to glorify God and to enjoy him forever.

———————

*Christianity Today,* May 12, 1967.

# 42

# Utilitarianism

Utilitarianism, dimly foreshadowed by Helvetius, Beccaria, and Hume, was perfected by Jeremy Bentham (1748-1842). The immediate stimulus was the imperfection of the British legal system. Utilitarianism was a theory to support reform.

The philosophical basis is psychological hedonism: "Nature has placed mankind under the governance of two sovereign masters, *pain* and *pleasure*. It is for them alone to point out what we ought to do, as well as to determine what we shall do."

If pleasure is the only human motive, it is plausible that we should aim for the greatest amount. To calculate the amount we must measure the intensity, the duration, the certainty, the propinquity, the fecundity, and the purity of the pleasure.

Then Bentham adds a seventh dimension: "the extent; that is, the number of persons to whom it extends."

Now, psychological hedonism surely means that a man is

motivated by his own pleasure. The pleasures of others are not pleasures and therefore not motives to him. Thus Bentham seems to have made a fallacious inference from psychological hedonism to utilitarianism—the theory that the good life is the one that produces the greatest good for the greatest number. Yet if the greatest good of the greatest number prevents a man from getting the greatest good for himself, what reason can be given to convince him to sacrifice his own good? Surely not psychological hedonism.

Bentham tries to minimize this conflict by a theory of four sanctions. The physical sanction is merely the natural consequence of one's action. This has little to do with inducing us to seek the pleasure of others. The political sanction is the power of the state. Such a sanction by imposing penalties can make one's personal pleasures result in pain and so produce a certain amount of harmony in the state. The social sanction still further makes it painful to seek personal pleasure at the expense of the greatest number. The religious sanction, *i.e.*, God's inflicting pain in order to harmonize private and universal pleasure, would guarantee the result, if only these punishments could continue into the world to come. But Bentham rejects this solution: God is supposed to operate only in this life and only through the powers of nature. Since these four sanctions do not produce a perfect harmony, utilitarianism is left without a justification of its principle of universalism.

The principle of the greatest good for the greatest number envisages at least some people, the smaller number, who must suffer. Thus utilitarianism justifies massacre. To be sure, Henry Sidgwick in the late nineteenth century tried to avoid justifying massacre by replacing the notion of the greatest good of the greatest number with the assumption that the greatest sum of pleasures for any one individual actually contributes to the greatest sum for every other individual. Thus a murder could never be beneficial to anyone. But there is no empirical evidence to support this assumption.

Bentham's original principle of the greatest good "on the whole" is quite consistent with Stalin's murder of millions of Ukrainians, his slaughter of the captured Polish officers, and his suppression of the Hungarians. These actions caused considerable pain to many people; but they will all be overbalanced by the pleasures of the greater number of happy communists in the centuries to come.

This is true, of course, provided that the calculation is correct —provided, of course, that the calculation is possible. The possibility of measurement depends on the identity of a unit. In order to measure heat, a degree of temperature had to be invented. No one has yet invented a unit of pleasure; therefore there can be no sum. There must also be a unit of pain, and this unit must be commensurable with the unit of pleasure. One cannot add an inch to a degree to an ounce and get a total. It is doubtful that pains and pleasures are commensurable, and at any rate there is no unit. Therefore the required calculation is impossible.

If it were possible, the question would still remain whether the calculation could be complete and correct. To count the pleasures, not only of all people living today, but also of all future generations all over the world, is a superhuman task. For example, how much pleasure or pain will my action today produce for a Chinese peasant a few hundred years from now? Must morality depend on my knowing this amount before I decide between two proposed decisions?

God and immortality, though in one way or another they may avoid the difficulty of conflicting goods, cannot help one to calculate. Practicability as well as consistency is needed. This requires a verbal revelation, such as the Ten Commandments. Only these can inform us which decisions are right and wrong.

---

*Baker's Dictionary of Christian Ethics,* Carl F.H. Henry, editor. Grand Rapids, Michigan: Baker Book House, 1973, pp. 690-692.

# 43

# Values

Value theory or axiology is a general theory based on the assumption that aesthetic value, moral value, political value, and (consistently) physical value or health, are all species of one genus.

A distinction must be made. The criteria for judging a work of art, the criteria of good health, and the criteria of moral action are not plausibly species of one genus. How often have we heard the aesthetes decry moral norms in art! On the other hand, a combination of health, wealth, morality, and art may define the good life. In this sense Aristotle's ethics is axiology, for his good life has the proper proportion of each. However, this is not axiology in the modern sense of making every value a species of an inclusive genus.

As a distinct modern movement axiology first came to notice in the neo-realist school of [Franz] Brentano [1838-1917] and [Alexius] Meinong [1853-1920]. Values as well as chairs and tables exist independently of consciousness. Green exists in a chair; good exists in a proposition. Whether or not minds exist or bodies exist, the *proposition* "a diseased appendix ought to be removed" is a good proposition. But one wonders whether a proposition can exist without a mind or an appendix without a body.

Meinong was followed by [Max] Scheler [1874-1928] and [Edmund] Husserl [1859-1938]. In America axiology was popularized by Ralph Barton Perry, John Dewey (though not a realist), S.C. Pepper, and others. C.I. Lewis uses the term *value* in a narrow sense and approximates Aristotle by subsuming axiology under ethics; but most make ethics a subdivision of axiology. In some cases a good amount (or is it a bad amount?) of pedantic linguistics is mixed in.

Neo-realism seems to imply a theory of valuation that is both cognitive and empirical. Absolute idealism and Calvinism are both cognitive, but not empirical. The emotive theories of A.J. Ayer, Charles L. Stevenson, *et al.*, are empirical, but noncognitive. These latter make valuation arbitrary and irrational, and remove it from the sphere of discussion. Ayer and [Jean Paul] Sartre are good examples.

The great difficulty with the cognitive, empirical view is its empiricism. Appendectomies, lies, and wars are as natural as plants and planets. None of them comes with a tag, saying, "I am valuable." An example is the war in Vietnam from 1962. The American effort was widely denounced as immoral and bad. But some of the denouncers thought that riot, arson, murder, and treason are moral and good. Anti-communists hold a different view. The difficulty is how to determine by empirical observation which view is right.

The same difficulty occurs in music. Some people value Bach, Beethoven, and Brahms; but others prefer ear-drum-splitting rock.

Empiricism is incapable of establishing norms. Perry may say that "any object, whatever it be, acquires value when any interest, whatever it be, is taken in it." But this may make heroin as valuable as, or even more valuable than chocolate ice cream. To avoid this embarrassment Perry tries to show how one value is better than another. The better value is the one that harmonizes many interests. But though this definition complicates the observation, it is of no help to empiricism. There could be several harmonies, each of ten different values. How then shall we choose one from among them? Or, again, one harmonious combination might integrate five values, while a second includes twenty. But could not a life of five values be better than a life of twenty? The example of drug addiction prevents the theory from advocating a highest value that includes all. Therefore observation cannot decide among combinations; empiricism justifies no *ought*.

Various empiricists have tried to defend their theory against this charge. But there can be no value in their arguments because it is always and everywhere fallacious to insert into the conclusion a concept that nowhere appears in the premises. The observational statement, X values rock, does not imply that X ought to value rock, that Y and Z should value rock, or that Bach and Brahms are disvalues. If the rock example is not convincing, try heroin.

---

*Baker's Dictionary of Christian Ethics*, Carl F.H. Henry, editor. Grand Rapids, Michigan: Baker Book House, 1973, pp. 292-293.

# Scripture Index

# Index

# The Crisis of Our Time

Historians have christened the thirteenth century the Age of Faith and termed the eighteenth century the Age of Reason. The twentieth century has been called many things: the Atomic Age, the Age of Inflation, the Age of the Tyrant, the Age of Aquarius. But it deserves one name more than the others: the Age of Irrationalism. Contemporary secular intellectuals are anti-intellectual. Contemporary philosophers are anti-philosophy. Contemporary theologians are anti-theology.

In past centuries secular philosophers have generally believed that knowledge is possible to man. Consequently they expended a great deal of thought and effort trying to justify knowledge. In the twentieth century, however, the optimism of the secular philosophers has all but disappeared. They despair of knowledge.

Like their secular counterparts, the great theologians and doctors of the church taught that knowledge is possible to man. Yet the theologians of the twentieth century have repudiated that belief. They also despair of knowledge. This radical skepticism has filtered down from the philosophers and theologians and penetrated our entire culture, from television to music to literature. *The Christian in the twentieth century is confronted with an overwhelming cultural consensus—sometimes stated explicitly, but most often implicitly: Man does not and cannot know anything truly.*

What does this have to do with Christianity? Simply this: If man can know nothing truly, man can truly know nothing. We cannot know that the Bible is the Word of God, that Christ died for the sins of his people, or that Christ is alive today at the right hand of the Father. Unless knowledge is possible, Christianity is nonsensical, for it claims to be knowledge. What is at stake in the twentieth century is not simply a single doctrine, such as the Virgin Birth, or the existence of hell, as important as those doctrines may be, but the whole of Christianity itself. If knowledge is not possible to man, it is worse than silly to argue points of doctrine—it is insane.

The irrationalism of the present age is so thorough-going and pervasive that even the Remnant—the segment of the professing church that remains faithful—has accepted much of it, frequently without even being aware of what it was accepting. In some circles this irrationalism has become synonymous with piety and humility, and those who oppose it are denounced as rationalists—as though to be logical were a sin. Our contemporary anti-theologians make a contradiction and call it a Mystery. The faithful ask for truth and are given Paradox. If any balk at swallowing the absurdities of the anti-theologians, they are frequently marked as heretics or schismatics who seek to act independently of God.

There is no greater threat facing the true Church of Christ at this moment than the irrationalism that now controls our entire culture. Totalitarianism, guilty of tens of millions of murders, including those of millions of Christians, is to be feared, but not nearly so much as the idea that we do not and cannot know the truth. Hedonism, the popular philosophy of America, is not to be feared so much as the belief that logic— that "mere human logic," to use the religious irrationalists' own phrase—is futile. The attacks on truth, on revelation, on the intellect, and on logic are renewed daily. But note well: The misologists—the haters of logic—use logic to demonstrate the futility of using logic. The anti-intellectuals construct intricate intellectual arguments to prove the insufficiency of the intellect. The anti-theologians use the revealed Word of God to show that there can be no revealed Word of God—or that if there could, it would remain impenetrable darkness and Mystery to our finite minds.

## Nonsense Has Come

Is it any wonder that the world is grasping at straws—the straws of experientialism, mysticism and drugs? After all, if people are told that the Bible contains insoluble mysteries, then is not a flight into mysticism to be expected? On what grounds can it be condemned? Certainly not on logical grounds or Biblical grounds, if logic is futile and the Bible unintelligible. Moreover, if it cannot be condemned on logical or Biblical grounds, it cannot be condemned at all. If people are going to have a religion of the mysterious, they will not adopt Christianity: They will have a genuine mystery religion. "Those who call for Nonsense," C.S. Lewis once wrote, "will find that it comes." And that is precisely what has happened. The popularity of Eastern mysticism, of drugs, and of religious experience is the logical consequence of the irrationalism of the twentieth century. There can and will be no Christian revival—and no reconstruction of society—unless and until the irrationalism of the age is totally repudiated by Christians.

## The Church Defenseless

Yet how shall they do it? The spokesmen for Christianity have been fatally infected with irrationalism. The seminaries, which annually train thousands of men to teach millions of Christians, are the finishing schools of irrationalism, completing the job begun by the government schools and colleges. Some of the pulpits of the most conservative churches (we are not speaking of the apostate churches) are occupied by graduates of the anti-theological schools. These products of modern anti-theological education, when asked to give a reason for the hope that is in them, can generally respond with only the intellectual analogue of a shrug—a mumble about Mystery. They have not grasped—and therefore cannot teach those for whom they are responsible—the first truth: "And ye shall know the truth." Many, in fact, explicitly deny it, saying that, at best, we possess only "pointers" to the truth, or something "similar" to the truth, a mere analogy. Is the impotence of the Christian Church a puzzle? Is the fascination with pentecostalism and faith healing among members of conservative churches an enigma? Not when one understands the sort of studied nonsense that is purveyed in the name of God in the seminaries.

## The Trinity Foundation

The creators of The Trinity Foundation firmly believe that theology is too important to be left to the licensed theologians —the graduates of the schools of theology. They have created The Trinity Foundation for the express purpose of teaching the faithful all that the Scriptures contain—not warmed over, baptized, secular philosophies. Each member of the board of directors of The Trinity Foundation has signed this oath: "I believe that the Bible alone and the Bible in its entirety is the Word of God and, therefore, inerrant in the autographs. I believe that the system of truth presented in the Bible is best summarized in the Westminster Confession of Faith. So help me God."

The ministry of The Trinity Foundation is the presentation of the system of truth taught in Scripture as clearly and as completely as possible. We do not regard obscurity as a virtue, nor confusion as a sign of spirituality. Confusion, like all error, is sin, and teaching that confusion is all that Christians can hope for is doubly sin.

The presentation of the truth of Scripture necessarily involves the rejection of error. The Foundation has exposed and will continue to expose the irrationalism of the twentieth century, whether its current spokesman be an existentialist philosopher or a professed Reformed theologian. We oppose anti-intellectualism, whether it be espoused by a neo-orthodox theologian or a fundamentalist evangelist. We reject misology, whether it be on the lips of a neo-evangelical or those of a Roman Catholic charismatic. To each error we bring the brilliant light of Scripture, proving all things, and holding fast to that which is true.

## The Primacy of Theory

The ministry of The Trinity Foundation is not a "practical" ministry. If you are a pastor, we will not enlighten you on how to organize an ecumenical prayer meeting in your community or how to double church attendance in a year. If you are a homemaker, you will have to read elsewhere to find out how to become a total woman. If you are a businessman, we will not tell you how to develop a social conscience. The professing church is drowning in such "practical" advice.

The Trinity Foundation is unapologetically theoretical in its outlook, believing that theory without practice is dead, and that practice without theory is blind. The trouble with the professing church is not primarily in its practice, but in its theory. Christians do not know, and many do not even care to know, the doctrines of Scripture. Doctrine is intellectual, and Christians are generally anti-intellectual. Doctrine is ivory tower philosophy, and they scorn ivory towers. The ivory tower, however, is the control tower of a civilization. It is a fundamental, theoretical mistake of the practical men to think that they can be merely practical, for practice is always the practice of some theory. The relationship between theory and practice is the relationship between cause and effect. If a person believes correct theory, his practice will tend to be correct. The practice of contemporary Christians is immoral because it is the practice of false theories. It is a major theoretical mistake of the practical men to think that they can ignore the ivory towers of the philosophers and theologians as irrelevant to their lives. Every action that the "practical" men take is governed by the thinking that has occurred in some ivory tower—whether that tower be the British Museum, the Academy, a home in Basel, Switzerland, or a tent in Israel.

## In Understanding Be Men

It is the first duty of the Christian to understand correct theory—correct doctrine—and thereby implement correct practice. This order—first theory, then practice—is both logical and

Biblical. It is, for example, exhibited in Paul's epistle to the Romans, in which he spends the first eleven chapters expounding theory and the last five discussing practice. The contemporary teachers of Christians have not only reversed the order, they have inverted the Pauline emphasis on theory and practice. The virtually complete failure of the teachers of the professing church to instruct the faithful in correct doctrine is the cause of the misconduct and cultural impotence of Christians. The Church's lack of power is the result of its lack of truth. The *Gospel* is the power of God, not religious experience or personal relationship. The Church has no power because it has abandoned the Gospel, the good news, for a religion of experientialism. Twentieth century American Christians are children carried about by every wind of doctrine, not knowing what they believe, or even if they believe anything for certain.

The chief purpose of The Trinity Foundation is to counteract the irrationalism of the age and to expose the errors of the teachers of the church. Our emphasis—on the Bible as the sole source of truth, on the primacy of the intellect, on the supreme importance of correct doctrine, and on the necessity for systematic and logical thinking—is almost unique in Christendom. To the extent that the church survives—and she will survive and flourish—it will be because of her increasing acceptance of these basic ideas and their logical implications.

We believe that the Trinity Foundation is filling a vacuum in Christendom. We are saying that Christianity is intellectually defensible—that, in fact, it is the only intellectually defensible system of thought. We are saying that God has made the wisdom of this world—whether that wisdom be called science, religion, philosophy, or common sense—foolishness. We are appealing to all Christians who have not conceded defeat in the intellectual battle with the world to join us in our efforts to raise a standard to which all men of sound mind can repair.

The love of truth, of God's Word, has all but disappeared in our time. We are committed to and pray for a great instauration. But though we may not see this reformation of Christendom in our lifetimes, we believe it is our duty to present the whole counsel of God because Christ has commanded it. The results of our teaching are in God's hands, not ours. Whatever those results, his Word is never taught in vain, but always accomplishes the result that he intended it to accomplish. Professor Gordon H. Clark has stated our view well:

> There have been times in the history of God's people, for example, in the days of Jeremiah, when refreshing grace and widespread revival were not to be expected: the time was one of chastisement. If this twentieth century is of a similar nature, individual Christians here and there can find comfort and strength in a study of God's Word. But if God has decreed happier days for us and if we may expect a world-shaking and genuine spiritual awakening, then it is the author's belief that a zeal for souls, however necessary, is not the sufficient condition. Have there not been devout saints in every age, numerous enough to carry on a revival? Twelve such persons are plenty. What distinguishes the arid ages from the period of the Reformation, when nations were moved as they had not been since Paul preached in Ephesus, Corinth, and Rome, is the latter's fullness of knowledge of God's Word. To echo an early Reformation thought, when the ploughman and the garage attendant know the Bible as well as the theologian does, and know it better than some contemporary theologians, then the desired awakening shall have already occurred.

In addition to publishing books, of which *Essays on Ethics and Politics* is the thirty-second, the Foundation publishes a bimonthly newsletter, *The Trinity Review*. Subscriptions to *The Review* are free; please write to the address below to become a subscriber. If you would like further information or would like to join us in our work, please let us know.

The Trinity Foundation is a non-profit foundation tax-exempt under section 501 (c)(3) of the Internal Revenue Code of 1954. You can help us disseminate the Word of God through your tax-deductible contributions to the Foundation.

*And we know that the Son of God is come, and hath given us an understanding, that we may know him that is true, and we are in him that is true, in his Son Jesus Christ. This is the true God, and eternal life.*

John W. Robbins

# Intellectual Ammunition

The Trinity Foundation is committed to the reconstruction of philosophy and theology along Biblical lines. We regard God's command to bring all our thoughts into conformity with Christ very seriously, and the books listed below are designed to accomplish that goal. They are written with two subordinate purposes: (1) to demolish all secular claims to knowledge; and (2) to build a system of truth based upon the Bible alone.

## Philosophy

**Behaviorism and Christianity**, Gordon H. Clark $6.95
Behaviorism *is a critique of both secular and religious behaviorists. It includes chapters on John Watson, Edgar S. Singer Jr., Gilbert Ryle, B.F. Skinner, and Donald MacKay. Clark's refutation of behaviorism and his argument for a Christian doctrine of man are unanswerable.*

**A Christian Philosophy of Education**, Gordon H. Clark $8.95
*The first edition of this book was published in 1946. It sparked the contemporary interest in Christian schools. Dr. Clark has thoroughly revised and updated it, and it is needed now more than ever. Its chapters include: The Need for a World-View, The Christian World-View, The Alternative to Christian Theism, Neutrality, Ethics, The Christian Philosophy of Education, Academic Matters, Kindergarten to University. Three appendices*

*are included as well: The Relationship of Public Education to Christianity, A Protestant World-View, and Art and the Gospel.*

**A Christian View of Men and Things,** Gordon H. Clark   $10.95
*No other book achieves what* A Christian View *does: the presentation of Christianity as it applies to history, politics, ethics, science, religion, and epistemology. Clark's command of both worldly philosophy and Scripture is evident on every page, and the result is a breathtaking and invigorating challenge to the wisdom of this world.*

**Clark Speaks From The Grave,** Gordon H. Clark     $3.95
*Dr. Clark chides some of his critics for their failure to defend Christianity competently.* Clark Speaks *is a stimulating and illuminating discussion of the errors of contemporary apologists.*

**Education, Christianity, and the State**     $7.95
J. Gresham Machen
*Machen was one of the foremost educators, theologians, and defenders of Christianity in the twentieth century. The author of numerous scholarly books, Machen saw clearly that if Christianity is to survive and flourish, a system of Christian grade schools must be established. This collection of essays captures his thought on education over nearly three decades.*

**Essays on Ethics and Politics**     $10.95
Gordon H. Clark
*Clark's s essays, written over the course of five decades, are a major statement of Christian ethics.*

**Gordon H. Clark: Personal Recollections**     $6.95
John W. Robbins, editor
*Friends of Dr. Clark have written their recollections of the man. Contributors include family members, colleagues, students, and friends such as Harold Lindsell, Carl Henry, Ronald Nash, Dwight Zeller, and Mary Crumpacker. The book includes an extensive bibliography of Clark's work.*

**John Dewey**, Gordon H. Clark                                      $2.00
   *America has not produced many philosophers, but John Dewey has been extremely influential. Clark examines his philosophy of Instrumentalism.*

**Logic**, Gordon H. Clark                                           $8.95
   *Written as a textbook for Christian schools,* Logic *is another unique book from Clark's pen. His presentation of the laws of thought, which must be followed if Scripture is to be understood correctly, and which are found in Scripture itself, is both clear and thorough.* Logic *is an indispensable book for the thinking Christian.*

**The Philosophy of Science and Belief in God**                      $5.95
Gordon H. Clark
   *In opposing the contemporary idolatry of science, Clark analyzes three major aspects of science: the problem of motion, Newtonian science, and modern theories of physics. His conclusion is that science, while it may be useful, is always false; and he demonstrates its falsity in numerous ways. Since science is always false, it can offer no objection to the Bible and Christianity.*

**Religion, Reason and Revelation**, Gordon H. Clark                 $7.95
   *One of Clark's apologetical masterpieces,* Religion, Reason and Revelation *has been praised for the clarity of its thought and language. It includes chapters on Is Christianity a Religion? Faith and Reason, Inspiration and Language, Revelation and Morality, and God and Evil. It is must reading for all serious Christians.*

**Thales to Dewey: A History of Philosophy**          paper $11.95
Gordon H. Clark                                      hardback $16.95
   *This volume is the best one volume history of philosophy in English.*

**Three Types of Religious Philosophy**, Gordon H. Clark    $6.95
   *In this book on apologetics, Clark examines empiricism, rationalism, dogmatism, and contemporary irrationalism, which*

*does not rise to the level of philosophy. He offers a solution to the question, "How can Christianity be defended before the world?"*

# Theology

**The Atonement**, Gordon H. Clark          $8.95
   *This is a major addition to Clark's multi-volume systematic theology. In* The Atonement, *Clark discusses the Covenants, the Virgin Birth and Incarnation, federal headship and representation, the relationship between God's sovereignty and justice, and much more. He analyzes traditional views of the Atonement and criticizes them in the light of Scripture alone.*

**The Biblical Doctrine of Man**, Gordon H. Clark          $6.95
   *Is man soul and body or soul, spirit, and body? What is the image of God? Is Adam's sin imputed to his children? Is evolution true? Are men totally depraved? What is the heart? These are some of the questions discussed and answered from Scripture in this book.*

**Cornelius Van Til: The Man and The Myth**          $2.45
John W. Robbins
   *The actual teachings of this eminent Philadelphia theologian have been obscured by the myths that surround him. This book penetrates those myths and criticizes Van Til's surprisingly unorthodox views of God and the Bible.*

**Faith and Saving Faith**, Gordon H. Clark          $6.95
   *The views of the Roman Catholic church, John Calvin, Thomas Manton, John Owen, Charles Hodge, and B.B. Warfield are discussed in this book. Is the object of faith a person or a proposition? Is faith more than belief? Is belief more than thinking with assent, as Augustine said? In a world chaotic with differing views of faith, Clark clearly explains the Biblical view of faith and saving faith.*

**God's Hammer: The Bible and Its Critics**                    $6.95
Gordon H. Clark

*The starting point of Christianity, the doctrine on which all other doctrines depend, is "The Bible alone is the Word of God written, and therefore inerrant in the autographs." Over the centuries the opponents of Christianity, with Satanic shrewdness, have concentrated their attacks on the truthfulness and completeness of the Bible. In the twentieth century the attack is not so much in the fields of history and archaeology as in philosophy. Clark's brilliant defense of the complete truthfulness of the Bible is captured in this collection of eleven major essays.*

**Guide to the Westminster Confession and Catechism**        $13.95
James E. Bordwine

*This large book contains the full text of both the Westminster Confession (both original and American versions) and the Larger Catechism. In addition, it offers a chapter-by-chapter summary of the Confession and a unique index to both the Confession and the Catechism.*

**The Incarnation,** Gordon H. Clark                          $8.95

*Who was Christ? The attack on the Incarnation in the nineteenth and twentieth centuries has been vigorous, but the orthodox response has been lame. Clark reconstructs the doctrine of the Incarnation building and improving upon the Chalcedonian definition.*

**In Defense of Theology,** Gordon H. Clark                   $9.95

*There are four groups to whom Clark addresses this book: the average Christians who are uninterested in theology, the atheists and agnostics, the religious experientialists, and the serious Christians. The vindication of the knowledge of God against the objections of three of these groups is the first step in theology.*

**The Johannine Logos,** Gordon H. Clark                      $5.95

*Clark analyzes the relationship between Christ, who is the truth, and the Bible. He explains why John used the same word to refer to both Christ and his teaching. Chapters deal with the*

*Prologue to John's Gospel, Logos and Rheemata, Truth, and Saving Faith.*

## Logical Criticisms of Textual Criticism $3.25
Gordon H. Clark
*In this critique of the science of textual criticism, Dr. Clark exposes the fallacious argumentation of the modern textual critics and defends the view that the early Christians knew better than the modern critics which manuscripts of the New Testament were more accurate.*

## Pat Robertson: A Warning to America, John W. Robbins $6.95
*The Protestant Reformation was based on the Biblical principle that the Bible is the only revelation from God, yet a growing religious movement, led by Pat Robertson, asserts that God speaks to them directly. This book addresses the serious issue of religious fanaticism in America by examining the theological views of Pat Robertson.*

## Predestination, Gordon H. Clark $8.95
*Clark thoroughly discusses one of the most controversial and pervasive doctrines of the Bible: that God is, quite literally, Almighty. Free will, the origin of evil, God's omniscience, creation, and the new birth are all presented within a Scriptural framework. The objections of those who do not believe in the Almighty God are considered and refuted. This edition also contains the text of the booklet,* Predestination in the Old Testament.

## Scripture Twisting in the Seminaries. Part 1: Feminism $5.95
John W. Robbins
*An analysis of the views of three graduates of Westminster Seminary on the role of women in the church.*

## Today's Evangelism: Counterfeit or Genuine? $6.95
Gordon H. Clark
*Clark compares the methods and messages of today's evangelists with Scripture, and finds that Christianity is on the wane*

*because the Gospel has been distorted or lost. This is an extremely useful and enlightening book.*

**The Trinity,** Gordon H. Clark                                    $8.95
  *Apart from the doctrine of Scripture, no teaching of the Bible is more important than the doctrine of God. Clark's defense of the orthodox doctrine of the Trinity is a principal portion of a major new work of Systematic Theology now in progress. There are chapters on the deity of Christ, Augustine, the incomprehensibility of God, Bavinck and Van Til, and the Holy Spirit, among others.*

**What Do Presbyterians Believe?** Gordon H. Clark          $7.95
  *This classic introduction to Christian doctrine has been republished. It is the best commentary on the Westminster Confession of Faith that has ever been written.*

## Commentaries on the New Testament

**Colossians,** Gordon H. Clark                                   $6.95
**Ephesians,** Gordon H. Clark                                    $8.95
**First Corinthians,** Gordon H. Clark                           $10.95
**First and Second Thessalonians,** Gordon H. Clark               $5.95
**The Pastoral Epistles** (I and II Timothy and Titus)            $9.95
  Gordon H. Clark
  *All of Clark's commentaries are expository, not technical, and are written for the Christian layman. His purpose is to explain the text clearly and accurately so that the Word of God will be thoroughly known by every Christian.*

# The Trinity Library
*We will send you one copy of each of the 34 books listed above for the low price of $175. The regular price of these books is $260. You may also order the books you want individually on the order blank on the next page. Because some of the books are in short supply, we must reserve the right to substitute others of equal or greater value in The Trinity Library. This special offer expires June 30, 1994.*

# Order Form

Name _____

Address _____

_____

Please:  □ add my name to the mailing list for *The Trinity Review*. I understand that there is no charge for the *Review*.

□ accept my tax deductible contribution of $_____ for the work of the Foundation.

□ send me _____ copies of *Essays on Ethics and Politics*. I enclose as payment $ _____.

□ send me the Trinity Library of 34 books. I enclose $175 as full payment for it.

□ send me the following books. I enclose full payment in the amount of $ _____ for them.

_____

_____

_____

_____

_____

_____

_____

Mail to:      **The Trinity Foundation**
              **Post Office Box 700**
              **Jefferson, MD 21755**

Please add $2.00 for postage on orders less than $10. Thank you.
For quantity discounts, please write to the Foundation.